# SPINOZA BEYOND PHILOSOPHY

# SPINOZA BEYOND PHILOSOPHY

Edited by Beth Lord

EDINBURGH
University Press

Edinburgh University Press Ltd
The Tun – Holyrood Road
12 (2f) Jackson's Entry
Edinburgh EH8 8PJ

www.euppublishing.com

First published in hardback by Edinburgh University Press 2012

This paperback edition 2015

Typeset in 10.5/13 Sabon
by Servis Filmsetting Ltd, Stockport, Cheshire, and
printed and bound in Great Britain by
CPI Group (UK) Ltd, Croydon, CR0 4YY

A CIP record for this book is available from the British Library

ISBN 978 0 7486 4480 3 (hardback)
ISBN 978 1 4744 0472 3 (paperback)
ISBN 978 0 7486 4481 0 (webready PDF)
ISBN 978 0 7486 5607 3 (epub)

# Contents

# Acknowledgements

This book is the outcome of the research activities of the Spinoza Research Network, a two-year project funded by the Arts and Humanities Research Council (AHRC; www.ahrc.ac.uk) in 2008 to 2010. The project developed a network of over 200 people working on Spinoza in multiple disciplines, within and outside academia, and continues to be an active group of Spinoza researchers (http://spinoza-researchnetwork.wordpress.com/). The chapters in this book were first presented at two Network conferences at the University of Dundee: *Spinoza and Bodies* and *Spinoza and Texts*. The editor and authors are grateful to the AHRC for its support. The image on page 69 is reproduced with the permission of AA Publications. The images on pages 108–14 are reproduced with the permission of the artists.

# *Abbreviations*

The chapter authors use different editions and translations of Spinoza's works, as indicated in the bibliography to each chapter. However, the following abbreviations and referencing system are used throughout the book for Spinoza's texts.

E    *Ethics*; references are to part number in Roman numerals, followed by Proposition (or other) number in Arabic numerals, as follows: D = Definition; A = Axiom; P = Proposition; Dem. = Demonstration; C = Corollary; S = Scholium; Exp. = Explanation; L = Lemma; Post. = Postulate; Pref. = Preface; App. = Appendix; Def. Aff. = Part III 'Definitions of the Affects' (e.g. E IVP18S = *Ethics* Part IV, Proposition 18, Scholium).

KV    *Short Treatise on God, Man, and his Wellbeing*; references are to part number in Roman numerals and chapter number in Arabic numerals.

*Letters* are referenced by number, correspondent and date (where known).

TIE    *Treatise on the Emendation of the Intellect*; references are to paragraph number.

TP    *Political Treatise*; references are to chapter and paragraph number.

TTP    *Theological–Political Treatise*; references are to chapter number and page number in the translation used.

# *Introduction*

## BETH LORD

Baruch Spinoza is often assumed to be a philosopher's philosopher – one whose system is so metaphysically complex and so distant from everyday life that it is read by very few, and understood by even fewer. Those who read Spinoza know this not to be true. Obscure though Spinoza's ideas may be, there is no doubt that he was deeply committed to elucidating our everyday experience. Spinoza's metaphysics and epistemology make way for a kind of anthropology: a philosophy of human nature and a theory of how human beings relate to one another. Spinoza gives us tools for understanding ourselves and strategies for living well, something that few philosophers since the Greeks have attempted to provide. Further, Spinoza wants us to understand ourselves as beings immersed in a world of things that affect each other constantly. While human nature is unavoidably the central concern of humanity, and thus of philosophy, it is shown not to be the central feature or purpose of the universe. His is a non-anthropocentric anthropology, or a 'non-humanist humanism'.

This complex aim – to understand that and how humanity is 'part of nature' – has made Spinoza one of Western philosophy's most popular figures, and one who is studied and known outside of the philosophy classroom. The difficulty of Spinoza's thought – its extreme 'philosophicality' – is no barrier to its being used and enjoyed by those who do not consider themselves students, teachers or writers of philosophy. People enjoy Spinoza because they feel that living a good life and taking a holistic perspective on oneself and the world *should* be philosophy's focus. That is, philosophy should ground not only anthropology, but also politics, ecology, history, and other systems that organise human thought and endeavour. Spinoza's texts make it clear that thinking philosophically leads to clearer thinking about these systems.

This book is, in part, motivated by the conviction that philosophy has not just a duty but also an inner *necessity* to become myriad other ways of thinking. The relationship between philosophy and other subjects is not one of grounding, but rather, truer to Spinoza's style, an *immanent* relation wherein other subjects are formed in the activity of philosophical thinking itself. Through and in philosophical thinking, multiple other ways of thinking come to be. This is what emerges in Spinoza's major work, the *Ethics*, where 'pure' philosophical thinking about being becomes, through an inner necessity, thinking about scientific knowledge and imaginative fiction, embodiment, relations to other things, and the complex systems of relations that are ethics and politics. To use the term that Deleuze found so productive in Spinoza, philosophy *expresses* these other subjects; they are immanent in it, and philosophy remains immanent in them.

This book aims to follow some of the routes taken by the *expression* of Spinoza's philosophy, routes that have not been followed before. Take, for instance, Spinoza's so-called 'parallelism' thesis: the view that mind and body are one thing, expressed in two different ways (E IIP7). This thought leads to surprising philosophical conclusions, including those about the limitations of knowledge and the impossibility of free will (see, for example, Della Rocca 1996). But in this book, it is also seen to generate new ways of thinking about political subjectivity (Chapters 1 and 2) and different modes of musical and literary analysis (Chapters 5 and 9). Spinoza's theory of the emotions (the neuroscientific plausibility of which has been recently explored by Damasio 2004) is here seen to inform thinking about architectural design (Chapter 4) and ecological activism (Chapter 3). Various schools of political thought in the twentieth century have drawn on Spinoza (see Althusser 1973, Negri 1991 and Balibar 1998 on the Marxist side; Feuer 1958 and Smith 1997 on the liberal side; and Gatens 2009 for feminist interpretations). In this book, Spinoza's political texts are considered not only in terms of their potential for thinking about individual and institutional power (Chapters 1 and 6), but also in terms of the narrative power that texts have to generate social cohesion or disruption (Chapters 2, 4, 7 and 8). The role of religion in Spinoza's thought is not restricted to questions of atheism and pantheism, but is treated here in terms of its connections to law (Chapter 7) and literary history (Chapter 10).

In taking Spinoza beyond philosophy, it is important to recognise the extent to which he is himself an 'interdisciplinary' thinker. This term, based on the nineteenth-century separation of 'natural philosophy' into different scientific disciplines, and the gradual estrangement of the sciences from poetry, history and moral philosophy, can only be used retrospectively of a seventeenth-century thinker. All philosophers were 'interdisciplinary' in the seventeenth and eighteenth centuries in the sense that their focus was not typically restricted by subject-matter (though it often was restricted by beliefs about what constituted suitable material for rational thought). However, not all such thinkers are of interdisciplinary relevance now, in the sense of informing thinking in areas outside philosophy. Spinoza's philosophy is interdisciplinary in both these senses: his thought, while expounding a complex metaphysics and epistemology, ventures into physics, politics and hermeneutics; and while Spinoza is studied mainly as a philosopher today, he is widely read and cited by many others. Categorising his work as 'philosophy' is restrictive, for he is interested in truth, wherever that may be found. It is not Spinoza's contention that truth is discoverable only through pure reason. Imagination has a central role to play, in building true understanding, in representing it, and in limiting and obfuscating it. It is this pursuit of truth *through* various ways of knowing – rational and imaginative – that keeps Spinoza's thought open to various disciplines today.

The search for truth, or more specifically, for a method of true understanding, is the theme of the *Treatise on the Emendation of the Intellect*, Spinoza's earliest text (begun 1658). In this text Spinoza presents a rudimentary distinction between four types of 'perception': from hearsay, from casual experience, from inference, and from knowledge of essences (TIE 19). These are specified as 'hearsay, experience, belief, [and] clear knowledge' in the *Short Treatise* (begun 1660; KV II.4), and are transformed into the first two kinds of knowledge, imagination and reason, in the *Ethics* (written 1662–5; E IIP40S2). Throughout Spinoza's development of these ideas, imaginative knowledge from hearsay, signs, experience and inference is contrasted with rational knowledge of essences and causes.

Significantly, the examples Spinoza gives of this latter kind of knowledge are mathematical, for mathematics 'gives us another standard of truth' from experience (E IApp., cf. TIE 22–4). Experience is particular to each individual and is bound up with the bodily and mental states of that individual; it tells us more about the perceiver than about the things perceived (E IIP16C2). Mathematics, by contrast, is a way of 'seeing' things in terms of their eternal truths; the geometric relations that work the same way in all things are 'common notions' between them. It is for this reason (among others) that Spinoza's *Ethics* is written in the geometric style, through the demonstration of propositions, to inculcate in the reader a habit of seeing the world in terms of its geometric commonalities and eternal truths: 'the eyes of the mind, by which it sees and observes things, are the demonstrations themselves' (E VP23S). Spinoza shared this view with followers of the new mechanical philosophy of Descartes and, in 1663, published an exposition of this, the *Principles of Cartesian Philosophy*, also demonstrated in geometric order.

While a purely mathematical understanding of the world may be closest to the truth in an absolute sense, such an understanding would miss what is crucial to being human (and would, in any case, be impossible for us as long as we are embodied): sensory and affective knowledge of ourselves and the world around us. From his early writings through to the *Ethics*, he stresses that humans are complexly affective: we feel and sense a great variety of things, we cause feelings in other beings, and these feelings cannot be avoided or entirely overcome. Our self-awareness and knowledge begin with our feelings (E IIP19), and the majority of our adequate ideas and common notions are formed *through* our experiences. Thus while reasoning is a 'truer' way of knowing than imagining is, reason cannot be separated from imagination, or held out in contrast to it. There is no either–or between imagining and reasoning for Spinoza; they form a single continuum of understanding. We are more rational as we understand things better, and more imaginative as we are more affected by our experiences. At no point can we ever be wholly rational (for then we would feel nothing) or wholly imaginative (for then we would know nothing truly).

A number of chapters in this book stress this point and its implications. Michael Mack (Chapter 2) comments that Spinoza was the first philosopher to break down the separation between reason and imagination, and suggests that this leads to a view of human being as that which is rational but not defined by its rationality – and therefore not punishable for its irrationality (whether natural or socially constructed). Peg Rawes (Chapter 4) uses the term 'sense-reason' to suggest, with Spinoza, that rational knowledge is always inflected by sensuous, imaginary, 'aesthetic' knowledge, and that our sensing the world has an always-already rational and geometrical outlook. Both Rawes and Simon Calder (Chapter 9) show that Spinoza helps us to break down the separation between rational (geometric or scientific) and imaginative (aesthetic, affective, sensuous or fictional) form in architectural design and literary writing.

This is why the experimental sciences are so important for Spinoza, and why he cannot be taken to advocate any system that would reduce knowledge to mathematics (as Badiou 2004 seems to suggest). By increasing our exposure to different things, and by varying the ways we affect, and are affected by, their different materials and properties, we are likelier to hit on the properties they have in common. The organised experience of an experiment will be more effective in gaining knowledge than looking at random events, just as an organised life will be more effective at reaching virtue than one that relies on happenstance. Science is the best way for humans to pursue knowledge, not because it is some purely rational pursuit, but because it brings together rational knowing – the deductive unfolding of adequate ideas – with imaginative knowing from experience and affects. Anthony Paul Smith (Chapter 3) draws out the importance of the affects in coming to understand the contemporary science, and political potential, of ecology.

Because Spinoza is interested in truth, he must take account of the representation of truth. This is another way in which our human finitude restricts our knowledge of eternal truths. We know little, if anything, in an eternal or 'intuitive' way (E VP29). In many cases, truth becomes known to us through language, but true ideas, for Spinoza, are not linguistic in form. Language does not express truth but merely represents it, usually badly. Not only do words lack any intrinsic connection to true ideas, they are connected to our experiences only by association and convention. Words 'are merely symbols of things as they are in the imagination, not in the intellect' (TIE 89; see Savan 1958). Writing is therefore several removes from the truth. Another reason for writing the *Ethics* geometrically rather than discursively (and, some argue, in Latin rather than Dutch) is that Spinoza takes the 'cumbersome geometric order' (E IVP18S) to be the best way of representing true ideas in writing, where 'best' means least prone to error and obfuscation. The geometric style might also be thought to be less prone to interpretive disagreements, though the huge variety of ways of interpreting Spinoza that has developed since the eighteenth century would suggest otherwise (see Norris 2011).

To understand the limitations of language, and the specific errors and interpretive possibilities to which a particular language is prone, one needs to understand its workings (TTP Ch. 7, p. 463). The incomplete *Hebrew Grammar* (likely begun 1669) is Spinoza's contribution to a long tradition of commentaries on this subject, one that focuses on the use of Hebrew as a living language. As Michael L. Morgan comments in his introduction to this rarely read text, 'Spinoza deserves to be called a philologist and grammatical scholar as well as a philosopher and scientist' (Spinoza 2002: 584). Yet Spinoza is interested not only in the structure of language, but also in its functions and uses. The fact that language and writing merely approximate the truth is productive and interesting in itself. The *Theological-Political Treatise* (published 1670) is concerned with the relationship between true ideas and written words in the Bible, and between true ideas and the spoken words of prophets and clerics. The representational nature of language, its intrinsic variance with the true nature of God, becomes crucial for Spinoza's critique of religion and the ways it mobilises words and images to its ends.

Words are no less powerful for being imaginary symbols, including the words written by Spinoza himself. Indeed, the fact that words are known imaginatively means their power lies in their capacity to affect us. The *Ethics* aims to engage the reader in the geometric deduction of true ideas from one another, a process that might well involve the rational joy of understanding (see E IVP52). Yet the reader cannot get there without feeling certain passions: frustration at the difficulty of the arguments, delight in the prose of the scholia, or shock at the definition of God as nature. Similarly, the *Theological-Political Treatise* makes different readers feel different things: it causes fury in the cleric, joy in the dissident, and fear in the common man (see Spinoza's comments on this at the end of the Preface: TTP Pref. pp. 393–4). Spinoza reflected on the affective power of his own texts because he is fascinated by the power of texts – particularly the Bible – to determine feelings and actions. Textual power is explored in very different ways by Dimitris Vardoulakis on law (Chapter 7) and Nick Nesbitt on freedom (Chapter 8). Vardoulakis argues that it is the form of law, as a linguistic and textual presence (rather than its content) that is important in Spinoza's analysis in bringing about social cohesion. Nesbitt argues that the true inheritors of Spinoza's political writings are neither contemporary Marxists nor contemporary liberals, but the thinkers and agents of revolution in the late eighteenth century.

'Fictions' have a particular textual power for Spinoza. Fictions are organised systems of words and images (see TIE 51–65), including scientific hypotheses, history and literature, all of which may be more or less useful depending on the extent to which they help us reach true understanding. Spinoza regularly makes use of fictions in his own writing, including the story of Adam and Eve, the history of the Hebrew people, the poetry of Ovid, and his own thought-experiments and (assumedly) memories. The scholia of the *Ethics*, which in Deleuze's phrase (1998: 146) 'interrupt the chain of demonstrative elements', contain discursive and often lyrical elaborations on the propositions and their proofs. We should not be surprised that the *Ethics* interweaves geometric proofs with imaginative and affective stories, for as a properly *scientific* study, it shows how eternal truths, understood mathematically and expressed geometrically, come to light through imagination, and how the imaginary stuff of experience and fiction, expressed in the scholia, is clarified through rational knowledge. This theme is touched on by Mack (Chapter 2), Rawes (Chapter 4) and Calder (Chapter 9).

Spinoza is, finally, concerned with the power to transmit and obfuscate truth. This happens everywhere that humans come together, and is a particular feature of the systems organising human communities: politics and religion. The *Theological-Political Treatise* is Spinoza's investigation into and critique of these systems, containing his argument for the separation of religion from truth-oriented pursuits. Religion does not aim at discovering truth, Spinoza argues; it aims at obedience, and so for peaceful and stable relations between people at a specific historical juncture (TTP Ch. 14). The socio-political utility of religion is thereby drawn out, and its philosophical and scientific misuses castigated. If there is a human practice that is excluded from Spinoza's project of truth-seeking, it is religion. Yet this did not stop Spinoza's readers from working to reconcile his philosophy with Christian doctrine. The attempts of German Enlightenment thinkers such as Moses Mendelssohn and J. G. Herder (members of the first generation able to read Spinoza without risking their positions) to resolve the 'pantheism controversy' with such a reconciliation are fairly well known (see, for example, Lord 2011). That Samuel Taylor Coleridge made a related attempt to identify Spinozism with Christianity in the early nineteenth century is less familiar and more puzzling in its motivation, as Nicholas Halmi explains in Chapter 10.

Depending on the distribution of power in a given political system, our ability to know things truly will fare differently. Good governments facilitate the pursuit of true knowledge and virtue, and relegate religion to its proper role of promoting social cohesion through obedience; bad ones obstruct true understanding and utilise religious and other fictions to provide explanations and control human affects and activity. Spinoza's *Political Treatise* (begun 1675) has a different aim from the *Ethics* and the *Theological-Political Treatise* in that it reveals how political life is lived, rather than demonstrating how to live or criticising current conditions. Spinoza's political philosophy must be understood in the context of his view of human being introduced earlier. Not only is the human being not defined by its rationality; it is not defined by the boundaries of its interior mind. Affectivity means we are intermeshed with things outside our physical and mental boundaries – things that affect and change us constantly. Our individuality is a composite of many lesser individuals, and a component of greater ones, each of which acquires its character from its encounters and relations with others (E IIL7S). As Caroline Williams argues in Chapter 1, this implies that our subjectivity extends beyond the traditional notion of the 'subject' and its 'identity', and should be thought instead as an impersonal, affective process. Mateusz Janik continues this discussion

in Chapter 6, suggesting that thinking about collective political agency
and the move to democracy must be grounded in material processes
rather than the liberal concept of the autonomous individual.

The visual arts appear to be one area in which Spinoza thinks truth
is unlikely to be found. Scholars have stressed Spinoza's view that true
ideas are not, and cannot be encapsulated in, images (see Morrison
1989). In so far as art is representational, it is as inadequate as language
as a conveyor of truth; a historical or allegorical painting has the same
status, for Spinoza, as the story or moral lesson it represents, and is
nothing more than that by virtue of being expressed visually. In so far
as it is non-representational, art may be decorative and pleasing (and
therefore of utility to a varied life; see E IVP45S), but it cannot be the
bearer of meaning or power except by arbitrary convention or personal
association.

Yet despite the impossibility of claiming Spinoza as a thinker of
the arts, Spinoza's philosophy may be more relevant to the visual arts
today than it has been at any point in the past. No longer centrally concerned with representation (or its denial), narrative or symbol, today's
modes of artistic practice are often 'experimental' in the sense of an
ordered investigation into present experience, one that is informed by
true understanding and that seeks new knowledge. Experimental art is,
like experimental science, based on combining ordered thought with
affective experience; it explores processes of making and relating things
together in order to understand the world more clearly. In addition to
the cover art, this volume contains an 'interlude' of four artworks. They
should not be regarded as illustrations of Spinoza's thought, but, like
the chapters, as attempts at using Spinoza non- (or extra-)philosophi-
cally. The other aesthetic subjects represented here are architecture
(Chapter 4) and music (Chapter 5). In the latter, Amy Cimini discusses Spinoza's utility for taking music away from models of celestial
harmony and mind–body dualism, and towards 'sonic materiality' that
can affect us with joy.

The chapters in this book, though wide-ranging, are drawn together
by four themes: affectivity, materiality, textuality and the ethical.
Affects for Spinoza are feelings, including sensations, the images associated with them, and the emotions attached to them; the term also refers
to changes that result in a body from its being affected by another. As
we have seen, it is a key tenet of the *Ethics* that bodies affect, and are
affected by, other bodies constantly and necessarily; from breathing
and eating to our complex interactions with other people, we are *affec-
tively* part of nature. *Affectivity* might be defined as the ways physical
bodies (and, in parallel, minds) interact and combine with one another

through feeling. Spinoza has a unique way of demonstrating that the ontological basis for affectivity is epistemologically, ethically and politically significant. This theme runs strongly through the chapters in the first half of the book, which show how this idea leads to new thinking about human subjectivity (Chapters 1 and 2), ecology (Chapter 3) and architecture (Chapter 4). It also figures in Chapter 9, where a particularly Spinozan view of affectivity is seen to operate in the fiction of George Eliot.

*Materiality* does not refer to any modern variant of materialism, since to call Spinoza a materialist would ignore the central place of immaterial ideas in his system. Instead, it refers to Spinoza's refusal to reduce matter to thought, and, *contra* Descartes, his refusal to subordinate bodies to minds. Placing equal significance on the bodily-material and the mental-ideal, and maintaining that they are different expressions of the same being (different attributes of one substance, in Spinoza's words), allows for ways of thinking that depart from the Cartesian model without falling into either materialism or idealism. This theme figures in the middle chapters of the book. Materiality dominates the discussion of musicology in Chapter 5 and political collectives in Chapter 6. It is also significant for the three artists whose work is presented in the 'interlude' between these chapters.

The last four chapters of the book have *textuality* as their central theme. This theme in one sense combines the first two, for what is meant by this term is the affective impacts that texts have, as material objects, on human passions and actions. We have seen already that Spinoza is particularly interested in the affective and material impacts the Bible has had throughout its history. Chapter 7 considers how texts of political theology make us understand the operation of power. In the last three chapters we see the impacts that Spinoza's texts have had historically: on the French and Haitian revolutions (Chapter 8), on George Eliot and the ethical potential of her literature (Chapter 9), and on Samuel Taylor Coleridge's ecumenical thinking (Chapter 10).

Finally, *the ethical* is a theme linking together all ten chapters of the book. Ethical philosophy concerns how to live (as opposed to moral philosophy, which concerns transcendent values of good and bad). All the book's authors consider how Spinoza's thought helps us to find new ways of living, and thereby explore the ethical dimension of their own disciplines. The authors come from different disciplinary backgrounds, but all converge on the significance of Spinoza's thought for addressing contemporary problems. Taking Spinoza *beyond* philosophy is not, however, a matter of closing off his metaphysics and epistemology. Rather, it is a matter of seeing how his deeply philosophical thought immanently contains the resources for new thinking about the arts, the sciences and the social sciences. It is a matter of seeing how *any* philosophical thinking necessarily generates other kinds of thinking.

# BIBLIOGRAPHY

Althusser, Louis (1973), *Essays in Self-Criticism*, London: New Left Books.

Badiou, Alain (2004), *Theoretical Writings*, ed. and trans. Ray Brassier and Alberto Toscano, London: Continuum.

Balibar, Etienne (1998), *Spinoza and Politics*, trans. P. Snowdon, London: Verso.

Damasio, Antonio (2004), *Looking for Spinoza: Joy, Sorrow, and the Feeling Brain*, London: Vintage.

Della Rocca, Michael (1996), *Representation and the Mind–Body Problem in Spinoza*, Oxford: Oxford University Press.

Deleuze, Gilles (1998), *Essays Critical and Clinical*, trans. Daniel W. Smith and Michael A. Greco, London: Verso.

Feuer, Lewis Samuel (1958), *Spinoza and the Rise of Liberalism*, Boston: Beacon.

Gatens, Moira (ed.) (2009), *Feminist Interpretations of Benedict Spinoza*, University Park: Pennsylvania State University Press.

Lord, Beth (2011), *Kant and Spinozism: Transcendental Idealism and Immanence from Jacobi to Deleuze*, Basingstoke: Palgrave Macmillan.

Morrison, James (1989), 'Why Spinoza Had No Aesthetics', *Journal of Aesthetics and Art Criticism* 47(4), pp. 359–65.

Negri, Antonio (1991), *The Savage Anomaly*, trans. M. Hardt, Minneapolis: University of Minnesota Press.

Norris, Christopher (2011), 'Spinoza and the Conflict of Interpretations', in D. Vardoulakis (ed.), *Spinoza Now*, Minneapolis: University of Minnesota Press, pp. 3–37.

Savan, David (1958), 'Spinoza and Language', *Philosophical Review* 67(2), pp. 212–25.

Smith, Steven B. (1997), *Spinoza, Liberalism, and the Question of Jewish Identity*, New Haven, CT: Yale University Press.

Spinoza, Benedictus de (1994), *A Spinoza Reader*, ed. and trans. E. Curley, Princeton: Princeton University Press.

Spinoza, Benedictus de (2002), *Complete Works*, trans. S. Shirley, ed. M. L. Morgan, Indianapolis: Hackett.

# 1. 'Subjectivity Without the Subject': Thinking Beyond the Subject with / through Spinoza

CAROLINE WILLIAMS

The problematisation and reconfiguration of the concept of the subject has long been a central preoccupation of philosophy. It also continues to orient discussions beyond philosophy, from neuroscience, ethics and philosophy, to aesthetics, architecture and science. Indeed, in recent years, a number of contemporary writers have returned to Spinoza in order to pursue such reconfigurations. They have done so primarily because Spinoza's political and philosophical writings offer many interesting reflections upon the affective composition of 'subjects' – although I admit to using this term rather cautiously since here I begin to question its precise theoretical utility and conceptual shape. What might it mean to discuss such a concept in the context of an early modern thinker who rarely utilises the term, and whose ontology, it may be argued, precludes the kind of metaphysics that historically accompanies philosophical reflections upon subjectivity?[1]

Without, at this stage, naming any philosophical approaches or proper names, we can observe the many acrobatic conceptual feats that have, in recent years, been performed by or through the *medium* of the subject. Deconstructed and displaced, distributed along chains of signification, interpellated via discursive and / or ideological formations, invoked at another place, present only in its absence, or through its effects, or as a lack, we might concur that the fate (indeed, the *necessary fate*) of the subject has been to *persist* in our philosophical grammar (albeit via new theoretical inflections), and yet to *desist* or *escape* our grasp (a somewhat slippery, as well as a *ticklish*, subject (see Žižek 1999)). Perhaps we might even be able to agree, in the wake of post-structuralism, that what we call the concept of the subject can only be utilised in critical thinking with due regard to the philosophical paradox which frames its ontological and political emergence.[2]

This paradox can take many different forms and shapes. One of its best-known formations is to be found in the Kantian problematic so aptly described by Foucault in *The Order of Things*: namely, the idea of the empirico-transcendental doublet – where the subject as the condition of possibility for knowledge is doubled as the subject in the world with all the inherent limits placed by finitude upon thought (Foucault 1970). Whatever the form of this paradox, however, in contemporary post-structuralist thought the essence of the problem is clear: the concept of the subject must be radically *displaced* from philosophical thought and yet it remains a *requirement* of analysis. In other words, references to the problem of *the* subject often seem to assume the existence of some form of subjectivity to be worked upon or undone, even though it is precisely this 'subject' which is open to question. We often embrace a critical rendering of the subject, then, even in approaches that endeavour to destabilise it. The nature of this paradox has been nicely captured in Althusser's deployment of the spectre of the subject as *always-already* a subject: moreover, a subject whose emergence is perpetually bound up with its subjugation to ideology (see Althusser 1971). Indeed, the history of this aporia inherent in the subject has been traced recently by Etienne Balibar, where 'the introduction of *subject* into philosophy is doubled with the avatars of *subjectum* and *subjectus*' (Balibar 2006: 16). On the one hand, this has a logico-grammatical and philosophical function, where the subject is a laying forth or a lying under, as in a ground, support or predicate for knowledge; and on the other hand, it has a politico-juridical function: under a rule, submitted, subjected. This mechanism has been radicalised further by Judith Butler, for whom the subject carries this paradox *within* itself, where subjection is presented as a general trope or retroactive 'turning' of the subject back upon itself to delineate the very possibility of subjectivity. There is, then, an attachment or relation to the outside (as power, language), some activity or form that incites the subject to take its place as the bearer of a language, a right or a norm, to become a political subject (see Butler 1997, Introduction).

It is partly the aim of this chapter to begin to excavate the ground of this labyrinthine paradox of subjectivity and to explore the theoretical and ethico-political consequences implied by this *redoubling* process of subjectivation, which produces both the subject and its subjection. Its stronger contention, however, is that a thinking of the *space* of the subject, and its complex conditions of production and existence, can perhaps only be advanced once we begin to question the precise theoretical and political *utility* of the concept of the subject. This is not a naïve request for a return to structuralism, if we understand by this move a theoretical decision to erase the subject and the question of experience from philosophy. Neither is it an evocation to erase the paradox of the subject itself. Rather, as I suggest here, a more measured reflection is called for: one that acknowledges the myriad ways through which the subject has been untangled by post-structuralism and rendered ambivalent at its site of production, and one that also stays close to the *productivity* of the paradox. In his *Philosophical Fragments*, Kierkegaard identifies the paradox as the passion of thought 'wanting to discover something that thought cannot think,' something without foundation or presupposition (Kierkegaard 1985: 37). As troubling burden and as passion, the form of the paradox offers the movement of thought a chance or opening through which to think new figures and concepts of political subjectivity.

It is in this context that I propose to think about subjectivity *without* the subject (whether this be without borders, identity, interiority, ground or destiny): that is, as an anonymous, generic process with varying qualities or functions (in contemporary thought this has been variously presented as a truth event, a plane of immanence, a game of truth), which itself subjectivises and produces something of the order of a 'political subject'. The term I develop here – namely, 'subjectivity as a process without a subject' – is a variation of Althusser's formulation of history 'as a process without a Subject or Goal', but this discussion will not return us to a structuralist paradigm, which is overly reductive of the richness of Althusser's writings (extending from structural contingency and overdetermination in his early writings to philosopher of the aleatory encounter in his later ones; see, for example, Althusser 1990, 2003). Despite the many tensions framing the respective projects of Althusser and Badiou (and I think there are also many fertile connections that I have begun to explore elsewhere; see Williams 2012b), Badiou still credits Althusser with the opening up of 'this enigma of subjectivity without a subject as the intra-philosophical mark of politics' (Badiou 2005: 64). It is to this kind of discussion that I wish my paper to contribute. To this end, I aim to utilise Spinoza, by placing his philosophical claims in dialogue with contemporary efforts to think subjectivity without a subject, whilst remaining mindful of the paradoxical status of this formulation.

First, however, a brief note on my reading of Spinoza: My aim here is to think *with* and *through* Spinoza, rather than attempt to interpret, for a contemporary audience, aspects of his philosophy and political thought. The degree to which I am faithful to Spinoza might, of course, be questioned; I do not consider the *Ethics* and related writings as having a single aim, and in a broader project I aim to unravel the effects of various concepts, identifying some of these as 'limit-concepts' that may subvert and disrupt the consistency of his argument (these concepts are *conatus* and imagination, which together point to the richness of Spinoza's political ontology). Following Pierre Macherey, I intend to think Spinoza's 'philosophical actuality' (Macherey 1998: Ch. 9). I hope to demonstrate the ways in which Spinoza's thought is deeply relevant for a thinking *beyond* the subject. This key contribution can be briefly indicated now and will be elaborated in the course of the discussion. Central to my argument is a reading of the twin concepts of encounter and relation in Spinoza's ontology that allows one to theorise consciousness and subjectivity as impersonal *processes without a subject*, as well as to give prominence to the question of our ethico-political existence. Being both *extensive* (its field recognises no distinction, difference or opposition between the human and non-human, the natural or the cultural) and *intensive* (it draws our attention to the fluidity, vacillation and intensity of affective relations flowing between all things), this ontology of encounter precludes ideas of containment and boundary and allows us to think the agency of bodies (understood in *broad* physico-corporeal terms) in new and exciting ways.

## SPINOZA AGAINST THE SUBJECT?

Significantly, we find very few (only two) direct references to the subject in Spinoza's philosophy (and yet its central theme is our freedom and knowledge of causality).[3] On the one hand, this is clearly because the empirico-transcendental doublet had yet to crystallise in thought, had yet to master the elements governing its formation and hence find its way – and its voice – in philosophical discourse. There is, arguably, no grammatical 'I' in Spinoza's philosophy. On the other hand, it is simply because both Spinoza's view of the world as substance, coupled with what I have called above his ontology of encounter, *require* no theory or faculty of consciousness as interiority, since their very starting point precludes the kind of containment or identity that generally accompanies such a theory. Indeed, much of the contemporary interest in Spinoza has tended to view him 'as an adversary of subjectivity' (see Balibar (1992) for discussion). We need only recall, for example, Althusser's insistence, in his *Essays in Self-Criticism*, that he was a Spinozist and not a structuralist; and again, that his rejection of humanism was, like Spinoza's, a *strategic* rejection of the various anthropocentric (for Althusser, ideological) perspectives governing their respective times of writing (Althusser 1973, 1997). In contrast, Badiou's quite challenging textual reading finds in the *Ethics* the surging forth of a subject or subject-effect, a supposition that is without ground, undecidable and atypical in form (Badiou 2006).[4]

If Spinoza is no subjectivist (at least not in any straightforward sense), then neither is he an objectivist. Such a one-dimensional, epistemological reading of Spinoza would be detrimental to the kind of project initiated here. To view his philosophy as seeking objectivity is also to render it incoherent in some respects, since a *disregard for the problem of the subject does not necessarily entail a subsequent disregard for the problematic and effects of subjectivity itself*. Indeed, this latter concern emerges through several dimensions in the *Ethics*, where the discussion of individuals, bodies, ideas, affect, desire, power (*potentia*) and imagination takes place. This is not the place for a detailed discussion of the ontological themes of the *Ethics*, many of which have generated intricate and lively debates within Spinoza studies (and are also broached by other chapters in this volume). However, it is important to situate briefly, within the broader context of Spinoza's philosophy, the kind of reading of subjectivity (without the subject) that I propose to develop here.

## SPINOZA: 'THE FIRST THINKER OF THE WORLD' (NANCY 1998: 54)

As Jacques Derrida reminds us in one of his brief, yet provocative, remarks on the philosopher, it is Spinoza who 'disturbs the schema of philosophical thinking'; he does not narrate a story about the history of philosophy, nor does he insist upon putting things in a teleological framework (Derrida cited in Bernasconi 1987: 96). His is a strategic, political engagement, which aims to overturn all political, religious and philosophical logics of transcendence. Hegel's reading of the Spinoza who develops a determinist and all-embracing view of Substance, within which the dynamic of agency is ontologically fixed and foreclosed, fails to appreciate the attention given by Spinoza in the *Ethics* to the relational character of Substance, as well as to the *finite* mode of existing in the world. Drawing upon the more nuanced readings of Deleuze, Macherey and others,[5] I wish to present a view of Spinoza's concept of an infinite and infinitely variable, non-teleological Substance expressed *perpetually* in the infinite forms of being (by which Spinoza means the attributes, of which mind and body are but two). There is no loss of power for finite things here, including the human being, since Substance (by which Spinoza understands *Deus, sive Natura*) is an immanent structure producing complex relations and events through which finite being is constituted. All individual things in the world (whatever species or form) must be understood as *modifications* of the infinite variability of substance; but they must not be viewed as simply its reflections or determinations. If they might have substance as their immanent *cause*, they will none the less interact with other finite things in diverse ways (according to their unique composition and disposition), generate their own specific effects and, over time, recompose or degenerate in structure. The human mind (and, as we shall see below, consciousness too) is precisely such a finite mode flowing from the immanence of substance yet also being determined to act through the mediation of other finite modes. Understood according to an immanent causality – that is, as giving rise to both the totality of causes *and* their effects, substance is an inexhaustible, relational system folded into – and out of – natural and human life. There is no brute nature, no clear division between natural and cultural, biological and social realities; we may better think of these realities on the model of a continuum, of the becoming culture of nature, or the virtual field of the socio-political. When, in IP29S, Spinoza distinguishes between *Natura naturans* (literally, nature *naturing*) and *Natura naturata* (that is, nature *natured*), he has in mind what Georges Canguilhem has called the 'poetic horizon of *natura naturans*' (Canguilhem 1994: 311), which takes note of nature's generativity and movement rather than focusing upon some quasi-agentic (and hence anthropomorphic) *capacity* of nature / Substance. It is this dynamic formulation that underscores Spinoza's view of a complex, layered materialism and informs the qualified account of the subject developed here.

Now, if Spinoza's point of reference is not the anthropocentric subject (which is deconstructed in the Appendix to Part I of the *Ethics*), then it is crucial to underscore the classical conception of 'individual' embraced in his approach. An *individuum* is a composite of differential relations between bodies / things, and it can refer to human and non-human forms alike. Indeed, an important aspect of Spinoza's ontology (that is, in addition to its radical thesis of the non-teleological and infinite variability of Substance) has to be the constitutive relationality established in his approach, which calls into question the existence of boundaries between individual things. Relation, here, must not simply be thought as a link, connection or association between two or more discrete objects; relation is literally a 'taking in hand' (see the discussion in Massumi 2002: Ch. 3), a production of something that did not exist before and which, through the process of relation, becomes an aspect of that thing's existence. Furthermore, when a body is in motion – and we might agree with this dynamic ontology that there is always the potential for variation, then the body will always exceed or overflow its current state. To be an individual is always to be composed of *other* bodies. The more complex a body, then, the more relations it will have with other bodies, and the more its identity will be compatible with a great many *different* entities. An individual can be a rock, an animal, a linguistic corpus, a collective, a storm, and, of course, all individuals are subject to infinite variability and possibility. A collective individual of a political kind, Spinoza noted, may under certain conditions become *demos* or recompose as *vulgas*, just as, in Steve Barbone's example, the mass of flowing water combines with other natural forces to become the storm (Barbone 2002). Jean-Luc Nancy makes a similar point, in *Being Singular Plural*, when he writes, although without allusion to Spinoza:

> I would no longer be human if I were not a body, a spacing of all other bodies and a spacing of 'me' in 'me'. A singularity is always a body, and all bodies are singularities (the bodies, their states, their movements, their transformations. (Nancy 2000: 18)

To be an individual, then, is to be a (shared) centre of action or *potentia* (or relations of motion and rest), and also to interact dynamically and in various ways with a network of other individuals. It is also to participate in a kind of virtual reality of possibility, that which Brian Massumi calls (after Foucault) an *incorporeal materialism* (Massumi 2002: 5). It is precisely these relations (which in turn give rise to an interdependency between parts – with, we might note, important ethical and communicative implications) that construct the individual. Individuals can be simple and more complex, from atoms and cells, to multi-cell organisms and institutions to, as Spinoza writes, 'the whole of Nature . . . whose parts i.e. all bodies, vary in infinite ways, without any change of the whole Individual' (E IIP13L7S): *the greater the order of complexity*, we might say, *the greater the power to interact with the rest of nature*. There can be, therefore, no view of the human individual as *imperium in imperio* (a kingdom within a kingdom), as somehow independent of nature. Instead, the individual must be conceived metabolically, as it was in Marx's *Paris Manuscripts* too, as 'part of nature', as intimately woven into a *natural, social and material* web of relations upon which it depends, and by which it is continually affected.[6] There is, then, a dynamic reciprocity between the unity of substance and the multiplicity of 'individuals' which is always more than the simple exchange between two parts.

It follows from this reading that to write in the *spirit* of Spinoza, in the context of this ontology of relation and encounter, one can have recourse to the subject only in an overdetermined sense: that is, only by recognising that the subject is not simply produced or constructed by an external structure, power, norm or ideology. Rather, what we might tentatively call 'the subject' only appears in this ontological scene as a temporary (that is, as variable, unstable and, with reference to Badiou, an always *rare*) form that is always *more than a subject*. The modern subject, on this reading, is that ontological excess generated through a specific series of relations and spacings constituting the modern age.

## BESIDE HERSELF WITH JOY

A prime example of the practice of the ontology of encounter and relation described in the previous section can be found in Spinoza's discussion of affect. The section heading above captures nicely the argument I wish to pursue here, since I understand affect, with Spinoza, as exceeding the subject. In a letter to one of his more enquiring readers, Spinoza remarks that it is to Epicurus, Democritus and Lucretius that he turns to locate the instruments to think about the experience of consciousness and imagination (Letter 56). In the Preface to Part III of the *Ethics*, we learn of his intention to understand the landscape of passion and action after the ancient atomists 'as if it were an investigation into lines, planes, or bodies' (E IIIPref.). Ethics thus becomes a kind of psycho-physics, for Spinoza, who proceeds in a materialist way by recognising the irreducible complexity of the passions that cannot be attributed to the agency or intentions of the will. This is not merely because, as Lucretius understands it in *The Nature of the Universe*, the mind is located in the central part of the breast (Lucretius [55 BC] 1994: Book III 135–45).[7] Neither is it, as neuroscientist and Spinozist Antonio Damasio notes, because much of our emotional experience takes place 'in the theatre of the body under the guidance of a congenitally wise brain designed by evolution to help manage the body' (Damasio 2003: 79). It is simply because affect cannot be housed by either body *or* mind and is often viewed as overflowing the subject who experiences it. Massumi describes it as a *'prepersonal intensity* corresponding to the passage from one experiential state of the body to another and implying an augmentation or diminution in that body's capacity to act' (Massumi 1988: xvi). As transitive links between states of affairs, affects pass through subjects communicating and unfolding images and intensities. They are, in a certain sense, *semiotic* as well as materialist. Spinoza describes them as images and corporeal traces (see E IIP17) that are eventually materialised in signs, norms, social and political practices, modes of living and ethical relations.[8] Denise

Riley underscores this impersonal and semiotic aspect of affect when she writes of the 'affect-soaked power of language', 'a forcible affect of language which courses like blood through its speakers' (Riley 2005: 5, 1). Thus affect passes *through, between* and *beyond* the subjects who remain, to all intents and purposes, its effects, its subversions and its point of torsion, anchoring identity (to varying degrees) though its normative displays and often *compelling* or inciting the subject to act, to take its place.

It is, then, according to a field of circulating flows and affective relations that we can best understand the passions that appear to become our own. Their composition, strength and power will be determined by the speed and slowness of interaction, the relations of agreement and disagreement surrounding them, and especially by the degree of intensity moderating their motion and mode of communication between bodies. In this way, affects are best understood as transitive states through which bodies pass; they meander through and between bodies, resting like 'foreign objects,' or excessive impersonal forces, awaiting transformation into the thought-imbued emotions of subjective experience.[9] Spinoza explores this field of possible experience, this force field, via the concept of the *conatus* as the *fractural* site through which affects have to pass. It is arguably the *conatus* which is the only concept in the *Ethics* able to account for the unfolding of affective life. It must be linked, in this final part of our discussion, to *imagination*, which in turn functions as the vehicle through which the experience of affect is galvanised. In place of the negative reading of Spinoza's imagination as a figment or error to be overcome by reason, I understand imagination as an anonymous *conductor* of affects circulating within and between bodies.[10] Indeed, it might be this very problematic that is alluded to by Althusser when he writes in his autobiographical reflections of finding in the heretical Spinoza not only the 'matrix of every *possible* theory of ideology' but also 'the *materiality of its very existence*' (Althusser 1997: 7, 10).

It is in Part III of the *Ethics*, entitled 'Concerning the Origin and Nature of the Affects', that the basis for the investigation into the physics of bodies and the various intensities that accompany them may be found. Here, Spinoza understands the human *conatus* as tied to desire; indeed, consciousness is not a *faculty* of the subject but a relational or transindividual *process* emerging out of this understanding of desire as conative striving. As such, it is a dynamic structure beset with tensions and possibilities ripe for transformation. In so far as the human body requires many other bodies to preserve and regenerate itself, and the affects are always turned towards others, the *conatus* is part of an intrahuman dynamic and in consequence will give rise to a matrix of psychic and social conflict, relations of agreement and disagreement that cohere to varying degrees in the imagination.

In Part II of the *Ethics*, Spinoza understands imagination as a form of corporeal awareness connecting the body's affects to understanding. His broad elaboration of imagination exceeds its presentation as a subjective faculty and emphasises instead its collective and anonymous structure. Given that the body retains *traces* of the changes brought about through interactions with other bodies, imagination will reflect the diverse ways in which bodies are affected by particular experiences, such that one is effectively many. Thus Spinoza writes that 'the human mind perceives a great many bodies together with the nature of its own body' (E IIP16C1). He further considers how the recollection of one experience may trigger imaginative associations with similar ones. In this way, imagination, image and memory are intimately tied to affective and corporeal existence. Furthermore, there will always exist an unconscious *affectus imitatio* within the process of imaginary identifications constituting a political body as citizens of a *demos*, a nation and so on. Thus, 'if we imagine something like us to be affected with the same affect, this imagination will express an affection of our Body like this affect' (E IIIP27). This dynamic psychic relation is at work in the composition (and decomposition) of individuals and groups alike. Whilst 'we *strive to further* the occurrence of whatever we imagine will lead to Joy, and to avert or destroy what we imagine is contrary to it, or will lead to Sadness' (E IIIP28) – that is, to strengthen the *active* affects – it is also the case that any common object or image of love or hope will be inseparable from hatred or fear caused by imagining a common evil opposed to this notion of goodness. In this way, the affects are subject to vacillation or ambivalence (*fluctuatio animi*), and the object or image of the other can be the cause of many conflicting passions (see E IIIP17S). Thus the mind can be drawn, *at one and the same time*, towards passive and active affects. Affects such as love may be built upon hatred, fears upon nascent hopes, and sadness upon hidden joys. The knot tied here between ignorance and knowledge, passion and turbulence, the dependence on others, objects, relations without which no persistence is possible, implicates desire in a structure of ambivalence that may deconstitute and unravel the subject who endeavours to persist in being. In this way, the power of the affects, whilst *appearing* to originate in the power of life or *conatus*, nonetheless *fold back upon this being and contribute to its very subjection*.

It should come as no surprise that contemporary thinkers of the political subject should find in Spinoza resources for theorising the process of subjectivity without the subject. For example, approaches to the discursive construction of power, knowledge, subjectivity and norms by Foucault and Butler (where norms are understood not only to discipline and seek mastery over the field of possible experiences but also, by creating affective ties, to activate and produce that very field) are certainly Nietzschean in many respects, but they also point – albeit somewhat elusively at times – to an interest in Spinoza's theory of immanent causality discussed above. Interestingly, as Butler's writings have developed a more nuanced account of the constitution of the subject and the internalisation of norms, she has increasingly fleshed out her ontological commitments with reference to Spinoza rather than Hegel and Lacan. Nonetheless, in drawing attention to Spinoza's concept of *conatus*, as 'passionate attachment to existence', a 'desire to be' or 'a striving to persist in being', a *potentia* or possibility that governs the subject, she also risks essentialising and naturalising it as subjective desire (Butler 2005: 43–4).

The reading here presents *conatus* as a fractural field of affective relations rather than a primary drive towards persistence and preservation. Together with the anonymous structure of imagination, it works to undo and decompose the subject. Understood through this relational site of production, which also twists and unravels that which it produces, the subject is a doubly inscribed register of being, moving back and forth across this affective terrain, perpetually affected by the encounters and practices surrounding it. The imitative structure discussed above is not simply induced *by* the subject; rather, this structure forms the mimetic process of identification for a subject. It is through the dispersal and circulation of affects (which simultaneously produces identity and unravels, or withdraws from its completion) that subjectivity is retroactively produced. In other words, there is no subject of the affect, because affect drives the subject towards identity and performance. This is not to say that the dispersed subject presented here harbours some ontological lack or negativity within itself. There is a sense in which (as Jean-Luc Nancy (1997: 33) also observes) Spinoza wants to think finite being in its immediate (immanent) relations without the mediation (transcendence) which ceaselessly re-opens a gap, or hole, in the subject. It is important to recall that, for Spinoza, philosophy is a meditation on life and not death (see E IVP67). Thus, when I argue that the *conatus* labours also to untie, to deconstitute, the subject, this is because the wider relations within which it circulates, and where it aspires, or strives, to seek unity, render it fragile and open to possible dissolution, as well as provisional states of unity.

## CONCLUSION

What might the fleshing out of this conception of *conatus* (along with imagination) bring to our thinking about, through or beyond, the 'subject'? Some liberal commentators have reduced this quantum of vital force to an egocentric appetite for survival or self-preservation, perhaps underestimating the way in which the *conatus* must also operate as a movement that goes constantly beyond the present, hence signifying an openness to the future: a condition of ontological expansion (see Jonas 1974; Yovel 1999). With reference to psychoanalysis, it has been argued strongly by Slavoj Žižek that Spinoza's concept of *conatus* is unable to conceive the 'elementary "twist" of dialectical inversion characterising negativity' and associated with Lacan's own theorisation of lack (see Žižek 2003: 33–41). If we follow the reading of Spinoza's ontology developed here, the *conatus* requires no internal (ontologically drawn) boundary or containment, no limitation or *Spaltung*, no deathly force, no negativity and no lack. Whilst one may draw parallels with psychoanalytic theory, given that the *conatus* in its human shape is a form of *desire*, this does not arise as 'a presence from a background of absence' as it does for Lacan. *Contra* Žižek, it may indeed be argued that Spinoza's philosophy certainly offers the conceptual resources to theorise an unconscious dynamic of ethico-political existence. That the *conatus* is an abundant and wholly *positive* energy that pulsates through bodies and is not wholly contained or controlled by them *does not* imply that it cannot be used to understand the decomposition, unravelling, in short, the ambivalent structure of subjectivity. What psychoanalysts call the death drive perhaps becomes in Spinoza a reaction to certain ethico-political states of being rather than an originary drive (see Williams 2010).

Indeed, the configuration of the *conatus* presented here allows one to respond (in three distinct ways) to those positions that attach a possessive or naturalistic formulation to it. First, it enables a consideration of how the *conatus* of complex individuals (or a higher-order composite like an ecosystem or a social organisation) might promote its persistence by actively tending towards greater interaction with its environment. It also follows that what we have called the human subject extends *infinitely* beyond the boundaries of the singular body, giving a whole new sense to what we might understand by the parallelism or identity of mind and body. If this ontological argument is taken seriously, one might suggest, to paraphrase Nietzsche, that the subject is an excessive multiplicity. What we understand by an individual's autonomy or freedom would be a function of this internal multiplicity, or external / internal relations – that which Deleuze, in his readings of the folding of subjectivation in Foucault, refers to as *folded force* (Deleuze 1988b). Second, the possessive formulation of the *conatus* appears to ignore how the relational character of bodies described above gives rise to a dynamic 'ratio of forces' which is incessantly modified and affected, hence underscoring the *communicative* aspects of the *conatus* that can be a source of conflict and disintegration in so far as disagreements between bodies occur (see also Balibar 1997). It also seriously underplays the linkage between the *conatus* and imagination. The *conatus* works upon and mobilises the imagination, which acts as a kind of impersonal conductor of affects in Spinoza's *Ethics*. It harbours the memory traces of experiences and reflects the diverse ways in which bodies are affected. Given the vacillations intrinsic to affective relations, the *conatus* will give rise to a matrix of psychic and social conflict with important political effects.

Finally, in assuming some kind of self-referential notion of preservation, the formulation ignores the sense in which non-human 'individuals' also have a *conatus*. Some readings of Spinoza's extension of the category of individual to, for example, the state argue that this translates, literally and illegitimately, Spinoza's 'ontological physics' into the political realm (Rice 1990). However, this translation of the term 'individual' makes perfect sense in the context of the argument developed here; it also bears interesting resemblances to the recent work of Bruno Latour (2004) and Jane Bennett (2004; 2010). However, in claiming that the analysis cannot be recast in this way (that the state, or indeed any other kind of 'body', cannot *act* as an individual), Spinoza's liberal critics collapse and reduce the rich resource of his ontology into a form of methodological individualism. Their reading also captures Spinoza's philosophy within an anthropomorphic circle where every collective form must be reduced to the discrete individuals who comprise it, or else be understood pejoratively as an organic whole.[11]

I have not said much about the kind of politics engendered by this reading of an anonymous process of subjectivation, and I will not do more than sketch out some of the implications (see Janik in this volume for further consideration). What can Spinoza contribute to this problematisation of the subject's simultaneous emergence and subjection, and how might this focus on relationality inform the paradox of the subject noted in my introduction?

I have tried to indicate a certain kind of genealogy of ideas from Spinoza to the present. For Spinoza, the subject emerges (in his time) as a result of multiple practices of despotic and religious power that feed on (but also nurture and incite) the ambivalence and vacillation characteristic of affective life. For Spinoza (as for Althusser, Foucault and Butler), is it precisely *bodies* that are at stake in practices of subjection, and a pluralised (or collective) body too, since the body *is* subject and contains its own complex twistings and turnings, which are part of power's modifications. But it is also *more than the subject*; it overflows the subject and thus expands the scene of agency. If affects are relations occurring in the space between individuals, traversing and composing singular knots of subjectivity *as their effect*, then interiority is constituted by these very relations. Spinoza, on my reading, is not quite the ethical optimist he is often presumed to be; his understanding and sensitive portrayal of human passivity and the mobility and ambivalence attached to affective life allow us to think the provisionality / openness of the subject, as well as the ethico-political relation between subjects in new and exciting ways.

## NOTES

1. Aspects of this argument have also been extensively developed in my recent article, 'Affective Processes Without a Subject' (Williams 2010), and my forthcoming article, 'Geographies of Consciousness: Reconfiguring the Subject in the Wake of Spinoza' (forthcoming 2013).
2. On the tension between structuralism and post-structuralist theories of the subject see Balibar (2003) and Williams (2012a).
3. We find only two direct references to the subject as *subjectum* in Spinoza's *Ethics*, both of which occur in relation to the first kind of knowledge, where an imaginative, self-consistent subject finds its freedom in *ignorance* of the nature of things, and the realm of causality (see E IIIP5; VA1).
4. One of the great controversies in Spinoza's philosophy concerns the relation between the infinite and finite. Badiou maintains that, because of his foreclosure of the void, Spinoza cannot account for this relation, producing a rift between the two and no adequate account of the sources of presentation, of world, in the empty set (the void). This precludes chance, excess and the subject. Badiou therefore argues that the priority of God / Substance fails and that it is here that the Subject surges forth. Badiou develops this argument in his *Theoretical Writings*, where the intellect, as a kind of singularity, the localised instance of God, occupies a fold / productive point of torsion, which acts back upon the structure.
5. Of particular influence upon my own interpretations have been Deleuze (1988a, 1990), Macherey (1987, 1998), Balibar (1997, 1998), Negri (1991), Montag (1999) and Morfino (2006).
6. See Klein (2003) for an interesting discussion of the theme of metabolism in relation to Spinoza and subjectivity.
7. It is well known that Spinoza's library contained a copy of this work by Lucretius.

8. Interestingly, in the *Four Fundamental Concepts of Psychoanalysis* and in one of his very few references to Spinoza, Lacan goes so far as to align what is sometimes read off (less often now) as Spinoza's pantheism with 'the reduction of the field of God to the universality of the signifier' (Lacan 1979: 275). For a fascinating reading of this relation, see Kordela (2007).

9. It should be noted that there remains an unevenness in definitional rigour adopted by theorists in discussions around affect. There still exists a tendency to treat affect as an emotional state rather than pointing to an important distinction between the two. Following Spinoza, Massumi rightly distinguishes between affect and emotion, where the former is bodily and autonomic while the latter is a qualified, subjective, situation-specific experience. Judith Butler refers to the agency of desire as a 'foreign object' in her analysis of Kafka's *The Punishment*. See Butler (2005: 74).

10. Here my analysis draws upon but seeks to press further the reading of imagination presented in the work of Balibar (1994) and Gatens and Lloyd (1999).

11. Of course, it is not just liberal theories that tend to follow this course; in many of its forms, structuralism too displaced humanism only by endowing some *other* order or system of rules with intentionality and unity. As I pointed out in the Introduction, my argument endeavours to go beyond a structuralist paradigm.

# BIBLIOGRAPHY

Althusser, Louis (1971), *Essays on Ideology*, London: New Left Books.

Althusser, Louis (1973), *Essays in Self-Criticism*, London: New Left Books.

Althusser, Louis (1990), *For Marx*, London: Verso.

Althusser, Louis (1997), 'The Only Materialist Tradition, Part 1: Spinoza', in W. Montag and T. Stolze (eds), *The New Spinoza*, Minneapolis: Minnesota University Press.

Althusser, Louis (2003), *Philosophy of the Encounter: Later Writings, 1978–1987*, London: Verso.

Badiou, Alain (2005), *Metapolitics*, London: Verso.

Badiou, Alain (2006), *Badiou: Theoretical Writings*, ed. R. Brassier and A. Toscano, London: Continuum.

Balibar, Etienne (1992), 'A Note on "Consciousness / Conscience" in the *Ethics*', *Spinoza Spinozana* 8, pp. 37–53.

Balibar, Etienne (1994), 'Spinoza, the Anti-Orwell: The Fear of the Masses', in *Masses, Classes, Ideas: Studies on Politics and Philosophy Before and After Marx*, London: Routledge.

Balibar, Etienne (1997), 'Spinoza: From Individuality to Transindividuality', *Mededelingen Vanwege het Spinozahauis*, Delft: Eburon.

Balibar, Etienne (1998), *Spinoza and Politics*, trans. P. Snowdon, London: Verso.

Balibar, Etienne (2003), 'Structuralism: A Destitution of the Subject', *differences* 14(1), pp. 1–21.

Balibar, Etienne, et al. (2006), 'Subject', *Radical Philosophy* 138, pp. 15–41.

Barbone, Steven (2002), 'What Counts as an Individual for Spinoza?', in Olli Koistinen and John Biro (eds), *Spinoza: Metaphysical Themes*, New York: Oxford University Press, pp. 89–112.

Bennett, Jane (2004), 'The Force of Things: Steps Towards an Ecology of Matter', *Political Theory* 32(3), pp. 347–72.

Bennett, Jane (2010), *Vibrant Matter: A Political Ecology of Things*, Durham, NC: Duke University Press.

Bernasconi, Robert (1987), 'Descartes in the History of Being: Another Bad Novel?', *Research in Phenomenology* 17, pp. 75–102.

Butler, Judith (1997), *The Psychic Life of Power*, Stanford: Stanford University Press.

Butler, Judith (2005), *Giving an Account of Oneself*, New York: Fordham University Press.

Canguilhem, Georges (1994), *A Vital Rationalist*, New York: Zone.

Damasio, Antonio (2003), *Looking for Spinoza: Joy, Sorrow and the Feeling Brain*, London: William Heinemann.

Deleuze, Gilles (1988a), *Spinoza: Practical Philosophy*, trans. R. Hurley, San Francisco: City Lights.

Deleuze, Gilles (1988b), *Foucault*, trans. Sean Hand, Minneapolis: University of Minnesota Press.

Deleuze, Gilles (1990), *Expressionism in Philosophy: Spinoza*, trans. M. Joughin, New York: Zone.

Foucault, Michel (1970), *The Order of Things*, London: Tavistock.

Gatens, Moira, and Genevieve Lloyd (1999), *Collective Imaginings: Spinoza, Past and Present*, London: Routledge.

Jonas, Hans (1974), *Philosophical Essays: From Ancient Creed to Technological Man*, Chicago: Chicago University Press.

Kierkegaard, Soren (1985), *Philosophical Fragments*, Princeton: Princeton University Press.

Klein, Julie (2003), 'Nature's Metabolism: On Eating in Derrida, Agamben and Spinoza', *Research in Phenomenology* 33, pp. 186–217.

Kordela, Kiarina A. (2007), *$urplus: Spinoza, Lacan*, New York: SUNY.

Lacan, Jacques (1979), *Four Fundamental Concepts of Psychoanalysis*, Harmondsworth: Penguin.

Latour, Bruno (2004), *Politics of Nature: How to Bring the Sciences into Democracy*, Cambridge, MA: Harvard University Press.

Lucretius (1994), *On the Nature of the Universe*, London: Penguin.

Macherey, Pierre (1987), 'The Problem of the Attributes', in W. Montag and T. Stolze (eds), *The New Spinoza*, Minneapolis: Minnesota University Press.

Macherey, Pierre (1998), *In a Materialist Way*, ed. W. Montag, trans. T. Stolze, London: Verso.

Massumi, Brian (1988), 'Translator's Foreword: Pleasures of Philosophy', in G. Deleuze and F. Guattari, *A Thousand Plateaus: Capitalism and Schizophrenia*, London: Athlone.

Massumi, Brian (2002), *Parables for the Virtual*, Durham, NC: Duke University Press.

Montag, Warren (1999), *Bodies, Masses, Power: Spinoza and his Contemporaries*, London: Verso.

Morfino, Vittorio (2006), 'Spinoza: An Ontology of Relation', *Graduate Faculty Philosophy Journal* 27(1), pp. 103–27.

Nancy, Jean-Luc (1997), *The Gravity of Thought*, Amherst: Prometheus.

Nancy, Jean-Luc (1998), *The Sense of the World*, Minneapolis: University of Minnesota Press.

Nancy, Jean-Luc (2000), *Being Singular Plural*, Stanford: Stanford University Press.

Negri, Antonio (1991), *The Savage Anomaly: The Power of Spinoza's Metaphysics and Politics*, trans. M. Hardt, Minneapolis: Minnesota University Press.

Negri, Antonio (1997), 'Reliqua Desiderantur: A Conjecture for a Definition of the Concept of Democracy in the Final Spinoza', in W. Montag and T. Stolze (eds), *The New Spinoza*, Minneapolis: Minnesota University Press.

Rice, Lee (1990), 'Individual and Community in Spinoza's Social Psychology', in E. Curley and P. F. Moreah (eds), *Spinoza: New Directions*, Leiden: E. J. Brill.

Riley, Denise (2005), *Impersonal Passion: Language as Affect*, Durham, NC: Duke University Press.

Spinoza, Baruch de (1985), *Collected Works of Spinoza*, vol. 1, ed. and trans. E. Curley, Princeton: Princeton University Press.

Williams, Caroline (2010), 'Affective Processes Without a Subject: Rethinking the Relation Between Subjectivity and Affect with Spinoza', *Subjectivity* 3(3), pp. 245–62.

Williams, Caroline (2012a), 'Structure and Subject', in Benoît Dillet, et al. (eds), *The Edinburgh Companion to Poststructuralism*, Edinburgh: Edinburgh University Press.

Williams, Caroline (2012b), 'Althusser and Spinoza: Thinking the Enigma of Subjectivity Without the Subject', in Sara Farris and Peter Thomas (eds), *Encountering Althusser*, London: Continuum.

Yovel, Yirmiyahu (1999), 'Transcending Mere Survival: From *Conatus* to *Conatus Intelligendi*', in Y. Yovel (ed.), *Desire and Affect: Spinoza as Psychologist*, New York: Little Room.

Žižek, Slavoj (1999), *The Ticklish Subject: The Absent Centre of Political Ontology*, London: Verso.

Žižek, Slavoj (2003), *Organs Without Bodies*, London: Routledge.

# 2. *Spinoza's Non-Humanist Humanism*

MICHAEL MACK

## INTRODUCTION: SPINOZA, LITERATURE AND THE HUMANITIES AND ARTS

This chapter continues the investigation into Spinoza's contribution to fields outside philosophy, developing and extending the preceding discussion about the relevance of Spinoza's work vis-à-vis a novel understanding of the imagination.

Further developing Spinoza's rationalist perspective on the imagination, I have recently delineated a new approach towards the ethical significance and social impact of literature and the arts (Mack 2011). This chapter shows how Spinoza's thought is helpful in formulating a nascent approach to the study of literature and the arts / humanities in general. I attempt to place emphasis on the active rather than merely receptive aspect of the humanities and arts. Here I creatively re-read Spinoza's term *conatus* as the striving or, in other words, the unending attempt to act within and perceive the world in radically new life-enhancing ways. The humanities and arts have traditionally been associated with the imagination. The imagination, in turn, has often been separated from the work of reason. Spinoza was the first philosopher to break down the separation between reason and imagination as well as between mind and body.

In order to understand Spinoza's philosophy of the *conatus* better, we must therefore attend to his novel approach to the mind–body problem. It will emerge from this discussion that bringing together literature, humanities and the arts with medicine, social sciences and science depends on Spinoza's post-humanist humanism. Spinoza does not deny humanity and human rationality. His reason is, however, that of the *conatus*: the striving to create and preserve ever-new forms of life. Rationality here consists in recognising the subjectivity of each form of life.

The first section will discuss what I call the ethics of literature: literature makes us conscious of the subjective and fictive ways of living which govern our day-to-day activities. This rationalist work of making us conscious of real fictions also provides the impetus to change our mode of action and interaction within society at large. The second section analyses one powerful fiction that has shaped various attempts to find an abstract measure of what is human. This is the fiction of biopolitics, the extreme variation of which determined the Nazi genocide. The last section analyses the ways in which the Spinozist thinker Gilles Deleuze comes to terms with philosophical repercussions of biopolitics and totalitarianism. This discussion will show that a literary mode of inquiry may prove to be closer to the ethics of living than Deleuze's ideational discourse. The radical wager proposed in this chapter is that literature, rather than philosophical discourse à la Deleuze, bridges the gap between the mental and the corporeal, between the humanities and the sciences. The bridging of these divides was a major concern of Spinoza's re-conception of the mind as the idea of the body.

## SPINOZA'S *CONATUS* AND THE NEW APPROACH TO LITERATURE, HUMANITIES AND THE ARTS

There is a certain parallelism between imagination and reason, between mind and body. What has been taken to be the receptive region of both the body and the imagination turns out to be connected to the more active or constructive workings of the mind. In the latter half of the twentieth century, Spinoza's radical revision of Descartes's mind–body dualism was scientifically substantiated by neurological experiments and research findings. By now it has become common neurological knowledge 'that the human mind and spirituality originates in a physical organ, the brain' (Kandel 2007: 9). Contemporary neurology has thus proved right Spinoza's materialism of the mind (Damasio 2003). The mind is not separated from the body but partakes of it. The mind is itself corporeal matter (the brain). These neurological findings overturn the traditional divide between body and mind which places the latter above the former. The predominance of Descartes's *res cogitans* has begun to disintegrate. Descartes's *res cogitans* 'gives rise to rational thought and consciousness, and it reflects in its nonphysical character the spiritual nature of the soul' (Kandel 2007: 117).

Our contemporary culture is, to a large extent, shaped by the biomedical assumptions of a materialism which was first advanced by Spinoza in his critique of Descartes's mind–body divide (Mack 2010: 11–29). Spinoza is, however, not a straightforward materialist, because he combines a biomedical (*avant la lettre*) understanding of our human-ity with an ethical perspective. Deleuze has analysed the ways in which ethics is different from morality. An ethical approach attempts to delineate ways of living, whereas a moral approach is concerned with conceptual issues or with representative models where questions of right and wrong are fixed and mutually opposed to each other (Deleuze 1988). Deleuze pinpoints the intellectual location of ethics within Spinoza's parallelism of mind and body:

> According to the *Ethics*, on the contrary, what is an action in the mind is necessarily an action in the body as well, and what is a passion in the body is necessarily a passion in the mind. There is no primacy of one over the other. (Deleuze 1988: 18)

The ideational name for such understanding of ethics is what Deleuze calls 'a philosophy of "life" in Spinoza; it consists precisely in denounc-ing all that separates us from life, all these transcendent values that are turned against life, these values that are tied to the conditions and illusions of consciousness' (Deleuze 1988: 26). In *How Literature Changes the Way We Think*, I have shown how Spinoza's ethics solves the problem of a divide between art and life, which has characterised traditional approaches to aesthetics.

Spinoza tried to delineate ways of living from the perspective of an active and preservative principle which he called *conatus*. This principle equally informs the body and the mind, as it does the imagination and reason. The imagination is not passive or simply receptive (of images and other sense data); it also acts upon reason in either beneficial or detrimental ways. Spinoza appreciates both desire and reason as being compelled by the *conatus*. In this way, 'desire is the very essence of man, that is, a striving by which a man strives to persevere in his being', and, in parallel, reason demands 'that everyone should strive to preserve his own being as far as he can' (E IVP18). Spinoza relates the imagination to desire, to the affects and to the body but also to morality, morality being determined by the concepts of good and evil. Spinoza submerges these concepts in a material or biological / corporeal realm. What we take to be morally good or evil varies according to what we desire, to what affects our body as either good or evil:

> And so knowledge of good and evil is nothing but an idea of joy or sadness which follows necessarily from the affect of joy or sadness itself. But this idea is united to the affect in the same way as the mind is united to the body, that is, this idea is not really distinguished from the affect itself, *or* from the idea of the body's affection; it is only conceptually distinguished from it. Therefore, this knowledge of good and evil is nothing but the affect itself, insofar as we are conscious of it. (E IVP8)

The concepts of good and evil denote cognition of what affects our bodies in either a beneficial or detrimental manner. Up to this point, Spinoza anticipates our biomedical age of materialism. Spinoza is, however, concerned with the discovery of a way of life where we are collectively able to reduce the politico-social exposure of individuals and minorities to harm. At this point, Spinoza counters the partial or ideological-moral-aesthetic discussions of good and evil or beautiful and ugly. The problem with bodily affects and perceptions or desires is that they can mislead us; they can make us confuse our subjective disposition with objective or universal states of affairs. In this way, we take our predilections to be universal facts rather than subjective entities.

Here we reach the point where Spinoza's thought critiques aspects of humanism. Out of our subjective notion of what is human we are prone to postulate an abstract and fixed notion of humanity in general. This form of humanism is quite moralistic; it defines its notion of humanity in accordance with the concepts of good and evil. As we have seen above, Spinoza removes these terms from the exclusively mental realm of morality – the domain of traditional humanism – and submerges them into a more fluid and less elevated element: that of biology, medicine and the corporeal. This is not to say that he abandons reason, intellect and the spiritual. His rationalist approach is, however, quite idiosyncratic and marks a difference in the history of rationalism. It is a rationalism that is aware of its dependence on, as well as exposure to, the illusions and misapprehensions of bodily sensations and impressions.

Our corporeality connects us to the outside world via the senses of sight, touch and smell. The way we interpret various sense information is, however, culturally conditioned. The corporeal work performed by the senses, its neurons and the transmission of this information to the neurotransmitters located in the brain does not exist in a neutral location. The work of how we interpret this information has to do with our culture and how we relate to it: whether we simply repeat or copy its interpretative framework or whether we differentiate ourselves from it. Medicine and biology cannot be separated from culture, and culture cannot be separated from the corporeal realm of medicine. As Sander L. Gilman has pointed out, 'medicine is a part of general culture and the general culture is shaped by medicine' (Gilman 2010: x). Spinoza's thought has solved the problem of a purported split between medicine and the humanities (the realm of culture); he argues that the mind is the idea of the body and that we therefore live within a parallelism of the mental and the corporeal. We inhabit the osmosis of mind and body. This collapse of the boundary between mind and body has serious implications for the validity of traditional humanism and, associated with it, rationalism and moral thought.

Significantly, Spinoza insists on both ethics and the rationalism of his thought. His is rationalism with a difference, however. Reason here does not work out abstract categories that are imposed on our life. Rather than ruling nature and the corporeal in a one-way manner, reason here listens to the medical realm of the body. It is an interconnection that reflects upon delusions of generality – such as the fixed notion of the human and, associated with it, the terms of good and evil – generated by the parallelism of mind and body which we inhabit.

Spinoza employs the term 'reason' for the opening-up of our perspective from our subjective lives to the larger, communal or universal map of our world: 'Insofar as the mind reasons, it wants nothing other than to understand' (E IVP26). The body, its affects and desires, are what the mind seeks to understand: 'the object of our mind is the existing body and nothing else' (E IIP13). In *How Literature Changes the Way We Think*, I have shown that literature does the work of Spinoza's reason; in different and related ways it seeks to understand the increasingly changing body of our world. Reason's work of understanding operates on different levels which are interrelated and depend on the imagination as one of its substantive parts.

## SPINOZA'S CRITIQUE OF HUMANISTIC ANTHROPOCENTRISM, THE NAZI GENOCIDE AND THE COLLAPSE OF ETHICS

This section analyses the ways in which Spinoza's critique of purportedly objective views which are intrinsically subjective contribute to solving the problem of humanity's centrality in our ecological structure, where – via industrial pollution and waste – the human has become a geological force (changing the ecosystem of the seas and the climate of our planet). In the following, we will first establish the larger cultural context for an examination of the relevance of Spinoza's thought to ecopolitical and medical problems through a discussion of the imagination and literature. The central argument focuses on an exploration of the problematic nature that characterises endeavours to define or 'measure' what it means to be human. This is all the more important in an age where the human has become an overweening and all-dominating force in the non-human life of our planet. The biopolitical definition of humanity in terms of species existence depends on certain conceptions of normativity and human essence.

Recent debates about the 'post-human' call these normative – or, in other words, moral – conceptions into question (see, for example, Žižek 2006). Is there a human essence and why should there be one? Definitions of human essence have been established with the understanding of humanity's centrality in the cosmos. Spinoza was the thinker who most explicitly and stringently analysed various humanistic and theological attempts to define the human in terms of anthropomorphic conceptions of God. This and the following section (focusing on Deleuze and Nietzsche) discuss how Spinoza's thought is of continuing relevance in an age that the Dutch chemist Paul Crutzen has described as anthropocene, as a new age 'defined by one creature – man – who had become so dominant that he was capable of altering the planet on a geological scale' (Kolbert 2005: 54). Through scientific-technological dominance, humanity is in the process of altering the conditions of life on Planet Earth. In our anthropocene age, humanity has thus become a geological force (see the discussion of Spinoza and ecology in the following chapter). Spinoza is helpful in a critique of the theological and scientific-historical ideas that prepared for such a predominance of humanity within the ecological system of our planet. As I have shown elsewhere (Mack 2010), he attempted to remove man from the centre of the philosophical, theological and scientific universe. He unmasked all grand human teleologies as theology that equates humanity with God / nature.

In this way, Spinoza is a non-humanist thinker. This does not mean that he is not concerned with the welfare of humanity. The following discussion explores how his critique of theology and normative strands of humanism may help us in a critique of current medical, theological and political attempts at reinforcing the anthropocene nature of what our planet has become. This analysis will shed light on how a normative conception of the human creates inhumane fictions of monolithic dominance and single-minded commercialism. One outcome of such developments is the anthropocene destruction of non-human life-worlds within the ecosystem of our planet. This shows that a normative conception of the human, which establishes abstract forms of what is normal, beautiful and good, does violence to the diversity of life (both within humanity and beyond). Normative conceptions of the human create fictions of truth, beauty and goodness, which can have inhumane consequences in the embodied world of both human society and the non-human life of our planet. A radically abstract and intransigently normative humanism can thus result in the collapse of the humanity which characterises traditional humanist ethics. The following will explore the ways in which Spinoza's thought assists us in solving a problem associated with the collapse of humanism: the absence of morality that can be remedied via a Spinozan re-appreciation of ethics and literature. Hannah Arendt and Martha Nussbaum are important thinkers who have struggled with the collapse of traditional humanist ethics. What is missing in Arendt's and Nussbaum's respective analyses is a Spinozist perspective on how the collapse of humanism is already part of a humanist intransigence regarding abstract norms, which Spinoza has famously (or infamously) unmasked as fictions of power.

In the latter part of the twentieth century, humanism has lost some of its ethical validity. Partly as a response to disturbing biopolitical practices within the twentieth century (Nazism, Stalinism and other forms of totalitarianism), traditional conceptions of humanity have been questioned (see Arendt 2004 and 1994). This has been the case because, as Arendt has argued, various forms of totalitarian rule made use of certain humanistic traditions of ethics while perverting these traditions. In her *Eichmann in Jerusalem* she attempts to describe 'the totality of the moral collapse the Nazis caused in respectable European society' (Arendt 1991: 125). The Nazis corrupted Biblical, Socratic and Kantian ethics while claiming to be their true heir. Here the infliction of harm, violence and mass death has become a duty. Acting unlawfully has become a law. Harmful acts have lost their traditional association with temptation. Instead harm, murder and robbery have transmogrified into the new content of an otherwise seemingly intact morality of duty and obedience.

Arendt's famous 'banality of evil' consists in the way cruelty has come to govern the normal way of social life. Eichmann and his fellow perpetrators were not abnormal or pathological. On the contrary, they represented normal and respectable German society. Evil has become normalised here; it has turned moral. Evil thus no longer denotes a temptation to break laws or a transgression of norms but the fulfilment of the law and an accommodation to the social norm:

> Evil in the Third Reich had lost the quality by which most people recognize it – the quality of temptation. Many Germans and many Nazis, probably an overwhelming majority of them, must have been tempted *not* to murder, *not* to rob, *not* to let their neighbors go off to their doom (for that the Jews were transported to their doom they knew, of course, even though many of them may not have known the gruesome details), and not to become accomplices in all these crimes by benefiting from them. But, God knows, they had learned how to resist temptation. (Arendt 1991: 150)

While breaking with the content of traditional ethics (Socratic, Biblical or Kantian), Nazism continued and even reinforced notions of respectability and of what is acceptable or normal. In this way, Nazism's corruption and distortion of traditional morality reinforced, as well as magnified, the normative dimension of traditional humanism. Indeed, the Nazis made it a duty to rob, deport and kill minorities (Jews, gypsies, people with a disability and homosexuals) by classifying them as abnormal, as carriers of infectious disease, and, worse still, as non-human and therefore not morally worthy to be alive. Jews, gypsies, homosexuals and people with a physical or mental disability were first deprived of rights. This loss of rights prepared for the legality of their being put to death. Arendt analyses this political process, which declared certain groups of people to be outside the realm of the political and the publicly useful. The exclusion from politics and the public good grows out of a normative or moralistic system which contrasts bare life, the mere fact of existence, with that of politics as the sphere of historical signification and public achievement. Arendt critiques the politics of normative exclusion that led to the division of humanity and, in the case of the Nazi genocide, the radical exclusion of certain groups from the category of humanity. Arendt examines the perversion and collapse of traditional politics and morality (here conflated with ethics). She attempts to understand this process of disintegration with a view to drawing consequences that could promote new beginnings for a non-exclusive approach towards politics and ethics in the post-war era. Arendt is especially concerned with the ways in which the re-enforcement of traditional practices of exclusion became the publicly valid form of ethical and political life under the Nazi regime.

In order to win public approval for its murderous norms, the Nazi propaganda machinery worked on the emotions of its audience. It provoked one emotion in particular: that of disgust. As Winfried Menninghaus has pointed out, 'the fundamental schema of disgust is the experience of a nearness that is not wanted' (Menninghaus 2003: 1). Disgust seems to work in an immediate manner; what is perceived as disgusting has a direct way of permeating our skin and entering into the information-gathering mind – the brain. The experience of a nearness that is not wanted is, however, culturally conditioned. It is not something that comes naturally but depends on memory and learning. Emotions such as disgust are part of our psychological constitution and 'aspects of many psychological problems are learned' (Kandel 2007: 116). So, to identify a group or groups of people with the immediate feeling of disgust requires some training. Martha Nussbaum has shown how disgust 'expresses a universal discomfort with bodily reality, but then uses this discomfort to target and subordinate vulnerable minorities' (Nussbaum 2010: xv). The identification of the abject body with a word denoting a group of people is clearly a form of cultural training or conditioning. This is what Nazi propaganda provided; it depicted Jews (and other minorities) in a way that made the word 'Jew' immediately identifiable with the feeling of disgust.

How is all of this relevant for today? Martha Nussbaum has recently shown how 'the politics of disgust continues to exercise influence, often in more subtle and unstated ways' (Nussbaum 2010: xiv). Whereas totalitarian societies are governed by a 'politics of disgust', in liberal democratic societies disgust has 'gone underground' (Nussbaum 2010: xv). Being hidden does not necessarily prevent disgust from exerting its harmful and often lethal political consequences. To counter the open or hidden influence of a politics of disgust, Nussbaum makes a strong case for a politics of humanity. Whereas a politics of disgust denies the humanity of the other, the politics of humanity acknowledges our shared human condition. The former is exclusive and the latter is inclusive. How, however, can we cultivate inclusion? Nussbaum argues that we can become more inclusive via the imagination: 'Disgust imputes to the other a subhuman nature. How, by contrast, do we ever become able to see one another as human? Only via the imagination' (Nussbaum 2010: xvii). Here Nussbaum's contemporary critique meets with Arendt's analysis of totalitarian terror. Both see the imagination as vital for ways of diminishing social exclusion, violence and genocide. Arendt makes a lack of imagination responsible for both Eichmann's lack of feeling of guilt and his inability to repent:

> It was precisely this lack of imagination which enabled him [i.e. Eichmann] to sit for months on end facing a German Jew who was conducting the police interrogation, pouring out his heart to the man and explaining again and again how it was that he reached only the rank of lieutenant colonel in the S.S. and that it had not been his fault that he was not promoted [. . .] He was not stupid. It was sheer thoughtlessness – something by no means identical with stupidity – that predisposed him to become one of the greatest criminals of that period. And if this is 'banal' and even funny, if with the best will in the world one cannot extract any diabolical or demonic profundity from Eichmann, that is still far from calling it commonplace. (Arendt 1991: 287–8)

As I have shown elsewhere (Mack 2009), Arendt does not understand by the word 'thoughtless' what it commonly means. Her usage of the term is uncommon in order to emphasise the non-communality of what the term describes. 'Thoughtless', in Arendt's usage here, does not mean absent-minded or stupid or dysfunctional. It rather denotes what its linguistic isolation performs: the loss of communality and the denial of humanity's interconnection. According to Arendt, Eichmann and his fellow perpetrators enacted such loss of our communality by declaring certain groups of people to reside outside of what they fixed in their racist nomenclature to be human.

Arendt assumes that such loss of communality goes hand in hand with the collapse of humanism. Spinoza, however, has already shown how such a collapse of humanism is potentially part of its normative intransigence that can do violence to the embodied world where we encounter a diversity of life forms that all strive to create and preserve their life (*conatus*). Arendt relates the imagination to understanding. Spinoza, as we have seen in the preceding section, defines reason as the work of understanding corporeal reality. The reality reason seeks to grasp is in constant flux and hence cannot be accurately depicted via static concepts of duty and obedience. Eichmann and his fellow perpetrators refer to such static concepts – even to Kant's categorical imperative (in Eichmann's case) – in order to move acts of mass murder into a detached or intellectual realm. The imposition of culturally determined standards of evil – the Jews, according to anti-Semitism, are 'evil' and thus evoke the bodily sensation of disgust – on the universe of matter is what happened during the state-sponsored reign of Nazi terror on the European continent.

Spinoza critiqued the fictions that come to shape socio-political reality. The most brutal fiction is the genocidal anti-Semitism which the Nazis enacted. Nazism thus brings to the fore the cultural or, in other words, subjective / fictive construction of the body; it fabricated the Jewish body as the non-human body. This harnessing of the term 'humanity' in order to exclude groups of people from the human highlights the importance of our cultural engagement with deleterious fictions that determine the empirical core of the social sciences and the sciences. In this way, Spinoza's analysis of humanist or moralistic thought about good and evil highlights the ways in which cultural inquiry – of which literature and the humanities partake – helps us tackle issues of violence, racism and other forms of stigmatisation in debates about and formulations of public policy. The Jews were certainly placeholders of evil for both Nazism and the quasi-scientific and quasi-theological racism that prepared its way (Mack 2003).

The following section analyses the predominance of a philosophical discourse that prioritises an abstract sphere of norms and ideas over and above the more fluid realm that characterises the ethics of literature. This will be accomplished in an exploration of how the work of twentieth-century Spinozist Gilles Deleuze and that of the contemporary philosopher Jacques Rancière come to terms with the collapse of humanist morality after the Holocaust.

## DELEUZE, NIETZSCHE AND THE TURN FROM ETHICS TO AESTHETICS

On an ideational level, Deleuze takes seriously Spinoza's critique of humanism and its concept-based morality of good and evil. He takes it so seriously that he decomposes the human body, which, in his thought, morphs into a body without organs. His work pivots around a reflection about indistinction that does away with hierarchy, with various hierarchies which have informed the moral system of humanism and traditional theological thought. It is important to emphasise that Deleuze's approach towards Spinoza's non-hierarchical vision is purely philosophical; it concerns Spinoza's philosophical term *attributes*. This is Deleuze's post-humanist / idealist take on Spinoza:

> Any hierarchy or pre-eminence is denied in so far as the substance is equally designated by all attributes in accordance with their essence, and equally expressed by all the modes in accordance with their degree of power. With Spinoza, univocal being ceases to be neutralized and becomes expressive; it becomes a truly expressive and affirmative position. (Deleuze 2004: 50)

According to Deleuze, Spinoza has philosophically / ideationally done away with the differentiations and hierarchies which characterise traditional humanism and theology. Instead of hierarchical differentiations, we find ourselves on an equal ideational playing field where every philosophical attribute has a right to engage in forms of expression. My concern is with human equality. Deleuze's philosophy does not bridge the divide which separates the ideational or mentalist world from the embodied sphere of human equality and public policy. My argument is that literature, rather than philosophical discourse à la Deleuze, bridges the gap between the mental and the corporeal, between the humanities and the sciences. The bridging of these divides was a major concern of Spinoza's re-conception of the mind as the idea of the body.

Deleuze's post-humanism has a decidedly idealist edge. His expressionism does not relate to the distinct individual of traditional humanism. It rather refers to a series of expressions that are impersonal and ontological. This emphasis on the non-distinct results in Deleuze's rejection of personalised representation in favour of impersonal repetition:

> The world of representation presupposes a certain type of sedentary distribution, which divides or shares out that which is distributed in order to give 'each' their fixed share (as in the bad game or the way to play, the pre-existing rules define distributive hypotheses according to which the results of the throws are partitioned). Representation essentially implies an analogy of being. However, the only realized Ontology – in other words, the univocity of being – is repetition. From Duns Scotus to Spinoza, the univocal position

has always rested on two fundamental theses. According to one, there are indeed forms of being, but contrary to what is suggested by the categories, these forms involve no division within being or plurality of ontological senses. According to the other, that of which being is said is repartitioned according to essentially mobile individuating differences which necessarily endow 'each one' with a plurality of modal significations. This programme is expounded from the beginning of the *Ethics*: we are told that the *attributes* are irreducible to genera or categories because while they are *formally* distinct they all remain equal and *ontologically* one, and introduce no division into the substance which is said or expressed through them in a single and same sense (in other words, the real distinction between attributes is formal, not a numerical distinction). (Deleuze 2004: 377)

On the basis of Spinoza's one-substance ontology, everything is more than interconnected or interrelated; it is univocally at one and all distinctions are simply formal rather than numerical. Deleuze's philosophy takes issue with representation because representation presupposes distinct entities; representation constructs concepts that do not do justice to the world they claim to depict. Distinct entities cannot exist (in an absolute sense) in a univocal world. One of the most striking distinctions is the one between good and evil, as has been discussed above. Whereas representation divides the world into spurious oppositions such as good and evil, the idea that, according to Deleuze, most accurately accounts for the univocal constitution of life is that of repetition. The concept of representation is premised on a humanist understanding of our lives being fixed in their proper place – proper according to the hierarchical coordinates of morality and theology. Deleuze's repetition, by contrast, is mobile; repetitions are on the move. Deleuze's repetitions enact infinite series of repeating movements which are not identical but differ as they move. His approach to repetition is thus via difference and contrasted with representation. Representation works through categories and concepts; repetition operates through the movement of ideas.

Representations are fictions whereas repetitions instantiate the truth of ideas. In contrast to Spinoza's, some aspects of Deleuze's thought attempt to do away with the imagination, which he equates with representation (fictions, non-truth) and which he contrasts with the truth of his ontological idea (repetition). Representation is the untruth of the imagination which violates the truth of the idea: repetition. Deleuze endeavours to propound a philosophy of difference. In order to do so, he distinguishes between repetition of the same (which is representation) and non-identical repetition. For non-identical repetition to work in a philosophy that attempts to combine Kantianism and Spinozism (Lord 2011: 130–54), the idea has to play a decisive role. Deleuze differentiates his understanding of the idea from the norms of tradi-tional humanism, which does its work via representation rather than non-identical repetition. Identical repetition depends on a standard or a norm of which it would be representative.

Deleuze denies that this origin of the normative exists in reality. In truth, reality consists not of originals but of simulacra:

> However, difference does not lie between things and simulacra, models and copies. Things are simulacra themselves, simulacra are the superior forms, and the difficulty facing everything is to become its own simulacrum, to attain the status of a sign in the coherence of the eternal return. (Deleuze 2004: 81)

Deleuze here combines Nietzsche with Spinoza and Kant. He affirms the primacy of the idea (idealism) by equating the idea with the reality of the senses (Spinoza's univocity), and then reads the product of this equation in terms of Nietzsche's eternal return. Nietzsche, as Alexander Nehemas's *Life as Literature* has shown, is concerned with turning life into literature. Deleuze's Nietzschean background is crucial for both his approach to Spinoza and his ideational reading of literature. Nietzsche's eternal return may well be a response to Spinoza but is one that diverges from and warps Spinoza's questioning of anthropomorphism. Spinoza argues that we should not conflate our idea of God or nature with God or nature. This conflation results from the mind's uncritical acceptance of information the brain receives from bodily sensations.

This confused knowledge is what characterises the imagination. In this sense, we imagine the sun to be in close proximity to us, because our senses are strongly affected by the rays of the sun. The mind, by representing bodily affects, sees the sun to be in the vicinity of the earth. This representation does not yield knowledge of the truth but, as Galileo showed, turns out to be a fiction: 'For we imagine the sun so near not because we do not know its true distance, but because an affection of body involves the essence of the sun insofar as our body is affected by the sun' (E IIP35). Spinoza does not berate us for our inadequacy; inadequacy here describes our proneness to believe rep-resentations or fictions to be true. On the contrary, he understands our representational dilemmas, writing that we 'can hardly avoid this, because [we] are continually affected by external bodies' (E IIP47). The point here is that we need to be aware that our knowledge derives from bodily inputs and represents our sense of being affected by external bodies. This awareness characterises reason; it is the mind's mindful-ness. Reason is the mind's mindfulness of its embodiment and, conse-quently, its imaginative tendencies. It puts our place in the universe in perspective. The cosmos is no longer anthropocentric and we are no longer its centre. Spinoza set out to make us love God or nature intellectually: to make us see how we are a small but significant part of the vast and, to us, in its totality, incomprehensible universe.

Nietzsche is not so much concerned with Spinoza's ethical and social thought as with the epistemological implications of a Spinozist critique of goal and God. What are the repercussions for our understanding of our cognitive powers, if we are only a small part of an infinite and impersonal universe which Spinoza calls *Deus sive natura*? Modern science operates on the basis of the ceaselessly renewed testability and thus falsifiability and re-visibility of its findings. In this sense, it has incorporated Galileo's and Spinoza's demotion of the earth and humanity as the centre of the universe and all this implies for human omniscience. On the other hand, our age is an anthropocene age and it is one that has been shaped by scientific discoveries for which Galileo and Spinoza have prepared the intellectual ground. How can we explain this discrepancy?

The welding together of our planet with the industrial waste of humanity (plastic in the sea and so forth) has to do not so much with the practice of science as with the ecological consequences of an ever-growing market economy based on consumption. Slavoj Žižek has famously called Deleuze 'the ideologist of late capitalism' (Žižek 2003: 184). Deleuze's Nietzschean idea of the eternal return finds a striking equivalent in the material sphere of infinite serialised production. Branding depends on the repetition, not of the same, but of the slightly different (in this way, the advertising industry reinvents branded products within a repetitive or serialised framework where the same forms become repeated in infinite variations). The basis of brand attachment is an affirmation of our worth and value which we attach to the brand and which we hope to see eternally returned to us with each purchase of the product. The point of Nietzsche's eternal returns is, indeed, the immanent affirmation of humanity's fate – *amor fati* – in the face of a deserted transcendent realm which traditionally provided such affirmation from above.

Nietzsche doubts whether we can be satisfied with Spinoza's, Galileo's and Darwin's demotion of our cognitive status from image of God to embodied part of the natural world. This may explain why he introduced the notion of the eternal return: to confirm rather than to question humanity's grandeur. As Nehemas has shown, Nietzsche equates life with literature. Such conception of life as repetition of literature – and vice versa, of literature as representation of life – is quite problematic. In Nietzsche's case, difficulties are compounded by the fact that a traditional understanding of literature as harmonious, coherent and whole underlies his concept of the eternal return. Nehemas has critiqued the internal coherence of Nietzsche's equation of literature and life as follows:

> And once we admit contents, we admit conflicts. What we think, want, and do is seldom if ever a coherent collection. Our thoughts contradict one another and contrast with our desires, which are themselves inconsistent and are in turn belied by our actions. The unity of the self, which Nietzsche identifies with this collection, is thus seriously undermined. (Nehemas 1985: 180)

Nietzsche's reading of life as literature is itself a fiction.

Whereas Spinoza critiques the fictitiousness that shapes aspects of our lives, Nietzsche's 'eternal return' encourages us to celebrate our lives as fictions: as stylised harmonisations or even deifications of our humanity. The point of Spinoza's critique of revelation is precisely to question this equation of life with an idealised concept of nature or God. So we can now come to see how Deleuze's reading of Nietzsche's eternal return fits into his attempt to submerge Spinoza's mind–body parallelism in Kantian and post-Kantian idealism. This combination eventuates in Nietzsche's eternal return, where we affirm what is and what has been and eagerly await its repetition with different internal constitutions. The primacy of Deleuze's idea of repetition sacrifices Spinoza's embodiment as ground of mental information to the Heideggerian thrownness (*Geworfenheit*) of the groundless as it separates memory from ideas. Deleuze's repetition does its work within a philosophical system 'where the ground was abolished in groundlessness, the Ideas were separated from the forms of memory, and the displacement and disguise of repetition engaged divergence and decentring, the powers of difference' (Deleuze 2004: 364). The separation of memory from the idea which is repetition brings to the fore a certain lack of remembrance which enables the serialised differences of Deleuze's philosophical system. His is a repetition out of amnesia:

> *One* repeats because one does not know, because one does not remember, etc: or because one is not capable of performing the action (whether this action remains to be performed or is already performed). 'One' therefore signifies here the unconscious of the Id as the first power of repetition. (Deleuze 2004: 368)

The driving force behind difference is the Freudian dialectic of disavowal or repression – the repression of a memory – and repetition. Deleuze discusses Freud with specific reference to the role of repetition and difference in the death drive:

> The turning point of Freudianism appears in *Beyond the Pleasure Principle*:
> the death instinct is discovered, not in connection with the destructive
> tendencies, not in connection with aggressivity, but as a result of a direct
> consideration of repetition phenomena. (Deleuze 2004: 18)

By 'death drive', Freud does not understand the state of being dead but
the wish to be so. This wish for the restfulness associated with death
is part of Freud's pleasure principle, which drives us to repeat actions
in different contexts and times that bring about states of rest and certainty. According to Žižek's recent interpretation, Freud's term denotes
the uncanny persistence, not of death, but of life:

> The paradox of the Freudian death drive is therefore that it is Freud's name
> for its very opposite, for the way immortality appears within psychoanaly-
> sis, for an uncanny *excess* of life, for an 'undead' urge that persists beyond
> the (biological) cycle of life and death, of generation and corruption. (Žižek
> 2006: 245)

Emotions are highly ambivalent and the desire to be dead is no exception, for what drives such desire is the fearful wish not ever to reach the
object of desire: death.

On an ontogenetic as well as a polygenetic level, we keep repeating
certain forms of action through which we attempt to increase our sense
of certainty, rest, respect and security, which makes us feel at home in
the world. Deleuze's notion of the simulacrum derives from Freud's
understanding of fantasy which determines our psychology (not only
the death drive but also the Oedipus complex):

> A decisive moment in psychoanalysis occurred when Freud gave up, in
> certain respects, the hypothesis of real childhood events, which would have
> played the part of ultimate disguised terms, in order to substitute the power
> of fantasy which is immersed in the death instinct, where everything is
> already masked and disguised. In short, repetition is in its essence symbolic;
> symbols or simulacra are the letter of repetition itself. (Deleuze 2004: 19)

Here we reach the point where Nietzsche's notion of life as literature
comes fully to inform Deleuze's idea of repetition.

What is repeated in ever-different shapes and forms is not the memory
of something that actually took place but a certain kind of fiction: in
short, an imagined storyline or literature (the Oedipus complex or
the primeval scene where the sons kill the alpha-male father figure).
This is why literature, theatre and cinema play such an important
role in Deleuze's work. Through Nietzsche's fascination with tragedy,
Aristotle's *Poetics* shapes Deleuze's notion of the non-identical action of
repetition that informs the world of theatre: 'play it and repeat it until
the acute moment that Aristotle called "recognition"' (Deleuze 2004:

17). By repeating the actions in a different context, we come to realise their signification and recognise their psychic meaning. This is Freud's approach to repetition and Deleuze describes it as follows: 'If repetition makes us ill, it also heals us; if it enchains and destroys us, it also frees us, testifying in both cases to its "demonic" power. All cure is a voyage to the bottom of repetition' (Deleuze 2004: 21). Deleuze does not, however, describe the ways in which such repetition of fantasy may free us.

According to Freud, the awareness of what we are repeating frees us from future repetitions. In this way, the re-enactment of the primal scene in *Moses and Monotheism* – where the Jews repeat the fantasy of the primal scene by killing their father figure, Moses (which is, of course, itself a fantasy) – frees the Jews from future repetition of such violence in different social, historical and political contexts. This moment of the breakaway from repetition is missing in Deleuze's philosophical system, because it is founded on the idea of repetition and thus cannot free itself from it. Instead, his philosophy relies on an infinite series of non-identical repetitions of simulacra which, as we have seen, are fantasies, storylines: in short, literature. Deleuze has banished one form of imagination – the concept of representation – from the truth of his idea of repetition. Yet, as we have seen, the substance of repetition is itself imaginative: simulacra, fantasy, art and literature. In Nietzsche's fashion, life turns out to be literature. This is where Deleuze diverges from Spinoza's account of the imagination. Spinoza does not attempt to exclude the imagination from our lives, because this would be an impossible undertaking (given that we do not live in an affect-less, disembodied sphere). He does, however, admonish us to be mindful of our mind's exposure to the misleading input of bodily sensations which gives rise to fictions of grandeur or fantasies of destruction. This mindfulness constitutes his ethics. Rather than abstract and superimposed concepts of good and evil, Spinoza's ethics of mindfulness is context-specific and requires ever-renewed awareness, as well as alertness in particular situations which vary according to a given time and space. Spinoza's ethics admonishes us to see our self-interest as bound up with that of others. Fantasies of one's superiority over others are harmful to the self, because the self relies on the communal in the same way in which the communal depends on the self. This mutual dependence is part of our embodied constitution, which is one of disease, neediness and mortality. In order to avoid harm and to alleviate the prospect of illness and death, we have to be mindful of re-enacting certain fantasies of immortality, predominance and auto-immunity. Whereas Deleuze's philosophy celebrates the repetition of various simulacra, Spinoza's (as well as Freud's) ethics attempts to break the circle of this and similar repetitions.

While Deleuze engages with Spinoza's critique of concepts (representation) as fiction, Deleuze himself clings to a fiction (repetition of simulacra) which he, in Nietzschean fashion, attempts to equate with everyday life: 'For there is no other aesthetic problem than that of the insertion of art into everyday life' (Deleuze 2004: 365). Developing and radicalising Deleuze, Rancière has recently described this as the aesthetic turn, which he distinguishes from the ethical turn that characterises the work of Derrida (Rancière 2010: 45–61). Rancière evokes Deleuze's Heideggerian notion of 'groundlessness' (Deleuze 2004: 364) when he attempts to do away with the ground of ethics in Spinoza's and Derrida's work. As I have shown elsewhere (Mack 2010), in different ways, the ground of ethics in Spinoza's and Derrida's thought is that of self and other. In contrast to Derrida, Spinoza focuses on the preservation of selfhood (*conatus*) and it is this preservation that depends on that of others. Derrida's ethics criticises the political prioritisation of the self over and above the other. In Rancière's aesthetic turn, we have lost all forms of differentiation between self and other, because otherness is the principle of democratic politics:

> Derrida argues that [. . .] democracy still holds fast to the same unexamined power of the *autos* or *self*. In a word, democracy lacks its Other, which can only come to it from the outside. Derrida thus set out to break with the circle of the *self* by weaving a thread from the pure receptivity of the *khora* to the other, or the *newcomer*, whose inclusion defines the horizon of a 'democracy to come'. My objection to this is very simple: otherness does not come to politics from the outside, for the reason that it already has its own otherness, its own principle of heterogeneity. (Rancière 2010: 53)

That democracy has its own principle of heterogeneity is true within an ideational context (à la Deleuze) but the actual politics of it may be quite different from its idea. Literature focuses on the ethical negotiation between ideas and the messiness of their performance in the embodied and thus affect-ridden context that shapes our actual lives. Rather than repeating various ideas (that of Rancière's groundless form of democratic equality or Deleuze's repetition of simulacra), literature and art change the way we think about the potentiality of ideas and the particular context in which various ideas or scientific discoveries are applied and played out. Here I have begun to delineate an alternative account of the imagination out of Spinoza's critique of representation. By focusing on the idea and by conflating the work of the imagination with that of representation, Deleuze perpetuates a mimetic account of literature from his perspective of philosophy. What I call the ethics of literature establishes the radical difference of creativity, which is not so much ideational but performative – in short, yet another shift of Spinoza's *conatus*.

# BIBLIOGRAPHY


Arendt, Hannah (1991), *Eichmann in Jerusalem: A Report on the Banality of Evil*, London: Penguin.

Arendt, Hannah (1994), *Essays in Understanding 1930–1954: Formation, Exile, and Totalitarianism*, ed. Jerome Kohn, New York: Schocken.

Arendt, Hannah (1998), *The Human Condition*, Chicago: University of Chicago Press.

Arendt, Hannah (2004), *The Origins of Totalitarianism*, New York: Schocken.

Damasio, Antonio (2003), *Looking for Spinoza: Joy, Sorrow, and the Feeling Brain*, London: Harcourt.

Deleuze, Gilles (1988), *Spinoza: Practical Philosophy*, trans. Robert Hurley, San Francisco: City Lights.

Deleuze, Gilles (2004), *Difference and Repetition*, trans. Paul Patton, London: Continuum.

Gilman, Sander L. (2010), *Obesity: The Biography*, Oxford: Oxford University Press.

Kandel, Eric R. (2007), *In Search of Memory: The Emergence of a New Science of the Mind*, London: Norton.

Kolbert, Elizabeth (2005), 'The Climate of Man', *New Yorker* (April).

Lord, Beth (2011), *Kant and Spinozism: Transcendental Idealism and Immanence from Jacobi to Deleuze*, Basingstoke: Palgrave Macmillan.

Mack, Michael (2003), *German Idealism and the Jew: The Inner Anti-Semitism of Philosophy and German Jewish Responses*, Chicago: University of Chicago Press.

Mack, Michael (2009), 'The Holocaust and Hannah Arendt's Philosophical Critique of Philosophy: *Eichmann in Jerusalem*', *New German Critique* (Winter), pp. 35–60.

Mack, Michael (2010), *Spinoza and the Specters of Modernity: The Hidden Enlightenment of Diversity from Spinoza to Freud*, New York: Continuum.

Mack, Michael (2011), *How Literature Changes the Way We Think*, New York: Continuum.

Malamud, Bernard (1966), *The Fixer*, London: Penguin.

Menninghaus, Winfried (2003), *Disgust: Theory and History of a Strong Emotion*, trans. Howard Eiland and Joel Golb, Albany: State University of New York Press.

Nehemas, Alexander (1985), *Life as Literature*, Cambridge, MA: Harvard University Press.

Nussbaum, Martha C. (2010), *From Disgust to Humanity: Sexual Orientation and Constitutional Law*, Oxford: Oxford University Press.

Rancière, Jacques (2010), *Dissensus: On Politics and Aesthetics*, ed. and trans. Steven Corcoran, London: Continuum.

Spinoza, Baruch (1996), *Ethics*, ed. and trans. Edwin Curley, London: Penguin.

Žižek, Slavoj (2003), *Organs Without Bodies: Deleuze and the Consequences*, London: Routledge.
Žižek, Slavoj (2006), 'A Plea for a Return to *Différance* (with a minor *Pro Domo Sua*)', *Critical Inquiry* 32, pp. 226–49.

# 3. *The Ethical Relation of Bodies: Thinking with Spinoza Towards an Affective Ecology*

ANTHONY PAUL SMITH

## SPINOZA AND ECOLOGY BEYOND IDEOLOGY

In the recent documentary *Examined Life*, directed by Astra Taylor, Slavoj Žižek repeats an argument he has been making for some years now: ecology has become the new opium of the people. In the film this argument is made quite vividly as he stands in the midst of a landfill clothed in a bright orange safety vest. The story he tells goes like this: ideologies arise as responses to real problems and real crises, but do so in a way that mystifies both the problem and its subjects by obscuring their reality. This act of obscuring happens by treating that crisis on the terms and conditions of an exchange of meaning that is dependent on the very system lying at the root of these problems. Žižek claims that ecology is an instance of such an obscuring ideology because it presents a view of Nature (the capital letter intended) that says what is natural is best and will form the best possible world. But the meaning of this 'natural' is very anti-political in so far as it is anti-human, for what is natural is that which happens without human intervention or even hubristic human interaction like the setting up of a city. Under this ideology Nature is a wise thing, even a wise being, which would exist in a perfect balance and only fails to achieve this balance because of the actions of a hubristic humanity. This harmonious whole of a Nature freed from humanity is sublime beauty itself. If this is the story that contemporary ecology tells, then it is nothing less, says Žižek, than a new instantiation of an old conservative trope that always warns human society not to violate a certain invisible limit. In the past this limit may have been the sanctity of the family or the nation, but now, in the age of ecology, it is the invisible limit of Nature's harmonious wholeness.

While Žižek locates a real danger here, one that scientific ecologists and ecological activists refer to as 'green-washing', his analysis is limited by his contrarianism. In the light of the environmental crisis which threatens the entire organisation of life on this planet, including human life, something more is required of theoretical engagement with ecology than Žižek's brazenly adolescent contrarianism. For, rather than engaging with the reality of the environmental crisis, Žižek is concerned with playing an all-too-philosophical game of annoying environmentalists by claiming that the truly radical act would be to exploit nature more! While the danger present in a conservative ecological ideology is rightly identified by Žižek, it is suggested that any engagement with ecology dooms a thinker to become one of the new court philosophers – sophists and propagandists, really – for the underlying ruling ideology. But that underlying ideology is anything but green because it disempowers human beings and presents the situation as completely decided. When the very possibility of a different form of social life is closed off, human beings will be unable to live intentionally in an ethical way, which, in the light of the environmental crisis, must mean living in an intentionally ecological way.

We must risk leaving the comfy confines of a contrarian philosophical act and think alongside ecology, not so that we can live as court philosophers, but because the environmental crisis is real and deeply connected with the most pressing ethical questions of human society. So, what is actually important for thinking through ecology now? First, I need to be clear about what I mean by the term ecology. Part of the weakness of recent ideological critiques of 'ecology', and I use the requisite scare quotes here, is the lack of a clear definition of what ecology is, often coupled with ignorance about how it actually operates as a science. Žižek appears to mean something akin to popular environmentalism (a middle-class moralism of buying carbon offsets or driving a Prius) or political ecology (which would include groups like Greenpeace who engage in direct action against corporate polluters, as well as more mainstream political activism by green parties in various nations). What I intend by the term ecology is an amalgamation of these political identities with its scientific identity.

This second aspect, ecology's scientific identity, is absolutely missing in most philosophical engagements with ecology, and so what Žižek gives voice to is a general mood in philosophy that shows it is unable to engage seriously with the science of ecology. A serious engagement by a philosopher with material outside of philosophy proper, like ecology, would mean that the philosopher is open to rethinking and re-conceiving ideas and practices on the basis of this engagement, without simply ceding everything to that outside of philosophy. Spinoza was an exemplary thinker in this regard, using the axiomatic style of mathematics in his *Ethics* and engaging with Jewish and Christian scriptures on the terms of those texts. In both cases we find neither a purely mathematical form of thought nor a purely religious form of thought, but a co-mutation of the two materials.

This aspect of Spinoza's thought is often missed when considering his relationship to contemporary ecology. It leads to a unilateral relationship in the mind of the philosopher where ecological issues are considered only through philosophy, leading to an overdetermination of ecology by philosophy. I will explain this below with regard to two different understandings of Spinoza: the determinist reading of Spinoza that sees his work as a forerunner to a reductionist form of scientific reason, and Arne Naess's reading of Spinoza as anticipating Naess's own 'deep ecology'. The focus in this section will be on the way that both the reductionist understanding of ecology and the holistic form appeal to Spinoza's grand metaphysical equivocation of God and Nature. I will offer a counter-reading of this equivocation. Yet the goal of this essay, shared by the other authors in this collection, is not simply to provide secondary material on Spinoza's philosophy, however helpful and interesting that material can be; it is to show how Spinoza's thinking can be used outside of philosophy for configuring a true interdisciplinary ecological thought. I will make the case that the truly powerful aspect of Spinoza's thought for an interdisciplinary ecological thought is not his grand metaphysics, but rather his theory of affect. This corresponds to what is most important now for a theoretical engagement with ecology, in both its political and scientific forms: first, a disempowering of the secular theology of Nature, and second, an understanding of the extra- or non-rational relationship of human beings and human societies to the wider biosphere, as well as how that relationship can become ethical despite its extra-rational status. Michael Mack has shown in Chapter 2 that, in Spinoza, the human can finally be understood to retain his or her dignity without being at the centre of the cosmos. This chapter will explore how Spinoza's theory of affect can help us to understand how the human and non-human can form an ethical relationship through a focus on affect.

## FORGET (FOR NOW) GOD (OR NATURE): THE THEOLOGICAL FORM OF ENVIRONMENTAL PHILOSOPHY

There are two dominant legacies of Spinoza's philosophy that can be traced to ecology: the reductionist and mechanistic form of science that arose out of the Radical Enlightenment, and the deep ecology movement that takes Spinoza as a main philosophical forebear. Both of these movements are strongly theological in form. They are theological not in the sense of the dogmatic theology of the various institutional faiths, but in the sense that they are concerned with the 'highest' within thought or the very possibility of beings. They concern themselves with big questions, and their answers are given along a theological model that largely negates, displaces or obscures the question of the ethical relation of bodies, and the corollary human question, that are vitally important for ecology. For both the reductionist and mechanistic scientistic thinker and the holistic deep ecologist there is an attempt to bring everything back to a cause that provides an order that finally explains how the diversity of all things hangs together. In both cases what we find is an overdetermination of ecology by philosophy (understood here to be operating as a secular form of theology).

Jonathan I. Israel has traced the importance of Spinoza's philosophy for the Radical Enlightenment and there his legacy appears as one of radical atheism serving as a precursor to modern eliminativist philosophies (Israel 2001). Israel shows that Spinoza's philosophy was put to use in radical ways throughout the development of European science, but does not exhaust the various plausible Spinozisms. In fact, in terms of how Spinoza's philosophy can be a powerful tool for contemporary ecology, it is a good thing that Spinoza's philosophy is not simply a reductionist and mechanistic one. For this mechanistic philosophy, which went hand-in-hand with a mechanistic practice of science, is not adequate to the reality of an ecosystem or to the practice of contemporary ecological science. So, if Spinoza's thought is not merely reduced to this position, it may still offer something to ecological practice and thought.

Those like Diderot and la Mettrie, whose work was not Spinozistic in the strict sense but for whom Spinoza paved the way, created the philosophy at the heart of the mechanistic image of Nature that, for some time, scientific ecology laboured under and whose effects are still felt at times within the science. Yet despite their own atheism, they carried a theological problem into ecology. Daniel Botkin has traced this image of nature in his book *Discordant Harmonies*, showing that under this image of thought the Earth is dead, as it is understood as a non-living machine instead of the living organism proposed by previous philosophies (Botkin 1990: 103). The death of the Earth in this mechanistic philosophy is not truly atheistic, meaning it has not escaped the theological forms of thought, because it is predicated on a theological perception of beauty: 'The mechanical view is constant with the idea of a divine order in most of its particulars and consequences, and thus the mechanical perspective simultaneously reinforced the ideal of divine order and was reinforced by that theological perspective' (Botkin 1990: 103). The theological perspective Botkin is here speaking of is, of course, the human search for a static vision of the cosmos where that stasis fosters a peaceful order that ultimately serves or can be manipulated to serve human ends. There is a deep connection here between an ecology guided by aesthetics and theological thinking:

> [T]he belief in aesthetically pleasing and theologically satisfying physical symmetries was replaced by a belief in an aesthetically pleasing and theologically satisfying conceptual order. While the belief in gross physical attributes of symmetry, balance, and order was no longer tenable following the new observations of nature, Newton's laws created a conceptual order. Subsequently, theologians used this conceptual order to justify their belief in a perfect world where a perfect order (the laws of nature) ruled our asymmetric and structurally imperfect world. (Botkin 1990: 109)

Like other theological images of nature that Botkin examines, the mechanistic image locates a simple, solid-state reality of nature despite the empirical findings of ecological fieldwork. Nature is not a great seventeenth-century machine that works according to an outdated physical model for the purposes of static predictions. The one truth that this image could give us has largely been occluded – nature is ultimately artificial at the same time as it is natural, or, in other words, human beings can act as engineers or custodians of this machine for the benefit of all of nature (human and non-human). Yet those who hold this view have tended to see nature as a divinely constructed machine that must either be left completely undisturbed to remain perfect as such, or be completely subjected to human mastery (Botkin 1990: 108). The mechanical image fails, not because it displaces God, but because it perpetuates a theological form of thinking that either negates one aspect of the Earth (humanity as the creator of unnatural artifice) or kills the whole of the Earth by refusing it life.

Deep ecology constitutes a radically different understanding of the world, but nevertheless operates along the same theological model: it sets up Nature, again with the capital N, as a secular divinity perfect in itself that has been unbalanced by the actions of humanity. This conception of nature is often confused with Spinoza's own project. Arne Naess, the leading intellectual figure in the movement of deep ecology, credits Spinoza with providing a philsophy that lays the foundations for a philosophy of deep ecology or 'ecosophia'. This is most explicitly expressed in the impressionistic article 'Spinoza and Ecology'. This article, while providing a very compact reading of Spinoza's philosophy in relation to ecology, connects philosophy and ecology via axioms and maxims. There is an image of ecology that determines Naess's reading of the fittingness between Spinoza's philosophy and ecology. That image is the notion that ecology allows us to see the interconnectedness of all things. Naess takes this interconnectedness to be both the main object of inquiry for ecology and the subsequent foundation for ethical thought.

This interconnectedness is related to the theological elements of Spinoza's thought, where Naess claims that, for Spinoza, nature is perfect in itself and exists outside time without goal. Both statements mirror classical theological positions on God, especially those notions found most forcefully in the medieval Scholasticism whose vocabulary and concepts Spinoza used and mutated. Naess, though, does not try to move beyond this theological element of Spinoza's work and instead, when Naess touches upon 'the human question' or the question of individual powers and affects (the aspects that I claim are more interesting and potentially powerful for uniting with ecology), he always does so within the wider goal of highlighting the big answer. Everything must ultimately be related to the 'all' or whole of interconnectedness, as when he writes: 'All beings strive to maintain *and gain* power. God or Nature has no other power than ours. [. . .] The freedom of the individual ultimately requires that of collectivity' (Naess 1977: 49). While this touches on smaller questions within ecology, of individual powers and affects that make up this collectivity, it does so wholly determined by the context of the larger question and the larger answer without much attention given to affects and power: which is to say, without much attention given to the human question.

This reflects a problem of scale common to deep ecology where the individual entities are lost in the big question concerning the whole of the biosphere. This problem of scale is good in some ways, for it rejects the usual division of philosophical domains like ethics and metaphysics that is found in mainstream Anglophone environmental philosophy. This separation of philosophical domains is all too often imposed on reality itself, such that ecology is brought before philosophy and asked to reveal its ethical status but to say nothing about metaphysics. Yet ecology presents certain challenges to these kinds of philosophical scissions, for the ontological status of an ecosystem and the ethical demand arising from its existence are not easily separable. Naess recognises this, writing that 'one's ethics in environmental questions are based largely on how one sees reality' and that it is 'important in the philosophy of environmentalism to *move from ethics to ontology and back*' (Naess 1989: 66, 67). But this issue of scale, where deep ecology operates at the theological level of the whole, also carries with it an implicit philosophy of science. The notion of a deep ecology would appear to suggest that Naess's philosophy is developed alongside concepts from scientific ecology, yet his real hope is to move from ecology to ecosophy. Ecology does not appear to set the agenda for the philosopher, but instead provides, as it so often does, a litany of facts about the destructive power of contemporary human society on the wider non-human world.

Rather than creating a unified practice of philosophy and ecology, which would require that the philosopher be challenged by ecological material, Naess provides environmental philosophy with a model that will be taken up by a plethora of other thinkers: Western philosophy, along with its complicity in the 'so-called scientific worldview', is to be challenged with Eastern philosophy (Naess 1989: 171–82). Naess does not do this in some naïve sense – he is not trading in a vulgar exoticism – but when it comes to concepts he finds problematic in the Western philosophical tradition, like the divide between objective and subjective qualities or the dominant form of the concept of the self, he draws on resources from the Eastern tradition combined with his own philosophical project rather than drawing on scientific ecology.

This is especially strange since he recognises that ecology 'has application to and overlaps with the problems of philosophy' (Naess 1989: 36). So what is it that keeps Naess from engaging deeply with ecological concepts? The answer is that ecology as a science is suspect precisely because it is a *science*; it operates with the suffix '-logy' rather than '-sophy'. Within Naess's ecosophy science must be controlled, including ecology; science must be placed within a normative – that is, philosophical – milieu that limits its power, or as Naess would rather say, that recognises the limits of its power. The impetus behind this ecosophical reining in of science is, in many ways, Spinozistic, for it suggests that while nature may have an infinite number of attributes, we know only two (E IP1, IIP1S), and so nature as such resists any total capture by human thought. Yet Naess uses this resistance to critique the post-Galilean scientific worldview, claiming that we must resist any kind of universalisation of one science, be it fostering biologism or ecologism, which generalises the concepts of the particular science too much (Naess 1989: 39).

What, then, are the limits to scientific ecology that Naess thinks are necessary to engender a 'profound' understanding of nature that undergirds a deep ecology? Against ecologism, the overgeneralisation of concepts from ecology understood simplistically, we can locate an ecological minimalism at work in Naess's ecosophy. We may even call this minimalism shallow ecologism, as it refuses a deep engagement with scientific ecology. This is operative in Naess's definition of ecology:

> The expression 'ecology' is infused with many meanings. Here, it will mean
> the interdisciplinary scientific study of the living conditions of organisms in
> interaction with each other and with their surroundings, organic as well as
> inorganic. For these surroundings the terms 'milieu' and 'environment' will
> be used nearly interchangeably. (Naess 1989: 34)

This is not a bad definition of ecology; in fact, it is quite close to the
generally accepted definition given in Michael Allaby's *Dictionary of
Ecology*: 'The scientific study of the inter-relationships among organisms and between organisms, and between them and all aspects, living
and non-living, of their environment' (2005: 146). However, it does not
delve into ecology's concepts with any depth either. Even the concepts it
touches upon, 'organisms' (populations, or the diversity of species that
populate the ecosystem), 'living conditions' (what we call the never-
living space and temporality of the environment), 'interaction' (energy
relations of exchange that arise out of the populations' interaction with
one another) and 'environment / milieu' (ecosystem), are not explored
in any depth in relation to philosophical issues.[1]

This lack of depth is related directly to the grand style of deep
ecology with its focus on the 'big questions' and 'big answers'. Naess
thinks that the science of ecology only provides us with recognition of
severely limited ecological knowledge, and that ecology tells us that
we do not yet understand the ecological consequences of change in a
particular ecosystem: 'the study of ecosystems makes us conscious of
our ignorance' (Naess 1989: 27). Indeed, the only truly positive notion
that Naess appears to take from ecology is the idea that 'all things hang
together', which he takes to be an ontological statement that is ethically significant (Naess 1989: 38). Naess points out that this does not,
in itself, explain how all things hang together, but instead of turning to
the very things that ecology is precisely not ignorant about, he turns to
another philosophy (Gestalt thinking) (Naess 1989: 57, 57–63).

Yet ecology could provide resources for understanding how things
hang together because it is not ignorant of the aspects mentioned above
(biodiversity, energy exchange, the spatial borders of an ecosystem and
so on); ecology has developed a number of tools for understanding the
various ecosystems and the wider biosphere. So what exactly is Naess
referring to by claiming that ecology reveals our ignorance? He says
that this has to do with a kind of political usefulness. No longer can
politicians appeal to science or instrumental reason to deal with the
pressing issues. Cost–benefit analyses will no longer be a substitute for
wisdom, and it is not as if Naess is wrong here; since writing this over
two decades ago, governments have not appeared to become any more
wise (Naess 1989: 26–8). If this were the case it would be laudable, but

there is a more nefarious effect of Naess's presentation of ecology, one that is often mirrored in other philosophical thinkers as well. In short, he is claiming that science, and ecology specifically, does not think; that only philosophy, in the guise of ecosophy, can provide the grand framework to make any practical sense of the statements of ecology. 'Without an ecosophy, ecology can provide no principles for acting, no motive for political and individual efforts' (Naess 1989: 41). Again, we are left with a split in reality between what we know *is* and what we think we *ought* to do.

In a strange way, then, Naess actually accepts the arrangement of philosophy and science that is unecological within thought. Not only does Naess not draw on scientific ecology to challenge and push philosophy on problems inherent to it and related to environmental issues; he does not attempt to mutate directly what he takes to be science's underlying *philosophical* split between primary and secondary qualities and objective and subjective reality. Rather, he continues the typical relationship of science and philosophy: philosophy is exalted over a science that does not think. At one point referring to the scientific study of the environment, he asks sarcastically, 'Are we getting any closer with the long scientific strides built upon the work of Galileo or Newton?' (Naess 1989: 48). If the goal of a deep ecology movement was to turn the tide of environmental destruction by fostering an ecosophy, can we not turn this question back on Naess? Are we getting any closer to an ecosophical relationship with the biosphere with the strides built upon his work?

The goal in this essay is obviously far more modest than Naess's, for I only aim to show that Spinoza's theory of affects can be useful for bringing together scientific ecology with environmental activism and public policy. That usefulness should tell us something about the importance of Spinoza beyond philosophy, as well as provide tools and new lines of research for theorists and activists directed by ecological concerns. This task requires subtlety. A full exposition of a unified theory of philosophy and ecology, suggested in the previous section, is beyond the scope of this essay, but while not directly challenging and adapting Spinoza's philosophical concepts and logic with scientific ecology, nothing in this essay should stand outside such a democracy of thought.

There are other restrictions as well, for the problem that arises from the theological form of environmental philosophy is one of attention, but to direct attention in a more ecologically productive manner we cannot simply foster an anti-theological form. While there may be comfort in playing the usual philosophical game of separating 'ought' from 'is', it is nothing more than a distraction from the real tasks of thinking through the ecological situation. With neither the theological form nor the anti-theological form as a real option, how can we direct our attention? Spinoza was dealing with the same impasse in his *Ethics* when he strove to move past the theological form of Descartes's philosophy as well as provide a philosophy that did not split reality. His tactic was to radicalise the theological form, not to direct attention to confused abstractions, but precisely to direct attention to material bodies.

Instead of pitching the material against the ideal (what the theological form of thought is concerned with), Spinoza creates a chimerical form of thinking where the genetic codes of the ideal flow with the codes of the material.[2] Philip Goodchild describes this radicalisation of the theological form as a method of immanent critique writing:

> Spinoza, writing at the cusp of modernity, pioneered a method of immanent critique through a cynical equivocation: *deus sive natura* [. . .] By taking this Calvinist piety to its logical extreme, attributing all that happens to God, Spinoza is able to identify God with nature [. . .] Spinoza's method of immanent critique is clear: he began from the ultimate principle, the Word or mind of God, and attributed to it all the properties required by piety, including unity, universality and infinite power. (Goodchild 2002: 73, 75)

What Goodchild means by cynical is helpful for understanding the radicalisation of the theological form Spinoza employs. The conception comes from Goodchild's reading of Diogenes the Cynic and the essence of cynicism is shown in the recounting of two stories. The first is Diogenes responding to Plato's definition of man as a featherless biped by bringing a plucked fowl into the lecture room, and the second is Diogenes drawing attention away from a set speech by eating lupins followed by his feigned shock that the assembly would be distracted from the speech by the simple eating of lupins. 'Such cynical gestures consist in responding to questions concerning the highest ideals with something material, edible and mortal' (Goodchild 2002: 71).

Even though the phrase 'God, or Nature' does not appear until the Preface to Part IV, late in the *Ethics*, the entirety of the work witnesses this intentional slippage between God and Nature. This equivocation is not a form of pantheism (Hegel's reading) or of esoteric naturalism (Leo Strauss's reading) but requires that the traditional conceptions of both God and Nature are transformed.[3] And this 'cynical equivocation' allows for attention to move outside the capture of the theological form that must always end in silence or poetry before the grandeur of nature for the Deep Ecologist. This is exactly the way it functions in the flow of Spinoza's text, allowing him to move from the usual discussions required by the theological form, residing as they do in the ideal realm, to a real understanding of the 'nature and powers [or abilities] of the affects' (E IIIPref.). Spinoza tells us that, at the time of his writing,

> Most of those who have written about the affects, and men's way of living, seem to treat, not of natural things, which follow the common laws of Nature, but of things that are outside Nature. Indeed they seem to conceive man in Nature as a dominion within a dominion. For they believe that man disturbs, rather than follows, the order of Nature, that he has absolute power over his actions, and that he is determined only by himself. And they attribute the cause of human impotence and inconstancy, not to the common power of Nature, but to I know not what vice of human nature, which they therefore bewail, or laugh at, or disdain, or (as usually happens) curse. And he who knows how to ensure more eloquently the weakness of the human mind is held to be godly. (E IIIPref.)

While there are those 'who prefer to curse or laugh at the affects and actions of men, rather than understand them', Spinoza is able to direct a clinical attention towards them: no longer as things that, in the light of the ideal, are nothing but crude jokes to be mocked and laughed at, but as things following from the universal laws of Nature (or God). Spinoza considers 'human actions and appetites just as if [they] were a question of lines, planes, and bodies' (E IIIPref.).

## SPINOZA'S THEORY OF AFFECTS AND THE POSSIBILITY OF AN AFFECTIVE ECOLOGY

Spinoza's theory of affects moves the attention of theory away from separating the 'is' from the 'ought', and instead directs it to the mixture of reason and passion, of the rational and those acts that lie outside of rationality, or what could be termed the extra-rational. Spinoza allows us to see that reason is not an absolute; it is placed within a wider relationship, and it is often strongly directed by the affect it relates to at any given time. While it is clearly necessary to approach ecological problems from a rational perspective, what Spinoza's theory of affects shows us is that such an approach must be carried out with an understanding of what lies outside of the rational perspective. For with such an understanding we may begin to foster more productive affects that would in turn strengthen the rational process. Of course, readers of Spinoza's *Ethics* will be familiar with his own description of each affect (joy, hatred and so on), and a project that takes the theory of affects seriously should be able to build on Spinoza's descriptions. But that is exactly what would be required: *building* on those descriptions. What is important to take from Spinoza's theory of affects is the model he gives of the relationship between affects. While historians of philosophy will be interested in the specificity of these descriptions, for a Spinoza beyond philosophy these specifics must be up for revision within a wider unified theory of philosophy and ecology. My claim is that the importance of Spinoza's theory of affects for such a project is to be seen by the place that theory finds within the *Ethics*, as a pivot between 'God or Nature' and the ethical place of humanity within nature, and within his discussion of the secondary nature of emotions (like guilt) to affects (like hatred).

So what is an affect, how does it fit within the wider schema of Spinoza's *Ethics*, and what does a theory of affect add to expanded ecological research? The questions are ultimately related, but let us start with the definition that Spinoza gives for affects in Part III of the *Ethics*, where the idea is first introduced. There he writes:

> By affect I understand affections of the body by which the body's power of acting is increased or diminished, aided or restrained, and at the same time, the ideas of these affections. *Therefore, if we can be the adequate cause of any of these affections, I understand by the affect an action; otherwise, a passion.* (E IIID3)

Affects are often waved away as *just* emotions or feelings. They are not often taken to be very important for theoretical work, which was classically more concerned with reason and those things that lie outside the realm of emotion. Spinoza's conception shifts thinking concerning affects by simply giving them attention and asserting the intention to understand them. So what is an affect? Simply put, it is a power acting either from the body or upon the body, and it is also the idea of that power. A joyful affect expresses an increase in power (the ability to effect change, not power in the sense of domination) and it can also increase power, both in oneself and in others. The opposite goes for sorrowful affects.

Importantly, affects are not something we consciously choose, but they happen to us in many ways. Spinoza uses the language of essence and 'of one's nature', but his use of these terms does not imply the same static state that these words tend to carry with them; in fact, it puts them into question. For while the reader of Spinoza's texts often finds what appear to be brazen assertions about the 'nature' or essence of a human being, they must be balanced with statements like:

> no one has yet determined what the body can do, that is, experience has not yet taught anyone what the body can do from the laws of Nature alone, insofar as Nature is only considered to be corporeal, and what the body can do only if it is determined by the mind. For no one has yet come to know the structure of the body so accurately that he could explain all its functions

> – not to mention that many things are observed in the lower animals which far surpass human ingenuity, and that sleepwalkers do a great many things in their sleep which they would not dare do awake. This shows well enough that the body itself, simply from the laws of its own nature, can do many things its mind wonders at. (E IIIP2S)

While we mistakenly think in our mind that we have control over ourselves, an affect is a kind of body or material thing that even our mind undergoes. For an affect is a state that either accords with our nature or does not. If it accords with our nature, our power increases, and if it does not, our power decreases.

Spinoza's theory of affect is central to the wider flow of the *Ethics* and reading it within that flow helps to elucidate its importance here. Part III of the *Ethics* is a pivot point between the abstract philosophy concerning God and Mind and the practical philosophy developed in Parts IV and V. Ultimately, the question of practice is centred on the question of affect, for affects have a dual identity. As touched on quickly above, either we may come under an affect of which we have an adequate idea, such that the affect becomes an action productive of an increase in power, or we come under an affect that is a passion that arises from an inadequate or confused idea. The question of these passions is treated at length in Part IV, where Spinoza writes,

> Man's lack of power to moderate and restrain the affects I call bondage. For the man who is subject to affects is under the control, not of himself, but of fortune, in whose power he so greatly is that often, though he sees the better for himself, he is still forced to follow the worse. (E IVPref.)

This means that the question of salvation treated in Part V is also ultimately concerned with the affects, where Spinoza praises the power of reason against the affects as passions. It would be easy for a reader to mistake Spinoza's intention here, reading him as advocating a Stoic life of coldness in the face of the passions, seeking freedom in detachment. But what we find in Part V is not a denigration of feeling, of love or joy, in favour of a cold mechanical reason, but instead what we can call a warm custodialism. There is no strict separation between reason and affects, for reason can act on an affect and change it from a passion to an action when we form a clear and distinct idea of it (E VP3), and an affect can arise from or be aroused by reason (E VP7).

I use the term 'warm custodialism' to describe the relationship between affects and reason in Spinoza's philosophy. This term avoids the negative connotations associated with managerialism, that confused, contradictory form of politics that aims to be apolitical, an apolitical politics, that is prevalent in the world today. Managerialism, especially within the circles of environmental activists, is usually associated with a certain kind of economic rationality that considers all aspects of human action as if they could fit into a cost–benefit analysis. So human beings' actions are tied to targets they must meet with the aim of increasing the power of the organisation. This can manifest itself in rather nefarious ways, but this managerialism is not present in Spinoza's conception of the relationship between reason and the affects. In the *Ethics*, reason is given the task of guiding the affects rather than ruling over them. This is a custodialism of affects such that they become acts through being known, rather than through passions that rule over reason through confusion. Custodialism can be differentiated from this sort of managerialism through a difference in relationship. A manager is hierarchically superior to those he manages, imagining himself to be a kind of imperium within an imperium, while a custodian is more embedded in the social relationships within which she dwells.

Why, though, would any of this matter for ecological research and activism? Naess is correct that ecology's conception of a single biosphere that includes humanity amongst other ecological actors shares much in common with Spinoza's propositions and subsequent deductions concerning nature (or God). While pre-ecological conceptions of nature that arose out of classical philosophical and theological research, described in the previous section, posited a relationship between humanity and the rest of non-human nature that was predicated on their separation, the ecological age has largely come to accept this fundamental relation. The real problem for thought in the age of ecological awareness is not the relation of humanity and wider non-human nature, but the production of this relation. Does this relation produce an artificial cession between the two? Such an artificial cession is not impossible from the viewpoint of the natural right of human beings to decrease their power through a short-term increase; nor is it, as existing, unnatural. Within the natural ability and thus right of human beings, can a relation be produced that is, in turn, productive of an ethical coupling that increases the overall power of the biosphere? This is the Spinozistic question that the avant-garde of scientific ecology is beginning, in its own way, to take up. It is a question that requires that we move our attention away from the grandeur of God or Nature and turn our attention instead to what could be provocatively termed 'the human question'.

Until very recently, ecology had not taken up this human question in a particularly ecological way. Instead, the human was a matter of peripheral interest, either because if humans were involved, it somehow was not truly natural (this is the stance of most nineteenth- and twentieth-century American nature writing), or because there was an impoverished understanding of the human within ecosystems. This was true not only at the physical level, since human-dominated ecosystems were not of particular interest to the early naturalists that paved the way for contemporary ecology, but also at the level of ideas. Ecologists have not, until recently, explicitly considered the complex relationships human beings have with their own thoughts on nature and the effects those ideas have on their actions within ecosystems. This is beginning to change within a somewhat heretical subset of ecology called 'urban ecology'. Urban ecology is forced to deal with the human question by virtue of being focused on an ecosystem more heavily determined by human beings. In turn, it must be concerned with the social form of common life amongst human beings, as well as the human desire and need for what we can call non-human natural areas (remembering that the city is also a natural area).[4]

Some ecologists have been calling for this new direction for some time. For example, the research of John F. Dwyer of the US Forest Service has shown the different relationships of differing social populations with forest preserves and how these relationships affect conservation efforts. There is also the turn towards considering human / non-human coupled ecosystems that is part of the general turn away from focusing on conservation towards a focus on resilience, as outlined brilliantly in Salt and Walker's recent book entitled *Resilience Thinking*. An exciting project has just begun in Chicago under the name 'Collaborative Research: Coupled Natural Human Systems in the Chicago Wilderness: Evaluating the Biodiversity and Social Outcomes of Different Models of Restoration Planning'. The project is funded by the US National Science Foundation, which is a hopeful sign, as it marks a truly interdisciplinary project that brings together scientific ecologists with those in the human sciences like sociology and anthropology. This team is, for the first time, posing the human question in a truly ecological way. In a move reminiscent of Spinoza's geometric method, the 'Coupled Natural Human Systems' project treats human ideas and attitudes towards nature, as manifested in the common lives of various communities, as a research variable that must be included within the wider research on the urban ecosystem. This is a revolutionary move within ecology. In addition to taking seriously the need for open and intelligent research into how best to restore and foster resilience in fragile and weak ecosystems, it considers the human interaction within that ecosystem, not as a matter of history, which some ecological studies have already done, but as a matter of the here and now. It is the first step towards understanding the strength of these ideas, their effects and how, if necessary, they can be changed.

This is precisely where Spinoza's theory of affect could be useful and bring the philosopher into the wider interdisciplinary effort. Spinoza, we have seen, identifies the power of 'ideas' and 'attitudes' in the affects. Emotions proper, like guilt, are secondary to affects. Yet, at the popular level of environmental politics, it is these emotions that are given attention. Mainstream environmental activists appear to think that, if they are able to convince others of their guilt, they will act 'green' out of contrition. Spinoza targeted this sense of guilt, for when we focus on guilt we are not acting intelligently, but instead blindly groping for true joy. Against the theological form, however secular, of popular environmentalism is Spinoza's ethical vision. That vision is given powerfully in the *Theological-Political Treatise*, where Spinoza argues against a voluntaristic God, for God did not make an arbitrary law against eating the fruit of the Tree of Good and Evil, but the law merely expressed the reality that, by eating of the body of the fruit, Adam would decompose his own body. Without thinking rationally, Adam confused this natural revelation with an arbitrary divine prohibition (see Deleuze 1988: 17–29).

Affect theory can be of practical use here. Consider Propositions 16 and 17 of Part III of the *Ethics*, where Spinoza writes,

> From the mere fact that we imagine a thing to have some likeness to an object which usually affects the mind with joy or sadness, we love it or hate it, even though that in which the thing is like the object is not the efficient cause of these affects [. . .] If we imagine that a thing which usually affects us with an affect of sadness is like another which usually affects us with an equally great affect of joy, we shall hate it and at the same time love it. (E IIIP16, IIIP17)

This can provide us with an insight into the impasse contemporary Western society has with its own ecological consciousness. For example, most of the already existing narrative of what it means to go 'green' is largely coded as white and upper middle-class, which, for those outside that social group, is an image caught up in other affects that have very little to do with practical changes that can foster a more rational and intentionally ecological dwelling. It also points to our ambiguous relationship with objects in the world like oil. Oil is necessary for our lives, it is productive of joyful affects as a necessary part of the freedom that comes from a car, but it also produces sadness, for its use leads to the guilt of knowing that our actions are part of the cause of global climate change. In Spinoza's terms, we are aware of the future weakening of our power that comes every time we fill up at the pump.

Looking at the affective conditions of different social groups will become an important area of research. For the already existing narrative of what it means to be 'green' is, in reality, only one expression of a single affective relationship. This affect is privileged in the media, but as we look to understand the nature of other social bodies we can begin to discover the tendencies of affects in those communities as well. Each community will hold within it a variety of different affects, some active and many passive, which can finally be understood in terms of the relations they produce. This is why, though urban ecologists may already know it, the city is a privileged site for ecological research into the human question, for the city is a site of ethical living. Spinoza says in the *Political Treatise* that 'Men are not born to be citizens, but are made so' (TP 5.2), and goes on to describe the formation of different cities by way of different affects – fear and anxiety, as well as hope for a greater good. The city is not *de facto* the site of reasonable human beings, of citizens, for cities must include the just and the unjust. The city becomes an ethical body in itself, depending on the relation of the subjects that form it. By focusing on the affects of the social bodies that make up the body of the city, urban ecologists can begin to understand what the affective health of that city is. This can be seen in so far as a joyful affect is tied directly to the ecological health of that city and the infrastructure which supports it (here we have to include agricultural areas, as well as those spaces reserved for non-human use). In this way, we will have a general sense of the ethical status of the whole of the ecosystem.

To close, what we have done here is move towards a Spinozist understanding of ecology where the theological form of environmental philosophy is radicalised. Practically, this means that metaphysics, ethics and politics are all given in one and the same vision as united under some relationship between affects. Thus a new relationship, one in the hope of a future joy, is fostered between philosophy and ecology. It is becoming increasingly clear that the health of an ecosystem and the health of the social communities of human beings are inseparable, revealing that there is an important parallelism between our ideas and our social bodies. This means that changes in the ecosystems we inhabit depend on our material actions, as well as our theoretical ideas. Or, to state that in clearer language, in order to address the ecological crisis, we must address the human question. Affects are powerful and, by looking to how they function, we may begin to find ways to foster more joyous relations with the rest of non-human nature. If we want to increase our joy in the light of the threat that faces not just an abstract quasi-divine Nature, but every actual living thing as well, then there is no alternative.

## NOTES

1. I have discussed these issues at length in Smith 2010.
2. For a longer discussion of the chimerical logic at work in Spinoza's philosophy, see Zourabichvili 2002: 218–26 and Gangle 2010: 26–43.
3. On these themes see Levene 2004 and Polka 2007. Levene is especially helpful in arguing against Strauss's reading of Spinoza as a writer of an esoteric text.
4. By non-human natural areas I mean parks, forest preserves, remnant prairies, and other places human beings may visit but do not dwell in, as well as the necessary green infrastructure required in cities to deal with the toxic pollution produced by human activity.

## BIBLIOGRAPHY


Allaby, Michael (2005), *Oxford Dictionary of Ecology*, 3rd edn, Oxford: Oxford University Press.

Botkin, Daniel B. (1990), *Discordant Harmonies: A New Ecology for the Twenty-first Century*, Oxford: Oxford University Press.

Deleuze, Gilles (1988), *Spinoza: Practical Philosophy*, trans. Robert Hurley, San Francisco: City Lights.

Gangle, Rocco (2010), 'Theology of the Chimera: Spinoza, Immanence, Practice', *After the Postsecular and the Postmodern: New Essays in Continental Philosophy of Religion*, ed. Anthony Paul Smith and Daniel Whistler, Newcastle upon Tyne: Cambridge Scholars.

Goodchild, Philip (2002), *Capitalism and Religion: The Price of Piety*, London: Routledge.

Israel, Jonathan I. (2001), *Radical Enlightenment: Philosophy and the Making of Modernity 1650–1750*, Oxford: Oxford University Press.

Levene, Nancy K. (2004), *Spinoza's Revelation: Religion, Democracy, and Reason*, Cambridge: Cambridge University Press.

Naess, Arne (1977), 'Spinoza and Ecology', *Philosophia* 7(1), pp. 45–54.

Naess, Arne (1989), *Ecology, Community and Lifestyle: Outline of an Ecosophy*, trans. David Rothenberg, Cambridge: Cambridge University Press.

Polka, Blayton (2007), *Between Philosophy and Religion: Spinoza, the Bible, and Modernity*, vol. I: *Hermeneutics and Ontology*, Lexington: Lexington Books.

Smith, Anthony Paul (2010), 'Philosophy and Ecosystem: Towards a Transcendental Ecology', *Polygraph* 22, pp. 65–82.

Spinoza, Benedict de (1994), *A Spinoza Reader: The Ethics and Other Works*, ed. and trans. Edwin Curley, Princeton: Princeton University Press.

Spinoza, Benedict de (2000), *Political Treatise*, trans. Samuel Shirley, Indianapolis: Hackett.

Zourabichvili, François (2002), *Spinoza. Une Physique de la pensée*, Paris: PUF.

# 4. *Spinoza's Architectural Passages and Geometric Comportments*

## PEG RAWES

Following the preceding examinations of subjectivity and environmental relations in Spinoza's writing, this chapter considers how his work provides an inventive approach for discussing important relational qualities in architectural drawings and spaces of inhabitation. In addition, I suggest that his intense study of the emotions underscores the capacity of geometry not just to embody the historically familiar forms of rational and technical reasoning with which it is normally associated, but how it has a more radical capacity for embodying temporal and sense-based modes of expression. As we have already seen in this collection, the *Ethics* is deeply concerned with the way in which the subject is constructed in process. This chapter connects with these discussions by considering how geometric reason and sense are brought together to produce diverse subjectivities. Moreover, if we transfer Spinoza's thinking about 'geometries of sense' into the discipline of architectural design, we see manifestations of these modes of expression where technical and sense-based geometric elements (such as human subjects and bodies, and geometric figures such as circles or triangles) constitute a uniquely processual method. In particular, I consider how these dynamic modes of geometric thinking are derived from a radical notion of 'nature' and 'substance' in the *Ethics*, which produce a special 'natural' kind of architecture. In this 'living' architecture or geometry, then, all modes of immaterial and material expression are imbued with substance and nature's irreducible powers of sense and reason. These include ordinary people and their desires and fears, everyday and common ideas or geometric principles, and aesthetic judgements that inform architectural design processes and the built environment.

The chapter begins by considering how Spinoza's geometric method resonates with the design and inhabitation of a Renaissance villa which the architect Robin Evans traces in the passage from its architectural drawings to the lived spatial experience of its interior organisation. I suggest that in both Spinoza's metaphysical text and Robin Evans's interpretation of Raphael's Villa Madama in Italy, lived modes of architectural space are generated in which sense and reason are intimately related. Spinoza's *Ethics* accords with the architectural passages of Villa Madama because each represents a special site of geometric process in which sense and reason are brought together to form particularly affective 'ways of life'.

The chapter also suggests that Spinoza's *Ethics* is itself a kind of architectural passage because of the diverse figures and passages of comportment that his geometric thinking enables. An intensive relationship between existence (that is, life) and geometric expression is constructed through the heterogeneous 'modes' and spaces of existence that compose the building and the text; for example, in the spatial and temporal inhabitations of the Villa, such as the comings and goings of its occupants and visitors that transform seemingly determined architectural drawings into a diverse range of encounters, bodies or spatiotemporal events; or the way in which Spinoza's text generates different kinds of subjects and lives; or the various dynamic modes of engagement and response that the *Ethics* provokes in the reader. In each 'architecture', then, diverse 'geometric subjects' are constructed. Together they enable subjects-in-process, that is, figures composed of sense and reason (sense-reason) in which architecture and the individual subject do not evolve from a series of pre-defined 'stagings' or plans, but from complex 'natural' geometric processes.[1] Generated out of the technical and aesthetic processes of geometry, drawing and design, as well as the desires and lives of the inhabitants and designers, the architectural design of Villa Madama may therefore be understood as a process in which geometry and human expression are brought into close proximity, in a manner similar to the way in which Spinoza's text operates. In turn, Spinoza's natural geometry might also be seen as a seventeenth-century kind of architectural passage.

Robin Evans's essays about the relationship between the 'everyday' social occupation and 'life' of buildings and geometric thinking offer valuable insights into how geometry in architecture can generate heterogeneous spatiotemporal experience.[2] In particular, his writing highlights how geometric thinking in architecture is a method through which buildings are transformed from drawn projections of space into everyday modes of psychic and physical interaction. In his 1978 essay 'Figures, Doors and Passages' for example, Evans addresses the widely held contemporary view that Cartesian geometry in architectural plans often results in rigid classifications, divisions and order in buildings, and consequently this also determines and restricts the behaviour and lives of the occupants in negative ways:[3]

> If anything is described by an architectural plan, it is the nature of human relationships, since the elements whose trace it records – walls, doors, windows and stairs – are employed first to divide and then selectively to re-unite inhabited space . . . Surely, though, if the circle were widened to take in material beyond architectural drawings, one might expect there to be some tally between the commonplaces of house-planning and the ordinary ways in which people dispose themselves in relation to each other. This might seem an odd connection to make at first, but however different they are – however realistic and particular the descriptions, pictures or photographs of men, women, children and other domestic animals doing what they do, however abstract and diagrammatic the plans – both relate back to the same fundamental issue of human relationships. Take the portrayal of human figures and take house plans from a given time and place: look at them together as evidence of a way of life, and the coupling between everyday conduct and architectural organization becomes more lucid. (Evans 2003: 56–7)

Evans notes that contemporary critiques of architectural plans question the tradition of populating architectural drawings with human figures which are merely 'emblematic signs of life' rather than 'substantial creatures'. He turns instead to consider Raphael's sympathetic treatment of the subject: in particular, the comportment of 'other' subjects and figures in his devotional paintings. Evans argues that there is much evidence of everyday life here, which also informs Raphael and his assistants' approach to designing the Villa Madama (1518–25). For Evans, Raphael's earthly paintings of religious figures, 'his particular *temperament towards others*', express the close proximity between 'commonplace' bodies and the geometric configurations in which they are situated (Evans 2003: 57). Raphael, he suggests, transforms the traditional lofty transcendental images of religious groups into images of intimate bodily relationships and spaces, especially between women and children (Mary and Jesus). Surely, Evans asks, the Villa's spaces might then also embody diverse 'ways of life' in which the relationship between the people who occupy the space and the geometry that composes it are interrelated so as to constitute everyday 'conduct'? His analysis is in contrast to the way in which traditional architectural history has overlooked these qualities in the Villa, in part because of its preoccupation with examining the technical and historical provenance of drawings in the design process.[4] Instead, Evans draws our attention to the sensible and aesthetic qualities of the human subjects and geometric figures in Raphael's paintings, and in his architectural drawing process, in order to highlight the importance of the 'commonplace' in

*Figure 1*  Antonio da Sangallo's plan of Villa Madama, Rome, redrawn by
Robin Evans (Evans 2003: 61)

his approach to geometric thinking, to architecture and, consequently,
in the production of subjectivity.

Focusing particularly on Raphael's apprentice Antonio da Sangallo's
translations of the original drawings into the more asymmetric plans
upon which the final building was based, Evans observes that the Villa's
interior is a progressively differentiated set of spaces which are open
to diverse passages of circulation. He notes, for example, the multiple
passages through the Villa that can be taken from the entrance at the
stairs of the south-western corner. In addition, this multiplicity is most
evident in the permeability of the walls, which are generated by the
large number of doorways designed into each of the 'discrete' rooms.
Sixteenth- and seventeenth-century domestic architecture represents a
highly perforated and dynamic kind of geometry, as its multiple doors
in rooms and walls allow for a range of passages through the various
living-rooms, vestibules and even, Evans notes, water-closets. He
observes the density of routes through the spaces and their multi-modal
points of access, which made it possible for occupants of all social
groups and classes to pass through the same rooms simultaneously from
different directions. In addition, he notes Alberti's praise of the 'ordinary practice' at the time for increasing the circulation in buildings by
designing in multiple doors, enabling access 'to as many Parts' as possible, and which made the house 'a matrix of discrete but thoroughly
interconnected chambers' (Evans 2003: 63–4). Unlike the later formal
spatial demarcation between the classes in the Victorian British house,
where passages become corridors that separate work from leisure and

patron from servant, and which therefore more exclusively divide the house into distinct class-based psychic and physical relations, Evans argues that the Villa's multi-modal construction produces passages that are available to all occupants and modes of life simultaneously, in close proximity.[5] Here, then, key elements that comprise the design of a building (that is, its rooms, walls and doors) generate geometric passages and enclosures. Those diverse modes of everyday existence, duration or encounter are retained which are lost in the later, more strongly demarcated, functional spaces of eighteenth- and nineteenth-century domestic architecture. For Evans, da Sangallo's drawings therefore represent especially strong embodiments of the potential for diverse comportments and modes of inhabitation in the Villa's social architecture.

Evans's observations about the everyday relations constructed between human bodies and geometry indicate the importance of life for geometric thinking in architectural design. Although he does not extend these discussions about the everyday to consider sexual and socio-economic difference, he does observe 'other' multi-modal and minor geometries. For example, in the closing paragraphs of his later influential essay, 'Translations from Drawing to Building' (1986), he explores the potential for the existence of different geometric thinkers, such as the female geometer. Rather than endorsing the traditional image of the male geometer or architect, or the God geometer, he notes the possibility of a history of the female architect-geometer in Giancinto Brandi's (1621–91) allegorical baroque painting of 'architecture' (Evans 2003: 186). Here, the figure of architecture is represented by the compass in the hands of an everyday woman: a woman who Evans identifies as 'other', yet who is both the corporeal and technical figuration of geometric reasoning. He does not elaborate further on what an 'other' sexed expression of geometry might be exactly, but his attention to Brandi's seventeenth-century figure is nevertheless evidence of the existence of geometric 'subject-figures' that express heterogeneous human subjectivity in aesthetic (that is, sensed), corporeal and technical modes of geometric comportment. Thus, as we will see in the discussion of Spinoza's *Ethics* below, Evans's analysis of the Villa Madama steps outside the circles of a reductive geometric method to examine the diverse lives of 'other' geometric subjects and figures. In addition, his attention to the 'other' in Brandi's female geometric subject-figure provides further evidence that there is a diverse biological and corporeal constitution to geometric thinking, which resonates with Spinoza's text.[6] In this respect, then, geometric subjects and figures are transformed from the divine, immaterial realm of reason into a 'natural' geometry of sense.

## GEOMETRIC EXPRESSION

Spinoza repeatedly uses the term 'expression' in the *Ethics* to indicate the immanent relationship between the various material and immaterial realms that construct the world. For Spinoza, this means geometric thinking connects human experience to absolute ideas, as well as to common ideas and bodies. Rather than operating merely as an idealised mathematical procedure, geometry is associated with modes of expression that range from the irreducible powers of God as 'substance' or 'nature' to everyday human powers of expression, such as the imagination and emotions, and the *conatus* (that is, the human endeavour to exist). The axiomatic structure of the *Ethics* is therefore a mode of classical geometric expression that Spinoza harnesses in order to emphasise the divine immanence of God / nature / substance in all its diverse modes and attributes. For example, in the opening Definitions of the text he writes: 'by God I mean an absolutely infinite being; that is, substance consisting of infinite attributes, each of which expresses eternal and infinite essence' (E ID6). In his preface to Deleuze's study of Spinoza's philosophy, Martin Joughin also observes the productive geometric diversification which the term enables. Expression denotes psychic and physical modes of production through which infinite and complex evolutions and involutions of time, space and matter are created.[7] We might therefore suggest that 'expression' is a finely tuned and highly productive geometric operation that allows Spinoza to identify the complex relationship between the body and mind, and their relationship to an originary geometric substance, within a single term.

In addition, Spinoza's retrieval of Euclid's classical geometric procedure, the *geometrico ordine*, provides him with a plenitude of 'common' geometric expressions.[8] By developing his analysis of God, nature and human existence through the classical elements of axioms, propositions, definitions, corollaries and scholia, Spinoza further underpins the capacity of geometric thinking to generate a densely woven examination of the relationship between human and other realms; for example, the step-by-step process of the *ordine geometrico demonstrata* enables him to account for the infinite discursivity of substance in multiple ways. An exceptionally genetic geometric discursivity is therefore expressed as a result of the highly developed axiomatic structure of the text.

However, Spinoza's text is unlike earlier commentaries on Euclid's geometry, such as Proclus' *Commentary on the First Book of Euclid's Elements* (410–85 AD), where geometric thinking remains firmly positioned within the realm of abstract disembodied ideas. Instead,

Spinoza's emphasis on the complex modalities of life – that is, substance or nature – promotes the importance of geometry for the construction of a sensible world. This is in contrast to Proclus's classical philosophy, which explicitly links geometric thinking to a discursive but immaterial spatial process of 'unfolding'. For Spinoza, however, the geometric diversification of the elements in the *Ethics* is derived from substance's genetic powers of expression, resulting, for example, in the complex interrelationships that link the modes and affects to the common notions. We might suggest that the heterogeneous passages through the modes, affects and common notions developed in Spinoza's 'biophysical' architecture are also, necessarily, expressions of a radical kind of sense-reason that exists in nature / substance.

Spinoza's unique technical and aesthetic labour in a metaphysical approach to geometric thinking is relevant for a discussion about architectural drawing because he brings together technical endeavour with aesthetic modes of expression. In both philosophy and architecture, therefore, life, nature and geometry are brought together to form complex multi-modal relations. Later, in his analysis of the affects, we will see how Spinoza directly addresses the nature of architectural design in an almost forensic study of the diversity of our emotions, and his evaluation of their capacity for enabling us to gain freedom of self-expression. In addition, the complex origin of these geometric relations as nature / substance highlights the scope for connecting architectural spatiotemporal relations, as well as philosophical thought, back to a radical sense-reason.

## SUBSTANCE

As I began to outline in the previous section, Spinoza's method is underpinned by his powerful theory of substance which does not merely designate extended matter, but is the idea through which he locates the complex (bio)diversity of life. Spinoza's theory of substance is central to his thinking, constituting a kind of proto-materialist theory (and reflects the materialist capacity in his work, which Chapters 5, 6 and 7 of this book also explore). Like 'expression', substance is another singularly complex term for the divine status of nature (that is, 'God-as-nature'). Spinoza defines this natural productive power through the terms *natura naturans* and *natura naturata,* which could be translated as 'constructing' and 'constructed' nature. Together, these generate the immanent and genetic plenitude of ideas, bodies and entities in the world. Substance is univocal, yet infinite. It is *the* primary 'cause' of all realities, the immanent 'life-force' in all things, including architecture and geometry. Yet, in itself, substance is also greater than all other causes because God's powers are limitless and irreducible. Once again, because substance is immanent in all modes of existence, whether they are physical, material, imaginary or highly abstracted forms of intellectual endeavour, geometry and its products are also always connected to this irreducible notion of life and to the ordinary material world. In addition, when geometric and spatial ideas exist as immaterial ideas or thoughts, rather than empirical examples, they are transformed from being understood merely as 'forms' into 'expressions' of existence. Geometry is therefore always immanently constituted by the absolute and genetic properties of substance. In addition, unlike methods that divide the world neatly into emotional and sensible realms and intellectual and mathematical realms, all are brought together into a kind of psychophysical architectural process that previews recent biophysical or materialist conceptualisations of difference.[9]

Spinoza brings together the singular and different qualities of human psychology and technical endeavour in a productive geometric principle of construction, resulting from the underlying foundation of an infinite substance or nature. In this respect, his argument once again resonates with earlier classical geometric philosophies: for example, the Stoic debates on Limit and Unlimit, in which fundamental immanent forces construct a metaphysics of relations (Proclus 1992: 70–8). But his metaphysics differs from this classical Greek thought on two counts: first, because it is an ontology of absolute affirmation, and second, because nature is not just subsumed to intellectual forms of discursivity. Spinoza therefore transforms the disembodied Stoic forms of intellectual geometric knowledge into embodied geometric figures (that is, bodies, emotions and corporeal experience) so that both the human subject and the geometric figure are understood to be *nature in process*. Geometric thinking in the *Ethics* is therefore aligned with life, and the reader's journey towards fulfilment or joy reflects this process as they make the step-by-step movement through the text's different elements, its axioms, definitions, corollaries, propositions and scholia.

Thus, Spinoza enables a radical materiality to come to the fore in geometric thinking, which is attributed with an immanent power of existence as a result of the 'univocity' that constitutes nature, substance and God. As such, immanence produces 'real' singularities or expressions of substance: for example, the general idea of nature or human life, or the particular embodiment of the natural world, such as trees, stones, horses or dogs; or the difference between human acts of endeavour and character, such as the distinction between the soldier and peasant, or feelings of delight, disappointment, rage or fear. Also, as explained previously, substance's genetic power underpins the particularly human mode of existence, the *conatus*, which is immanent in all human endeavour, including geometric and architectural modes of expression:

> Therefore, the power of any thing, or the conatus with which it acts or endeavours to act, alone or in conjunction with other things, that is (E IIIP6), the power or conatus by which it endeavours to persist in its own being, is nothing but the given, or actual, essence of the thing. (E IIIP7Dem.)

Philosophy and architecture are once again brought under the terms of a powerful 'sense-reason' which determines the nature of our existence, as well as our comportments and expressions. However, although God-as-nature, human existence and geometric thinking share the genetic power of substance, this immanent force remains distinct from human existence because of the limited life-force that constitutes the temporality of our bodies.

## GEOMETRIC PASSAGES

As outlined earlier, Spinoza employs the classical geometric figures of expression in order to demonstrate the originary heterogeneity of nature. For example, the axioms, together with the definitions, provide affirmative expressions of substance's irreducibility. Yet they also embody increasingly concrete forms of differentiation, even when the modes, affects and common notions are brought together in the passage towards a 'third kind of knowledge' and agency. In Part I, the axiomatic method affirms the singularly infinite expression of substance – that is, as God-or-nature; in Part II, it explicates the specific human attributes of thought and extension; in Parts III and IV, it defines the human powers of expression in the text's analysis of the emotions and affects; and finally, in Part V, Spinoza discusses how the active subject's self-knowledge (that is, their agency) represents an 'intuitive geometry' or fully embodied sense-reason. To put it another way, we might also say that Spinoza's axiomatic architecture creates a stunningly intense explication of diverse and singular geometric figures: the figure of God in Part I, the human figure in Parts II, III and IV, and the fully acting subject that embodies geometric intuition in Part V. Consequently, each of these figures is an affirmation of the fundamental heterogeneity in the architecture of the axiomatic process.

This tiring discursivity in the axiomatic method has been remarked upon by readers such as Bergson, who compared its relentlessness to a 'dreadnought', yet also notes the 'subtle lightness' of Spinoza's thought.[10] The axiomatic method underpins the scope of Spinoza's geometric thinking for constructing intense differentiations in life, the emotions and expression.

The heterogeneity of this geometric architecture is also generated by Spinoza's employment of other classical geometric elements; for example, his use of propositions increases the complexity of emotional realities available to the reader and the evidence of highly transitory expressions of substance or nature. Propositions therefore further intensify the scope of the method for generating discrete differentiations of geometric thought. By emphasising and expanding the 'clarity' of expression posited in the axioms and definitions, they contribute to the genetic evolution of the subject, highlighting both the modality of the method and their own singularity within the text's architecture. But, as we will see below, it is the scholia which introduce a particularly forceful intensity of expression within the method; their asides, commentaries, corrections, emphases and demonstrations multiply yet further the expressive power of the geometric method, adding weight to the complex multiplicity of embodied geometric figures which evolve, and the interrelationship between reasoned and sense-based modes of expression.

Spinoza's redeployment of these classical geometric figures operates in conjunction with his complex triad of interdependent capacities that express existence. These capacities – the attributes, modes and affects – constitute a radically productive and speculative architecture, as well as operating as singularly expressive figures within the geometric architecture of the text. Of these, affects constitute key sites of transformation. Intimately connected with sensibility and the imagination, they are particularly dynamic ways in which nature is expressed: for example, through everyday emotions of happiness, joy, delight, pride, sadness, fear or melancholy. Examined extensively in Parts III and IV, Spinoza's analysis of the affective powers of human emotions once again draws attention to the plenitude of this genetic architecture, and its significance for understanding the psychophysical nature of human experience in the world. For example, in Part IV, the modal nature of the emotions is explained within a particularly excessive form of axiomatic analysis, which moves from the preface, to eight definitions and an axiom, through to seventy-three propositions together with their accompanying proofs and scholia. Such a dense and forceful explanation underpins how these significant 'transitive' internal powers continuously produce different subjectivities. And, although Spinoza cautions that emotions which arise from reason are more powerful than those which exceed or ignore understanding, he also observes that affects are essential for our ability to be able to reach a 'joyful' life, even if the understanding may 'free' them from their mistaken judgements (see, for example, E IVP61 and E VP7). The emotions are therefore central to an architecture of natural geometry. In addition, their irreducible nature constructs subjects-in-process because they are always in transition and 'go forth' (as Deleuze has observed, additional modes of diversity are achieved as a result of the different 'speeds' in which they transform from one to another).[11] So, although we may experience the same emotions on more than one occasion, Spinoza is at pains to point out that the sequence of their transition and their duration is always different, and this affective kind of transformation represents a special 'third kind of knowledge' (E VP25Proof) or 'intuitive' geometry (E VP36S). Not only do the different passages between our emotional states provide necessary ways through which we can reach 'freedom', but also the movement between them is itself a kind of geometric reasoning, expressed in the dynamic nature of our emotional lives. Later in the chapter we will see how Spinoza brings these concerns to bear in his discussion about architectural design, but first it will be helpful to consider the work of the common notions and scholia in this process.

Like the affects, common notions are part of our psychophysical architecture in so far as they are 'certain ideas or notions common to all men' (E IIIP36). Common notions are important, not just because they are one of the ways in which qualitative differences between entities are established (for example, the difference between a man and a horse), but because they represent another form of diversity which can lead us towards a proper understanding of God / nature: 'those things that can lead us as it were by the hand to the knowledge of the human mind and its utmost blessedness' (E IIP40S9). The commonality of these singular embodied ideas further enables us to understand the perfection of God through their resolution of the step-by-step agreement between mind and body, and their expression of an embodied kind of human 'perfection' or unity: 'The more we understand particular things, the more we understand God' (E VP24). However, although they constitute examples of embodied knowledge or sense-reason, in so far as they unify adequate and inadequate states of human experience, their value is not just derived from the logical progression of the deductive step-by-step process through the text. Rather, they are singularities (that is, figure-subjects) in which particular expressions of nature / substance are brought into agreement with understanding God. In this respect they are similar to the 'all-in-one totality' of geometric intuition. However, unlike classical forms of geometric intuition which are exclusively immaterial, their irreducibility is derived from the corporeal and genetic nature of the geometric method. To an extent, therefore, common notions represent the most unified mode of geometric figure through which our senses and reason are brought together, and are key architectural passages in themselves. Yet, like the relationship between God and the transitory human expression of existence found in the emotions or the *conatus*, they are also always durational.

Spinoza's natural geometry is perhaps most strongly represented by the scholia, which introduce even greater ranges of comportment or expression into the text. Ranging from forceful logical explications of scientific procedures, to irritated appeals for attention from the reader, to scathing corrections of common misunderstandings, they construct a secondary architecture of 'interruptions' or interlocutor voices throughout the text.[12]

Occurring principally in Parts I and II in discussions of substance, limit and body, they are used to identify the ratio (that is, reason) between the infinity of God / substance and the qualitative modality of nature. In addition, Spinoza's use of classical mathematical and geometric examples in the scholia enables him to incorporate divine and empirical figures of sense-reason within one geometric textual element. They also frequently display more heightened emotional states of expression. Triangles, circles and geometric figures highlight the multi-modal nature of Spinoza's metaphysics because they oscillate between representing the particular and the divine in one singularity. Spinoza's strenuous commitment to scientific reasoning is brought together with corporeal bodies and clearly emotional 'voices'; for example, Spinoza uses the first scholium of the text as an extended proof that 'substance is necessarily infinite.' But here he also notes, with some irritation, confused, imagined or false beliefs about the natural world and substance which result in misunderstandings such as trees that talk and men who originate from stones (E IP8S2). Here, then, we find Spinoza developing the scholia in order to emphasise the necessity of nature's infinity, but also to correct mistaken beliefs about natural processes. Once again, the *Ethics* is not merely a text that attempts to 'solve' the relationship between reason and sense by means of an exclusively scientific method. Instead, it is an architecture of agreement and disagreement that challenges the reduction of geometric thinking to repetitive re-presentations of symbolic forms of science.[13]

The scholia represent a kind of geometric architecture that is significant not merely because of their capacity for technical or scientific expression, but because they embody diverse modes of sense-reason and infinite modes of difference, including abstract mathematical examples, empirical bodies and corporeal voices. As a result, they are significant operations within the text's architecture for constituting the genetic reality and ordinariness of Spinoza's natural architecture. In addition, like Evans's study of the Villa Madama's multiple routes of circulation through rooms, Spinoza's scholia perforate the boundaries of the classical geometric method because they are outsider voices (we might say a 'chorus' of affects) through which he appeals directly to his reader. The reader is consequently propelled psychically through the text so that it is not just a logical experience of understanding geometric order, proposition, analysis and argument, but an embodied act of reading that can endure in us as a 'practical' philosophy, or as a 'way of life'. The disruptive and reflexive nature of the scholia also emphasises the (bio)diversity that is immanent in their 'otherness'. They are singularities that reaffirm the scope for multiplicity in architectural geometries, rather than reducing architecture or geometry to universal abstractions that reproduce logics of self-sameness.

The act of reading the *Ethics* is therefore a demanding undertaking because the reader is expected to engage with a text that is technically intense, as both a scientific and an aesthetic experience. Its geometric conduct brings together the classical axiomatic scientific method with the affective agitation experienced in reading the text to generate a particularly aesthetic and embodied reader: that is, the ethical geometric subject. Both geometric expression and the reader are reconfigured through this highly affective aesthetic procedure because it generates a textual *and* technical engagement in different modes of geometric life. In this respect, Spinoza's method is an important precursor to Kant's eighteenth-century aesthetic theory in the *Critique of Judgment*, where we find another psychogcometric passage in the subject's experiences of pleasure and pain which form aesthetic judgement.[14] Also, if we recall the practical function of Euclid's *Elements*, which was written as an operational guide to geometry, Spinoza's animation of geometric figures, especially the scholia and common notions, enable the reader to be guided towards more fulfilling modes of existence or agency. The *Ethics* combines the practical value of a technical 'manual' together with a highly focused study of the emotions that enable diverse and productive expressions of sense-reason to be made accessible to the reader.

The heterogeneity of the geometric 'elements' represents an architecture of subjects-in-process. This establishes a significant shift away from logical and deductive mathematical geometric methods into a metaphysical approach which affirms the importance of psychic powers for geometric thinking and for understanding human existence. Thus, the *Ethics* is not merely a scientific hypothesis of axiomatic commonality and agreement, but a series of textual expressions of agreement, disruption or commonality which run side by side with the deductive scientific method, suggesting a shift away from idealised and exclusively immaterial accounts of geometry. Instead, Spinoza proposes an ethics of life in which geometric thinking, and the diverse geometric figures that constitute this 'living' architecture, are irreducible from their material, bodily expressions: in particular, because their unique powers of evolution are attributed to a univocal and multiplicitous substance / nature.

## AN ARCHITECTURE OF AFFECTS

In the Preface to Part IV, 'Of human bondage, or the strength of the emotions', Spinoza begins with an analogy about the process of constructing a building through which he considers the power of the emotions in establishing judgements of perfection and imperfection. He observes that a building designed in a recognisable style should not be considered inherently imperfect when it is still under construction because the final outcome is known, and hence any judgement about its perfection should be delayed until it is complete. However, he also notes that a building that is designed in an unrecognisable style to the viewer should not be assessed by its lack of perfection during the process because its final outcome is unknown:

> For example, if anyone sees a work (which I assume is not yet finished) and knows that the aim of the author is to build a house, he will say that the house is imperfect. On the other hand, as soon as he sees that the work has been brought to the conclusion that its author had intended to give it, he will say that it is perfect. But if anyone sees a work whose like he had never seen before and he does not know the artificer's intention, he cannot possibly know whether the work is perfect or imperfect. (E IVPref.)

He continues, observing that theories of design that are used to judge the perfection of a finished building against the original idea that underpins its construction are evidence of another modality in the design process. Furthermore, these questions of comparison and judgement are derived from the human emotions; for example, when connected to judgements about our environment, an analysis of the modality of the human emotions of pleasure or displeasure also reveals the modal nature of the built environment. This discussion about architectural design provides Spinoza with evidence of the diversity of substance, and of the relationship between different aesthetic modes of expression, leading him to caution the reader that if we also judge nature's 'work' to be imperfect, we mistakenly ascribe a final cause to it where there is none.

This discussion makes it clear that, for Spinoza, the relationship between human emotions and nature should not be seen in terms of exclusively opposing realities; he is not espousing a perfectly finished design against imperfect or incomplete modes of nature and human expression. Despite the potential for a teleological drive towards perfection in architectural design, Spinoza suggests that design is a heterogeneous and temporal process of construction and endeavour. As 'in reality', the architectural design process and the subsequent use of buildings are evidence of diverse 'modes of thinking' where nature and the human-built environment, together with their respective events, causes and characteristics, are brought together under a single notion of a complex nature / substance.

In the second part of his analysis of architecture, Spinoza observes that architectural design is even more closely linked to expressions of human desire or 'appetite'. Once again, he observes that our emotions constitute our psychophysical modes of endeavour, as well as reflecting the power and diversity of nature. Rather than considering architectural design to be merely a discipline that re-presents 'perfect' pre-existing natural and physical laws or ideas, Spinoza writes that it is an expression of human 'appetite' in which the desires and intentions of the builder express just one *mode* of nature's potential.

> So the reason or cause why God, or Nature, acts, and the reason or cause why he exists, are one and the same. Therefore, just as he does not exist for an end, so he does not act for an end; just as there is no beginning or end to his existing, so there is no beginning or end to his acting. What is termed a 'final cause' is nothing but human appetite in so far as it is considered as the starting-point or primary cause of some thing. For example, when we say that being a place of habitation was the final cause of this or that house, we surely mean no more than this, that a man, from thinking of the advantages of domestic life, had an urge to build a house. Therefore, the need for a habitation in so far as it is considered as a final cause is nothing but this particular urge, which is in reality an efficient cause, and is considered as the prime cause because men are commonly ignorant of the causes of their own urges; for, as I have repeatedly said, they are conscious of their actions and appetites but unaware of the causes by which they are determined to seek something. (E IVPref.)

For Spinoza, then, the architectural design process clearly comes under the terms of his inventive geometric exploration of the relationship between nature and our expression of this substance through our emotions. By placing architecture within a natural geometry of substance and human emotions, its methods, uses and defining characteristics (that is, its processes and techniques of construction) are considered to be examples of the diverse modes of aesthetic relations that constitute reality. Rather than defining architecture and geometry through a solely technical or rational mathematical analysis of geometric construction, proportion and application (whether these are derived from Euclidian, Cartesian, Vitruvian or even the contemporary 'non-standard' or 'biomorphic' geometries that are employed by today's architectural practices, but which are nevertheless still fundamentally formally driven), architectural thinking and practice under Spinoza's definition of geometry becomes a contiguous expression of complex physical and psychic human relations. Geometry in architectural design is therefore associated more with the processes of transforming human emotions from desires into complex relationships and environments, than with its function for constructing representations of perfectly idealised bodies, volumes and spaces. Rather, for Spinoza, architectural design, and our actual inhabitation of buildings, operate as diverse expressions of nature and the *conatus*. Spinoza's identification of perfection in the design process as a transformative psychophysical power that is immanent in life (rather than the desire for ideality) accords more closely with the aspirations of architectural designers who wish to construct multiple spatiotemporal passages for all in the built environment. In this respect, architectural design is much more strongly identified with a geometric ontology in which diverse living spatiotemporal relations are essential.

Figure and subject relations, geometric figures (such as architectural rooms, proportions or plans, and embodied subjects or lives), are key to this discussion because they populate both Spinoza's *Ethics* and Evans's architectural criticism. However, as has been shown, this is not a return to universal notions of subjectivity where the work of geometry excludes heterogeneous modes of expression and experience (especially in relation to 'otherness': for example, everyday spaces or occurrences, and sex difference), or where nature is idealised by symbolic forms of geometry that limit it to the realms of the physical and mathematical sciences. Rather, Spinoza inaugurates a diverse living geometry through which multiple, transformative subjects live out life. Geometric technical activities become aesthetic 'affective' agitations and diverse geometric figure-subjects are generated through the text's arguments and its demonstrations of 'ways of life'.

Spinoza's *Ethics* is therefore a geometric way of life or architecture for two reasons. First, it engages in an intense study of the relationship between geometric thinking and aesthetic experience in its expression of biophysical comportments of events, bodies and figures. Second, Spinoza's examination of these comportments reflects questions about the production of subjectivity, which are important to architects and artists involved in spatiotemporal practices. In both cases, new modes of subjective expression, new subjectivities and new subject-figures, are generated. Architecture is then understood as the relationships that are constructed between bodies, nature and geometries, and in this text, Spinoza's conceptualisation of this complex diversity is developed through his intense analysis of the geometric elements. As in the construction of a building with its elements of walls, passages and doors, Spinoza's building 'blocks' are the axioms, definitions, propositions, common notions and scholia. In addition, these generate a kind of architecture which enables movement and circulation through the text in a manner sympathetic to Evans's observations of the presence of everyday life in the design and inhabitation of the Villa Madama. In each, geometric figures are both transformative 'settings' or 'diagrams', and diverse subjectivities.

Spinoza's radical conceptualisation of a natural geometry, generated from the relationship between substance, nature and human modes of endeavour (especially the emotions), represents a fascinating kind of psychophysical architecture which informs questions about the construction of subjectivity and architecture, and the relationship between the two: how does architecture engage with, and respond to diverse subjectivities? Might Spinoza's natural geometry enable contemporary architects to design for these diverse needs: for instance, in contributing to contemporary critiques of agency or issues of designing public space, or the need for developing diverse cultures of dwelling? In addition, his examination of substance provides a radical material form of architectural diversity which can inform ecological questions in the discipline. Might his ethical thinking about nature and geometry also enable re-thinking the commercially driven digital fascination with formal geometric production that continues to dominate the discipline? In the face of these and other pressing questions of human difference and well-being, together with the need to protect ecological difference, this chapter suggests that Spinoza's philosophy may provide opportunities through which architecture can re-think and protect human and environmental biodiversity in the built environment.

## NOTES

1. See Adrian Forty's discussion of social space in the Royal Festival Hall as an example of an architectural historical discussion about 'settings' and 'life': 'And in this containment, architecture had special value, for architecture creates the settings in which life is lived – it is, in the French phrase, which does not bear translation too well, *la mise-en-scène de la vie*' (Forty 1995: 31).

2. Evans's use of the term 'everyday' also links to the work of contemporary post-structuralist architectural historians who affirm the significance of the ephemeral, domestic, ordinary and quotidian in understandings of the built environment and spatial practices (for example, Harris and Berke 1997, or Borden, et al. 2002). Henri Lefebvre's *The Production of Space* (1974) and Michel de Certeau's *The Practice of Everyday Life* (1984) are important post-Marxist references for these discussions.

3. Evans's discussion is distinct from Leonardo's Vitruvian Man (1487), which translates Vitruvius's architectural principles of proportion and harmony into the drawn human figure. Here the link between subjectivity and architecture is firmly established through a principle of proportion and deviation from standards or norm. However, Evans's and Spinoza's corporeal geometries are concerned with the capacity for geometry to generate diverse transformations in everyday existence, not the form of correspondence between the constituent parts of the subject. We might argue that this 'freedom' is also evident in the extent to which Spinoza frequently breaks the formal logic of the axiomatic method in the *Ethics*, especially in Parts IV and V.

4. David Coffin and Sabine Eiche's writings on the Villa Madama are examples of architectural historical scholarship that focuses on the process of the building's design evolution but which tends to dwell on the extent to which the original plans and subsequent iterations of these drawings were 'incomplete' (Coffin 1967 and Eiche 1992). Although this is interesting as a process of translation of the geometric idea to a realised building, Evans's observations shift traditional architectural historical analysis away from discussions about provenance and analyses of drawing techniques to a discussion about how the building's geometric relations operate as social and corporeal encounters.

5. It is important to note that Evans does not address the political and socio-economic issues of this kind of architecture for its occupants. Although servants would be able to pass through the same spaces as their patrons and guests, political, class and gender relations are not neutralised with this 'access'. Moreover, the Villa was commissioned by the Medici family and so, although it was used as a retreat from the political scene in Rome, social and spatial relations would have nevertheless been thoroughly imbued with the politics of the day at every level. The Villa's social architectural relations are therefore also produced out of political, cultural, artistic and economic processes.

6. Evans does not discuss nature in relation to the Villa, but David Coffin notes that it was 'the first appearance in Rome during the Renaissance of an attempt to weld together architecture and nature into one complex'. He also suggests that the Villa's gardens are designed to 'enhance' nature, rather than to 'pervert' or 'ignore' it. The Villa's design may therefore be seen as less hierarchical and deterministic than much Renaissance architectural and landscape design (Coffin 1967: 118).

7.  In the Preface to *Expressionism in Philosophy: Spinoza*, Martin Joughin
    writes:

    > Spinoza and Leibniz: two different expressions of 'expressionism in philosophy'
    > characterized in this book as a system of *implicatio* and *explicatio*, enfolding
    > and unfolding, implication and explication, implying and explaining, involving
    > and evolving, enveloping and developing. Two systems of universal folding:
    > Spinoza's unfolded from the bare 'simplicity' of an Infinity into which all things
    > are ultimately folded up, as into a universal map that folds back into a single
    > point; while Leibniz starts from the infinite points in that map, each of which
    > enfolds within its infinitely 'complex' identity all its relations with all other
    > such points, the unfolding of all these infinite relations being the evolution of a
    > Leibnizian Universe. (Deleuze 1992: 5)

8.  In his introduction, Seymour Feldman writes,

    > Spinoza's *Ethics* is perhaps the first purely philosophical treatise that presents its
    > conclusions consistently and completely in an axiomatic manner. In this respect
    > it is the paradigm of the hypothetical-deductive method suggested by Aristotle in
    > his *Posterior Analytics* as the model for a scientific theory, which until Spinoza
    > was only exemplified by Euclid's geometry. (Spinoza 1992: 7)

9.  See, for example, Gilles Deleuze's short book, *Spinoza*, or Moira Gatens's
    *Imaginary Bodies* (Deleuze 1988; Gatens 1995).

10. Bergson describes Spinoza's method as having the impact of a 'dread-
    nought' and the 'subtleness' of intuition in the essay 'Philosophical
    Intuition' in *The Creative Mind* (1933):

    > Nevertheless I know of nothing more instructive than the contrast between the
    > form and the matter of a book like the *Ethics*: on the one hand those tremen-
    > dous things called substance, Attribute and Mode, and the formidable array of
    > theorems with the close network of definitions, corollaries and scholia, and that
    > complication of machinery, that power to crush which causes the beginner, in
    > the presence of the *Ethics*, to be struck with admiration and terror as though he
    > were before a battleship of the Dreadnought class; on the other hand, something
    > subtle, very light and almost airy, which flees at one's approach, but which one
    > cannot look at even from afar, without becoming incapable of attaching oneself
    > to any part whatever of the remainder, even to what is considered essential,
    > even to the distinction between substance and Attribute, even to the duality of
    > thought and Extension. What we have behind the heavy mass of concepts of
    > Cartesian and Aristotelian parentage is that intuition which was Spinoza's, an
    > intuition which no formula, no matter how simple, can be simple enough to
    > express. (Ansell Pearson and Mullarkey 2002: 36–7)

11. Deleuze uses the concept of 'speeds' to register the multiple kinds of activ-
    ity that are generated in the body by the emotions. For example, of the
    modes, he writes: 'for, concretely, a mode is a complex relation of speed
    and slowness, in the body but also in thought, and it is a capacity for
    affecting or being affected, pertaining to the body or to thought' (Deleuze
    1988: 124).

12. Deleuze writes that the *Ethics* is a twice-written book; the first book is the

formal geometric method, the second 'subterranean' book is the 'broken chain of the scholia, a discontinuous volcanic line, a second version underneath the first, expressing all the angers of the heart and setting forth the practical theses of denunciation and liberation' (Deleuze 1992: 28–9).

13. Spinoza might therefore be seen as prefiguring the contemporary continental philosopher Isabelle Stengers, who discusses whether it is possible to think of an ethics of science that might reflect feminist practice or radical politics, and suggests re-thinking the scope of the scientific method towards an ethical and critical practice in a manner that recalls the (bio) diversity found in Spinoza's inquiry (Stengers 1997).

14. See, for example, Kant's discussion of the 'mental agitation' that arises from the imagination's unsuccessful attempts to comprehend the sublime (Kant 1987: 116).

# BIBLIOGRAPHY

Ansell Pearson, Keith, and John Mullarkey (eds) (2002), *Henri Bergson: Key Writings*, London: Continuum.

Borden, Iain, et al. (eds) (2002), *The Unknown City: Contesting Architecture and Social Space*, London: MIT Press.

Coffin, David R. (1967), 'The Plans of the Villa Madama', *Art Bulletin* 49(2), pp. 111–22.

de Certeau, Michel (1984), *The Practice of Everyday Life*, trans. S. Rendall, London: University of California Press.

Deleuze, Gilles (1988), *Spinoza: Practical Philosophy*, trans. R. Hurley, San Francisco: City Lights.

Deleuze, Gilles (1992), *Expressionism in Philosophy: Spinoza*, trans. M. Joughin, New York: Zone.

Eiche, Sabine (1992), *A New Look at Three Drawings for Villa Madama and Some Related Images*, Mitteilungen des Kunsthistorischen Institutes in Florenz, 36. Bd., H. 3, pp. 275–86.

Evans, Robin (2003), *Translations from Drawing to Building and Other Essays*, AA Documents 2, London: Janet Evans & Architectural Association.

Forty, Adrian (1995), 'Being or Nothingness: Private Experience and Public Architecture in Post-War Britain', *Architectural History* 38, pp. 25–35.

Gatens, Moira (1995), *Imaginary Bodies: Ethics, Power and Corporality*, London: Routledge.

Harris, Steven, and Deborah Berke (eds) (1997), *Architecture of the Everyday*, New York: Princeton Architectural Press.

Kant, Immanuel [1790] (1987), *Critique of Judgment*, trans. W. S. Pluhar, Indianapolis: Hackett.

Lefebvre, Henri [1974] (1991), *The Production of Space*, trans. D. Nicholson-Smith, Oxford: Blackwell.

Proclus [AD 410–85] (1992), *A Commentary on the First Book of Euclid's Elements*, trans. G. R. Morrow, Princeton: Princeton University Press.

Spinoza, Baruch (1992), *Ethics, Treatise on the Emendation of the Intellect and Selected Letters*, trans. Samuel Shirley, ed. S. Feldman, Indianapolis: Hackett.
Stengers, Isabelle (1997), *Power and Invention: Situating Science*, Minneapolis: University of Minnesota Press.

# 5. *The Secret History of Musical Spinozism*

AMY CIMINI

## INTRODUCTION

At the beginning of his *Spinoza and Politics* Etienne Balibar offers a strange wager, demonstrating how some unspecified interlocutors might respond to his project. Spinoza and politics, he says, what a glaring paradox (Balibar 1998: xxi)! A chapter on Spinoza and music might begin with similarly generative scepticism. If music belongs to the order of aesthetics or perception, Spinoza is a philosopher who seems uninterested in beauty, and whose epistemology aims to overcome the inadequate knowledge that sense perception yields. If music belongs to the order of the passions and affects, Spinoza is a philosopher who, like Descartes and Hobbes, wants to understand affective life 'in the geometric style . . . as if it were a question of lines, planes and bodies' (E IIIPref.). If music belongs to the articulation of subjectivity, community or political agency along axes of racial, ethnic, class and/or sexual difference, Spinoza is a philosopher whose non-anthropocentric ontology defines difference in terms of capacities and not on the basis of identity. What can a specifically Spinozistic approach tell us about these (and other) domains of musical knowledge and experience?

Although Spinoza's anachronistic contemporaneity with respect to music (and the other arts) has not been explored as extensively as parallel engagements with political theory, in the manner of Balibar, Spinoza's few discussions of art appear in support of some of the *Ethics*' central arguments. In these cases, art does not appear to be qualitatively different from other ethical activities conceived under the attribute of extension. In *Ethics* Part III, for example, Spinoza places architecture and painting on a par with sleepwalking as evidence that we do know what a body can do from its nature alone (E

IIIP2S). In Part IV, for example, he places listening to music alongside 'pleasant food and drink, scents, green plants and decoration' as ways to nourish the body that promote the mind's capacity to 'understand many things at once' (E IVP45S). In this chapter, I argue that it is precisely his emplacement of artworks within broader material networks that makes Spinoza a compelling *musical* thinker – a thinker whose anti-Cartesian view of matter and the mind–body union illuminates contemporary music studies' abiding commitment to bodies in new ways. Placing Spinoza's resolution of Descartes's dualism in musical perspective, I show that, although both Descartes and Spinoza opposed the cosmological approach to music that prevailed in their historical moment, only Spinoza's critique of musical cosmology facilitates a thinking of sonic materiality as a source of rational joy and bodily empowerment. How, I ask, might this reconstituted musical Spinozism be brought to bear on contemporary practices of listening and performance?

I situate this question within music studies' often-polemical commitment to the embodied dimension of musical experience over, say, the formal features of musical works or the biographies of composers, their patrons and audiences. Prioritising the body's role in the production and circulation of music and sound has been central to music scholarship since the music fields underwent tremendous disciplinary reconfiguration in the 1980s. At the urging of signal scholar Joseph Kerman (among others), musicology, in particular, took arms against its reputation for the production of positivistic knowledge about Western high art at the expense of insight into musical *experience*, which was typically left to criticism and popular music journalism (Kerman 1985). What was at stake here was the fields' very claim to understand the vital and complex connection of music to the social world; what resulted was nothing less than a new strain of musicological thinking, which came to be known as the 'New' (or 'Critical,' or 'Cultural') musicology, that sought to understand how power, pleasure and socio-political content circulate in and through musical sound.

Listening and performing bodies became the media through which the music fields were to affirm this commitment to musical experience, bringing with them the challenges of understanding music's relationship to gender, sexuality, race and ethnicity, complexly conjugated with progressive political and ethical directives of the New Left, post-countercultural movements and post-Civil Rights projects. Music studies' engagement with these challenges took shape according to two broad formations. On the one hand, theories of the body's discursive and performative construction, like the early work of Michel

Foucault and Judith Butler, became important for explaining how bodily materiality is itself a product of power relations and how music might intervene in that production. On the other, a new interest in the lives and practices of contemporary and historical performers posited the specialised actions of material bodies – like the weight of the arm that presses into the string, the training of small muscles to move at tremendous speed, and the coordination of the lungs, nose and mouth to create a continuous 'circular' stream of air – as the condition of possibility for the production of any musical meaning, ascribing an indubitable presence to bodies' materiality while moving that presence to the centre of musical inquiry (Hahn 2007; LeGuin 2006; Abbate 2004). It is in accounting for the effort of these moving, resting and ultimately *sounding* bodies that, as I will show, a musical Spinozistic intervention will register most powerfully. I unfurl this intervention by first examining the particularities of music studies' opposition to Cartesian dualism.

## THE MUSICO-POLITICAL EXPEDIENCE OF THE MIND–BODY PROBLEM

Both of these disciplinary approaches to musical bodies oppose the notorious denigration of the body associated with Descartes's *cogito*. Music studies rejected dualism's famous devaluation of the body, but retained its purportedly *antagonistic* relation between the mind and body in order to posit the body as a resistive site for a progressive ethics and politics. Taking arms against dualism's epistemological and moral indictments of the body, music studies set two principles in place: one, the body is an ineluctable site for the production of knowledge; and two, the body's actions form the very ground of progressive social and political life.

Following the Gilles Deleuze of *Expressionism in Philosophy* (Deleuze 1993: 255–72), I conceive music studies' attack on dualism to be essentially *moral* in character in so far as it rejects the notion that the body has to *suffer* in order for the mind to produce clear and distinct ideas. The considerable firepower behind this moral critique forecloses an engagement with dualism's celebrated *philosophical* problem – the challenge of mind–body interaction. By addressing the Cartesian mind–body union from the perspective of interaction, Spinoza resolves the *moral* problems against which music studies defines its interest in the body. The *moral* approach seeks redress for dualism's denigration of the body by stabilising a disciplinary programme that affirms its progressive capacities, while a Spinozistic *ethical* approach understands the body's value to the human subject as immanent to the actions and activities of which it is capable.

Almost twenty years after its publication, Suzanne Cusick's 'Feminist Theory, Music Theory and the Mind/Body Problem' (Cusick 1994: 8–27) is still frequently cited as an exhortation to do justice to performing bodies after years of disciplinary neglect by formal, hermeneutic and archival priorities (McMullen 2006: 61–83; Sanden 2009: 7–36). Cusick's article provides a well-rendered version of this moral anti-Cartesianism, binding that moral critique to a familiarly gendered version of the Cartesian mind–body relation. She recasts the Cartesian mind–body opposition as an opposition between composer/analyst and performer. She writes, 'the composer is masculine not because so many individuals in that category are biologically male, but because the composer has come to be understood to be the *mind – mind* that creates patterns of sounds to which other minds assign meaning' (Cusick 1994: 16). The composing mind asserts sovereign control over musical sound just as the Cartesian mind asserts sovereign control over the body. Formal analysis, then, documents the workings of that mind by attending to the details of *how* the composing mind exercises this power. And so, a tightly concentric collection of terms begins to aggregate around the concept of mind: composer, analyst, masculine, control, creation. This collection comes to threaten not only alternative approaches to musical analysis but also other musical subjectivities and activities. 'It is performers', Cusick writes, 'who are most ignored and dismissed by a mind–mind conception of music' (Cusick 1994: 18). The analytic models that Cusick indicts refuse to account for the bodily action that forms, in many ways, their condition of possibility.

But, as it turns out, Cusick's performers can achieve musical knowledge that is inaccessible by other analytic means. This claim emerges from a powerful account of what happens when performers are written out of the mind-centric analytic circuit. She writes,

> To deny musical meaning to things only the performers of a work will know implicitly denies that performers are knowers, knowers whose knowledge comes from their bodies and their minds. To deny musical meaning to purely physical, performative things is in effect to transform human performers into machines for the transmission of mind–mind messages between members of a metaphorically disembodied class, and because disembodied, elite. (Cusick 1994: 19–20)

Without mentioning Descartes by name, Cusick indicts the Cartesian conception of the body as automated, inanimate and machinic. Such a conception, she implies, makes performing bodies susceptible to exploitation and instrumentalisation by agential minds. Affirming bodies' power to resist this instrumentalisation, Cusick endows them with the capacity for knowledge production. This knowledge, as it turns out, is irreducible to formal analysis or hermeneutic interpretations. She explains, 'an embodied music theory, then, would include in its notion of musical meaning things which could not be heard by even the most attentive co-composing listener' (Cusick 1994: 20).

Cusick mobilises her own performance experience playing J. S. Bach's 'Aus tiefer Not' (*Clavierubung*, Part III, PWV 686) at the organ in order to drive a particularly powerful wedge between analytic and embodied approaches to musical meaning. In this case, the work's *meaning* rests in how it conveys a Lutheran conception of grace. The passage Cusick examines sets the phrase 'out of the depths, send me the grace my spirit needs.' Cusick interprets the presentation of this grace using a dualistic logic; on one hand, grace appears as a 'dance-like bass', which is both audible and analysable, and, on the other, grace appears through the score's inaudible demands on the performer. Holding fast to her programmatic opposition of embodied knowledge to analysis, Cusick allocates the first form of grace to the listening/analysing mind, the second to the performing body; in the first case, the listener registers this lithe bass, but in the second, the performer faces complex technical challenges.

Dramatising the disparity between listening and performing, she writes, 'for these terrifying moments, one might as well be floating in mid air, so confused and shifting is the body's center of gravity' – and yet, 'neither harmonic, nor contrapuntal analysis would identify this little passage as critical to the work's meaning' (Cusick 1994: 18). Subordinating the performer to the 'work's meaning' reinforces dualism's familiar economy of suffering; that is, the organist suffers for the work's audible integrity. As amelioration, Cusick cordons off a category of musical meaning that is only accessible to performing bodies, endowing the performer with epistemological secrets that silently undermine the adequacy of mind-centric analytic approaches. While empowering the body with a specialised form of knowledge production, Cusick's interest in opposing that specialisation to dominant modes of analysis forces her to re-inscribe dualism's structure despite reversing its values.

## DESCARTES, SPINOZA AND THE PROBLEM OF MUSICAL COSMOLOGY

Cusick turns dualism's apparent intractability to the body's advantage, although this affirmation retrenches its economy of suffering.

Placing Descartes's dualism in broader intellectual historical purview throws his engagement with Renaissance and early modern musical thought into stark relief, highlighting an important point of convergence between Descartes and Spinoza: a decisive rejection of Pythagorean and Neo-Platonic musical cosmology. Focusing on this rejection moves sound to the centre of both philosophers' works, taking an explicitly *musical* approach to their understanding of the mind-body union.

Both Descartes and Spinoza make strong interventions in the Pythagorean and Neo-Platonic approaches to music that persisted, in different forms, in European musical thought through to the early eighteenth century. Sounds – and musical intervals in particular – were not uniformly understood as material objects of empirical inquiry until around the turn of the eighteenth century. By the early eighteenth century, sound, along with electricity and light, came to constitute the vanguard of the empirical sciences because of its capacity for dramatic demonstration (Christensen 1993: 77). However, musical thinkers in the seventeenth century were tremendously uncertain about how to commensurate cosmological and empirical approaches to the study of musical sound. Consequently, seventeenth-century musical thought is strikingly heterogeneous in its methods and epistemic priorities: major–minor tonality commingles with the seven church modes; early acoustical and mathematical research about the nature of sound maps on to occult theories of sympathy and resonance; myth and scientific research slip freely into one another (Gouk 2002: 223).

To imagine how truly anachronistic musical thought may have been at this time, consider that the standard music textbook in liberal arts curricula from the twelfth to the mid-eighteenth century was Boethius's sixth-century treatise, *Fundamentals of Music*. In *Fundamentals*, Boethius, a Roman statesman and philosopher, divides music into three distinct hierarchical domains that are mathematically isomorphic. The same whole-number ratios (1:2, 2:3, 4:3) structure each domain despite their different priorities. Boethius's first 'music' is *musica mundana*, or simply the harmony of the spheres. *Musica mundana* has no sonorous form. It maintains primacy in this tripartite system because it describes God's structural relationship to the organisation of the cosmos. The second, *musica humana*, regulates the relationship between the human body and soul using these cosmic ratios. In the context of *musica humana*, cosmic intervals direct an ethical programme that 'brings the body and soul into harmony, [integrates] the rational and irrational parts of the soul and [balances] the disparate members of the body' (Kassler 1995: 20). The third, and lowliest, music is the only sounding music in this system. *Musica instrumentalis* is the domain of vocal and instrumental composition that generates music based on the ratios that govern *musica mundana* and *musica humana*. As historian of music theory Penelope Gouk summarises, 'underpinning this hierarchical division is the fundamental belief that cosmic music, or *musica mundana*, embodies 'true' music – or harmony – while instrumental music offers an imperfect approximation of these divine and unchanging proportions' (Gouk 2002: 225).

Boethius is typically credited with disseminating the origin myth of universal harmony in so far as he grounds his musical thought in the shadowy tale of Pythagoras's discovery of harmony based on whole-number ratios. As the myth alleges, Pythagoras was struck by the consonant sounds produced by the hammers in the blacksmith's forge and found, after further investigation, that the masses of the hammers that produced the most harmonious sounds were related to one another according to simple whole-number ratios like 1:2, 2:3, 4:3. When applied to vibrating strings, these ratios produced simple musical intervals like the octave, the perfect fifth and the perfect fourth. While experimenting with different tools for producing these intervals, Pythagoras and his followers also proposed that these whole-number ratios structure the universe itself.

Even the most cursory look at some iconic representations of universal harmony reveals how thoroughly seventeenth-century musical thinkers forgot the empirical basis for the Pythagoreans' speculations about musical, mathematical and cosmological correspondences. Robert Fludd's now-famous image of the Divine Monochord uses the acoustic monochord as a model for *musica mundana*. The hand of God descends from the clouds in order to tune the single string whose divisions determine the position of the Earth, its elements and all other cosmic bodies. In this geocentric model, the Earth sits at the bottom of the monochord, where the string connects with the box. The octave D-d represents the moon and planets, where the pitches A and B correspond to water and air. Each planet is assigned a tone: the moon, D; Mercury, E; Venus, F; the sun, G; Mars, A; Jupiter, B, and Saturn, C. The tones get higher the farther away they are from the Earth, while the sun sits exactly halfway between Earth and the hand of God, creating an octave between Earth and the governance of the divine agent.

In his rendering of *musica humana*, Fludd drew upon his colleague William Harvey's mobilisation of cosmic ratios to understand human physiology. On Harvey's view, 'the proportion of chest to belly is an interval of a perfect fourth (4:3), that of head to chest, a fifth (2:3), that of chest to stomach, a whole octave (2:1)' (Kassler 1995: 66). Fludd parses the human being using the 2:1 ratio that generates the octave. This upper octave describes the mental and spiritual aspects of the human being, which strive upward toward the godly source of all concord. The mind, in this image, stands in analogically for *musica mundana*'s hand of God as the musician who catalyses bodily action, animating an otherwise inert and passive extended substance. Because the human body is constructed according to universally harmonious ratios, certain *aural experiences* – say, of the perfect fourth over the minor seventh – are eternally and cosmically determined to support the health of the body. *Musica humana* presents the ethical care of the self as a specifically musical activity (Kassler 1995: 20–5).

## DESCARTES'S MUSICAL SECRET: CONTEXTUALISING THE *COMPENDIUM OF MUSIC* (1618)

Descartes's intervention in the system is decisive. Students and mature scholars alike tend to be surprised to learn that Descartes's first complete manuscript was a music theory treatise – the *Compendium Of Music,* completed in 1618.[1] Descartes wrote the *Compendium* during his tenure in the army of Prince Maurice of Nassau and it is dedicated to his friend and physico-mathematical interlocutor, Isaac Beeckman. In the very first sentence of the *Compendium*, Descartes declares *the basis of music is sound – its aim is to please and arouse various emotions in us* (Descartes 1961: 11). Though this claim may sound unremarkable to our ears, it is radical in the context of seventeenth-century musical thought. By declaring that music *as such* will henceforth be associated *only* with its sonorous instantiation, Descartes effectively dispenses with the moral and more broadly regulative functions that cosmological theory assigns to music. Descartes ontologises *musica instrumentalis* – the most degraded form of music in Boethius's hierarchy – as nothing less than music itself. While in cosmological perspective, sound is little more than a degraded instantiation of number, for Descartes, 'string segments [became] the true foundation of sounds and numbers only a description' (Christensen 1993: 77). By identifying pitch with sound and not number, Descartes replaced Neo-Platonic musical cosmology with an empirical and acoustical approach.

The *Compendium* hands what were once heavenly truths over to the senses, framing the thinking and sensing subject – not the divine agent – as the sole arbiter of music's affects. The hearing subject is now cleaved from the musical object, while *musica humana* once merged the two. While this creates important conceptual problems for Descartes, this emplacement of musical knowledge in *experience* unsettles traditional hierarchies in musical thought and practice. According to musicologist Kate Van Orden, 'Descartes disregards ancient Renaissance authorities, intellectual, social and moral hierarchies are largely banished, and even the class distinctions implicit in the elevated status of vocal polyphony crumble when he heaps praise on the simplest music around – military drumming' (Van Orden 2002: 19). While at the same time making strides towards aspects of his mature epistemology, Descartes's *Compendium* places the production and transmission of musical knowledge within the most mundane forms of bodily and aural experience.

Reading the *Compendium* in dialogue with Descartes's mature philosophical positions is not the most popular way to interpret the text. Scholarly reception of the *Compendium* seems to take three different forms: ignore it completely, treat it as a vestige of Renaissance metaphysics (thus separating it from Descartes's properly philosophical corpus), or read it as a rough, experimental prototype of Descartes's mature positions on the senses, the mind, mechanism and mathematics. I take a nuanced version of this position. Breaking with Aristotle's hylomorphic understanding of perception, the Descartes of the *Compendium* must account for how the senses (in this case, the ears) are related to the objects (in this case, the sounds) they perceive. When Descartes replaces secret affinities and substantial forms with motion and quantity, Bertrand Augst argues,

> it is not only the object, the phenomenon observed which comes under scrutiny, but also the possibility of the observer to perceive the object, and in 1618, unwilling to use the complex apparatus of Scholastic physics, Descartes could only rely on sense perception, his one *real* link between the observer and the object. (Augst 1965: 122)

This separation of subject from object requires a parallel account of the mathematical continuity by which, on the one hand, objects conform to the senses' perceptual abilities and, on the other, the senses meet the demands of their objects (Moreno 2004: 62).

But this is not exactly how things go for the Descartes of the *Compendium*. The senses' ability to represent things accurately emerges only secondarily to Descartes's interest in sensory pleasure in the *Compendium*. That is, the senses' link to the world appears, in this early manuscript, alloyed with what pleases them. He elaborates these conditions in the *Compendium*'s eight preliminary remarks. After confirming that 'all senses are capable of experiencing pleasure,' Descartes goes on to show that pleasure consists in a certain relation between the sensed object and our sensory capacities. 'For this pleasure,' he writes, 'a proportional relation of some kind between the object and the sense itself must be present' (Descartes 1961: 11). Descartes described these proportional relationships in four steps of increasing specificity, drawing, notably, on visual examples – not aural ones. First, discounting sense objects, like bright light or thunder, that injure the senses, Descartes examines the parts of the astrolabe (the 'net' as opposed to the 'matrix') in order to argue, not surprisingly, that it is easier to perceive regular than irregular patterns. We can perceive the former more easily when 'the differences between the parts are smaller.' Descartes then defines 'difference' though proportionality, asserting that parts of an object 'will be less different when there is a greater proportion between them', like 2:1 or 3:2 as opposed to 7:8. Finally, Descartes specifies that these proportions ought to be arithmetic (and not geometric), so that the parts will be equal in size.

By way of parsing these examples, Descartes writes, 'the proportion obtained between [arithmetic proportions] is easier to perceive *visually* than [the] geometric proportions' (Descartes 1961: 12, my emphasis). Descartes allows vision to function as a proxy for hearing, making what historian of music theory Jairo Moreno suggests is a lateral move between sense modalities (Moreno 2004: 67). We should be able to hear the difference between proportional parts as easily as we can see them. What we can see is taken as evidence of what we can hear when it comes to perceiving proportionality. While vision and hearing seem to be equivalent in terms of their perceptual ability, in this example vision gains the cognitive upper hand by virtue of its ability to represent hearing. Vision's subsumption of hearing, in the *Compendium*, presages two aspects of Descartes's mature thought. On the one hand, it intimates the emplacement of sense perception within the mind, and on the other, it underscores the robustly visual conception of thought that Descartes develops in the *Meditations* and *Optics* (Carriero 1999: 13–46).[2]

After enumerating the proportions that best accommodate things to our senses, Descartes turns to the soul in order to explicate what exactly constitutes sensory pleasure.

> Among the sense objects most agreeable to the soul is neither that which is perceived most easily nor that which is perceived with the greatest difficulty; it is that which does not quite gratify the natural desire by which the senses are carried to object, yet not so complicated that it tires the senses. (Descartes 1961: 13)

A number of important aspects of Descartes's view of sensory pleasure come into play here. First, while pleasure is contingent on what the senses are able to perceive without sustaining, say, bodily injury, pleasure really only registers in the immaterial domain of the soul. If pleasure is an affair of the soul, then it cannot explain how or what the ears perceive 'with ease' or 'with difficulty'. Indeed, Descartes takes on two seemingly opposed projects here: he is trying to demonstrate that the senses are materially yoked to sense objects, while at the same time explaining how the immaterial soul (or mind) takes pleasure in the senses' activities.

Cartesian musical pleasure, it seems, sits tenuously between the ear and the soul. Reading the *Compendium* in dialogue with Descartes's mature thought, I place this pleasure at the fraught union of mind and body – framing it, that is, as an important instantiation of the 'third notion' through which Descartes recommends that Princess Elizabeth affirm the mind's substantial unity with the body. Descartes's early conception of the body in the *Compendium* is automated through and through, much like the view he espouses in the sixth meditation. While the soul discerns how musical intervals challenge the senses, the body simply reacts automatically to sound's vibrational touch. In Descartes's hands, sound's material force animates human beings, animals and inorganic things in the same way. Because 'sound strikes *all bodies* on all sides,' movement becomes nothing more and nothing less than a physiological compulsion (Descartes 1961: 14–15). 'We accompany each beat of the music by a corresponding motion of our body,' Descartes writes, adding 'we are quite naturally compelled to do this' (Descartes 1961: 14). Precisely because our responses to rhythmic impetus are automated, Descartes explains, animals can be taught to dance just as easily as human beings; dance thus becomes less an expressive form than a mechanical activation of the body. Sound's vibrational force, it seems, illuminates the extent to which human bodies are like the rest of matter.

The strong argument of my reading of the *Compendium* is that Descartes's robust formulation of dualism is nascent within this early text. Sound affects the soul, the senses and body differently, emphasising their independence while, at the same time, gesturing toward the 'notions' by which Descartes will later try to make the mind–body union intelligible. Although the Descartes of the *Meditations* rejects sound (and, by proxy, music) as an object of epistemological certainty, the foundations of that certainty emerge through his initial attempt at an empirical and acoustic account of music's effects on the embodied, sensing and thinking subject.

## SPINOZA AND THE HARMONY OF THE SPHERES

Spinoza, too, addresses the harmony of the spheres, if only to reject it with considerably more vitriol than Descartes – and, importantly, to engage with its implications for ethical life and self-knowledge in a more comprehensive way. While Descartes cleaves music from cosmology by aligning it with sound, Spinoza attacks the anthropomorphic conception of God upon which that cosmology is based. In order to strip theodicy of its power over human life, in the Appendix of Part I, Spinoza unfurls a ferocious critique of the human presumption that God has made worldly things for their pleasure and welfare. This critique applies to revealed religion and sense experience in equal (if different) measure. Here Spinoza catalogues how mistakes about pleasure and value unfold in all five sensory domains. His discussion of hearing precipitates a compelling shift in register.

> The ignorant consider [the affectations of the imagination] to be the chief attributes of things, because, as we have already said, they believe all things have been made for their sake, and call the nature of a thing good or evil, sound or rotten and corrupt, as they are affected by it. Those which move the senses through the nose, they call pleasant smelling or stinking, through the tongue, sweet, bitter, tasty or tasteless, through touch, hard or soft, rough or smooth and the like; and finally, those which move the ears are said to produce noise, sound or harmony. Men have been so mad as to believe that God is pleased by harmony. Indeed, there are philosophers who have persuaded themselves that the motions of the heavens produce a harmony. (E IApp.)

The notion that things might be pleasing to us because they are pleasing to an anthropomorphised God emerges *only* through the sense of hearing. Thus, Spinoza opposes his conception of the divine nature, causality and ethics to the harmony of the spheres, intimating that a Spinozistic view of noise, sound and harmony would have diverged radically from the views that dominated his historical moment. In light of this striking opposition, this section works to reconstruct what a Spinozistic ethics of musical experience might have looked like.

When human subjects 'place themselves at the origin of every perception, every action, every object and every meaning', Spinoza argues, they fail to understand the network of causes that determine them to action, perception and the production of meaning (Althusser 1997: 6). Without such an understanding, human subjects believe themselves to be freely disposed towards one thing over another simply by virtue of being 'conscious of their volitions and appetite', thereby failing to 'think of what moves them to wanting or willing' (Sharp 2007: 732–55). Descartes's account of music pleasure fails along these lines. That is, by studying the nature of interval through its effect on the listening subject, Descartes offers an intractably anthropocentric view of sound – and it is precisely the variability of each subject's experience of sound that renders it unfit for the production of mathematically certain knowledge. By positing the harmony of the spheres as a paradigmatic instance of humans' mistakes about causality, Spinoza implicitly posits music and sound as rich sites for cultivating knowledge and responsibility for our mental and bodily relationships to substance and its modes.

Spinoza may have absorbed this position on the harmony of the spheres (and the rejection of a transcendent God that attends it) from Maimonides. Like Spinoza, Maimonides rejects the ascription of any human qualities to God. Maimonides also rejected the use of music in religious services because of its inflammatory and passionate effects. In what little he has to say about music, Spinoza is much more forgiving. Maimonides rejected the Greek notion of *harmonia* as a sonorous instantiation of celestial order. In their compelling article about Maimonides's 'silence' on the matter of cantillation and music more generally, Werner and Kravitz point out that he 'only cites passages where the "tremendous noise" of the sun or other celestial bodies is being marvelled at. The Greek concept of *harmonia*, i.e. fitting together in a cosmic or transcendental way, would have been totally alien to him' (Kravitz and Werner 1986: 179 201). Tracing Spinoza, here, to Maimonides further emphasises that what is at stake in his invocation of the harmony of the spheres is sound and hearing as such. So, how might a Spinozistic theory of sound – and a Spinozistic theory of aurality – unfold?

Understanding how matter is constituted forms the cornerstone of Spinoza's epistemology. Grasping modes' conative propensity to move and rest is essential for seeing how their 'agreements, differences and oppositions' operate within the infinite material expanse by which we are affected and determined (E IIP29S). Spinoza never presents a position on the materiality of sound, but his conception of matter sets him at odds with historically reified constructions of sound as immersive and hearing as passive and non-perspectival. In Spinoza's monism, sound cannot be qualitatively separated from the rest of matter, making *a priori* claims about passivity and immersion impossible. Rather, thinking sound through Spinoza's substantial unity demands that it be conceived – like the rest of matter – through what it shares in common with what it affects and is affected by. While Descartes relegates knowledge about sound to the domain of taste, Spinoza implicitly recognises sonic experience as a form of adequate knowledge.

## MATTERS OF EXPRESSION

While both Spinoza and Descartes reject the harmony of the spheres, only Spinoza's epistemology makes possible a re-emplacement of sound within the parameters of certain knowledge, even if he does not explicitly do so himself. In order to illustrate *how* that reconstruction might unfold, I turn to Gilles Deleuze. Music appears frequently in Deleuze's work (and in his work with Félix Guattari) as an exemplary agent of creative deterritorialisation. As Peter Hallward points out, music's creative capacity is, for Deleuze, only exceeded by philosophy itself (Hallward 2006: 104–26). I seek a robustly Spinozistic basis for Deleuze's (and Guattari's) interest in musical expressivity by reading their famous 'Of the Refrain' in the terms of Deleuze's early work on Spinoza, *Expressionism in Philosophy*. By so doing, I explicate *how* that expressivity depends on Spinoza's common notions, implicating sound in the production of adequate ideas in radical contrast to Descartes's dualistic exclusion of sound from epistemological certainty.

Spinoza's common notions constitute the building blocks of our reasoning. Through the common notions, we come to grasp material things through their causes and shared properties. As Deleuze explains, 'the common notions are so named not because they are common to all minds, but because they are common to bodies, either all bodies (extension, motion and rest) or to some bodies (mine and another)' (Deleuze 1988: 54). And so, understood through the common notions, sound will emphasise *something* that is common to both human bodies and sonic materiality. Unpacking the common notions' imbrication in bodily encounters, Moira Gatens writes, 'common notions arise when one body encounters another with which it is compatible, and so experiences joy' (Gatens 2009: 9). This encounter precipitates reflection on what constitutes compatibility amongst bodies, leading us to consider what bodies can and do share in common – through such consideration, we strive to understand the cause of joyful encounters with others (Gatens 2009: 7). 'From this it follows', Spinoza writes, 'that the mind is more capable of perceiving a great many things adequately as its body has many things in common with other bodies' (E IIP39C). The foundations of our reasoning rely, in this sense, on our bodily orientation towards others and other materialities.

Reading between Deleuze's soberly philosophical examination of expression in Spinoza's thought in *Expressionism in Philosophy* and his far wilder treatment of music in *A Thousand Plateaus'* 'Of the Refrain' yields a rich account of how the production of sound constitutes an expression of what bodies share in common. Deleuze initiates his expressive reading of Spinoza by unpacking the sixth definition from Part I of the *Ethics*. Identifying God with substance, Spinoza writes, 'By God, I understand a being absolutely infinite, that is, a substance consisting of an infinity of attributes, each of which expresses an eternal and infinite essence' (E ID6). The attributes we know (thought and extension) render two aspects of God's essence accessible to human subjects, thus 'constituting our reality and rendering it thinkable' (Macherey 1998: 125). Deleuze radicalises this reading by claiming that the attributes literally bring the essence of substance into knowable existence. He explains that 'the essence of substance has no existence outside the attributes that express it so that each attribute expresses a certain eternal and infinite essence' (Deleuze 1993: 42). Expression is a dynamic and productive action that brings substance's essence into being. Both Deleuze and Macherey schematise this production according to a three-part model. They identify something that expresses itself (in this case, substance), something that is brought into being through its expression (in this case, the essence), and the agent through which that thing is brought into being (in this case, the attribute). These three parts depend on one another while retaining their singularity.

In 'Of the Refrain', Deleuze and Guattari build their aesthetics on a recurring, mantra-like question: how can matter become expressive? In so far as extension is an attribute of substance (and thus expresses substance's essence), matter is always-already constitutively expressive in Spinoza's ontology. What Deleuze and Guattari are after here, however, is a highly specialised way in which modes can be made to maximise the 'certain and determinate way' they express substance's essence (E IID1). They apply the three-part model Deleuze proposed for the relation of substance, essence and attribute to matter. 'Material thus has three principal characteristics,' they write; 'it is a molecular-ized matter; it has a relation to forces to be harnessed; and it is defined by operations of consistency applied to it' (Deleuze and Guattari 1987: 345). Translating this formula into Spinozistic terms, we could simply begin by saying that *bodies exist*. They are 'molecular' in the sense that each simple body expresses substance's essence in its own 'certain and determinate' way. However, when bodies unify by coordinating, elaborating or complexifying the way they move and rest, they become *consistent.* It is in this becoming-consistent that bodies begin to articulate what they share in common.

Becoming sonorous is one way of becoming consistent. Just as Spinoza's monism effaces any principled line separating thinking and non-thinking things, so does this sonorous consistency unfold across normative distinctions between nature and culture or animate and inanimate things (Della Rocca 2008: 110). As Elizabeth Grosz elaborates, the Australian tooth-billed catbird, known colloquially as the stagemaker, is one of the most interesting creatures through which Deleuze and Guattari examine matter's expressivity (Grosz 2008). The stagemaker earns his name because he will sing only after turning the leaves in his immediate area upside-down. The glossy, light-coloured undersides of the leaves form a 'display court' upon which he presents his song. Here, the stagemaker and the leaves enter into a mutually affective relationship by which the leaves activate the bird's sonorous capacities and the bird implicates the leaves in the production of sound. The bird and the leaves are 'expressers'; they start out as co-existent singularities or 'molecularized' things. Their consolidation elaborates a mutual relation to sonorousness, which is then 'expressed' through the bird's song. The song expresses the sonic potential immanent to the bird's composite formation with the leaves; the sounding event of song makes that immanence a sensible reality.

In the case of the stagemaker, the sounding song belongs less to the bird himself than it does to the bird–leaf composite. The expressive relationship between the bird and the leaves becomes a thinkable reality through the event of song. The event of sound provides *evidence* of their shared capacities, but does not exactly illuminate how sound *itself* becomes expressive. How does the very *material* of sound operate as a matter of expression? American experimentalist Maryanne Amacher's *Third Ear Music* makes a stunning case for sound's capacity to instigate consistency within matter. The notion of the *third ear* bears a rich intellectual history, articulated through Nietzsche, Jacques Derrida, the psychoanalytic technique of Theodor Reik and the deconstructive feminist critique of Sarah Kofman (Reik 1949; Derrida 1988; Kofman and Dobie 1996: 173–89; Kofman and Lionnet-McCumber 1987: 39–55). In all of these cases, listening with the *third ear* describes a mode of listening that accesses affective content, secret wishes sand occulted directives from within the 'official' discursive content of speech. The third ear attends to the material features of speech (its timbre, contour, timing, articulation) over its signifying content. It gives us access to the truth of discourse through attunement to its paralinguistic features. As a locus for the production of secret knowledge, the third ear shares an affinity with Cusick's anti-Cartesian performing bodies. Though Amacher does not engage directly with its intellectual history, her musical instantiation of the third ear liquidates the distinction between content and materiality that underpins its interpretive responsibilities in psychoanalytic and deconstructive discourse.

Published on a 1999 Tzadik release alongside a set of site-specific compositions, the third ear music mobilises the psychoacoustic phenomena of 'otoacoustic emission' to produce sounds that originate within the listener's ear. The piece is made of rapidly oscillating patterns of high-register sine tones articulated by sharp, clear attacks. The effect is something like a highly amplified and accelerated music box or, as Amacher herself lightheartedly describes, like an 'ice cream man' (Amacher 1999). Applied to the cochlea in short bursts, the pure sine tones provoke the cochlea and cilia to amplify the tones' frequencies within the inner ear, creating the effect that the ear itself is producing sound. In my experience listening to, reflecting upon and teaching Amacher's *Third Ear Music*, otoacoustic sounds begin within the ear as a slight vibrational presence, as an itch, or a sense that the temperature within the ear has somehow risen. The gradual increase in intensity eventually presents itself as pitch, once I have acclimated to the harsh register and timbre of the sine tones. By way of guiding the listener through this process, she writes,

> When played at the right sound level, which is quite high and excited, the tones in the music will cause your ears to act as neurophonic instruments that emit sounds that will seem to be issuing directly from your head. In concert, my audiences discover music streaming out from their head, popping out of their ears . . . and converging with the sound in the room . . . These virtual tones are a natural and very real physical aspect of auditory perception, similar to the fusing of two images resulting in a third three-dimensional image in binocular perception. Produced interaurally, these virtual sounds and melodic patterns originate in ears and neuroanatomy . . . I believe such responses exist in all music, where they are registered subliminally and are certainly masked within more complex timbres. I want to release this music which is produced by the listener, bring it out of subliminal existence, make it an important sonic dimension of my music. (Amacher 1999)

The 'molecularized matter' that Amacher uses in this expressive effort is simple: sine tones, amplification, the inner ear, a room. The ear's propensity to *produce* sound remains latent until the sine tones make it a sensible reality; Amacher draws critical focus on the ear's sonorous capacity, emphasising what it shares in common with the sine tones that activate it. This transformation revises the allocation of activity to the eye (and mind), and passivity to the ear (and the body).

In so far as Spinoza's ethical and epistemological programme is premised on cultivating an *active* orientation toward the things that affect us (including our own affects), Amacher's *Third Ear Music* is stunning in its tactical passage from passive listening to active sonorousness. The ear's constitutive *openness* grounds the *active* production of sound within the inner ear. Interaural sound recasts and thus reconfigures the 'agreements, difference and oppositions' between sound and the listening body, positing the once-passive ear as a site of sonic production. As Genevieve Lloyd explains, Spinozistic knowledge 'is not direct attention to an intellectual object – there to be known, independent of awareness of the body. It is, rather, a refining of the direct sensory awareness of the body' (Lloyd 1994: 18). Amacher's *Third Ear Music* constitutes such a refinement, sensitising subjects to the inner ear's sonorous capacities. Amacher's expressive inner ear does not merge with the sine tones that activate it. Rather, the sine tones coax that ear to express its capacities with extreme specificity.

## CONCLUSION

Placed in Spinozistic perspective, music studies' commitment to dualism's political expedience gives way to an expressive approach to sonic materiality. This material focus illuminates both Descartes's and Spinoza's strategies for rejecting or reconfiguring Renaissance musical cosmologies. In order to unseat the harmony of the spheres, sound (and not number) had to become the basis for musical production. Descartes makes this transition, but does not go far enough – he posits sound as something that can be studied empirically, but not as something about which we can achieve certain knowledge. Spinoza's tack is lastingly radical. By undermining the metaphysical system that supports this musical cosmology, Spinoza implicitly includes sonic materiality within the epistemological and ethical systems that he derives from God's immanence to matter. As such, sound becomes a source of adequate knowledge and the active affects that attend that knowledge. Spinoza thus refigures the historically normative allocation of activity to vision and passivity to hearing (of which Descartes is an important part) as a matter of epistemological perspective and tactical practice. Amacher's *Third Ear Music* exemplifies precisely such a tactic in so far as it effaces the distinction between sounding and listening bodies by coaxing what they have in common into expressive sensibility. Considered through the parameters of Spinoza's common notions, material and bodily knowledge – once secret in Cusick's anti-Cartesian account – now becomes the condition of possibility for the production of rational life, active joy and the ethical sociability immanent to their transmission.

## NOTES

1. The *Compendium* was first published in 1650, and the first English translation of the *Compendium* appeared in London in 1653.
2. In this compelling article, Carriero argues that standard readings of the *Meditations* tend to neglect the long analogy between thought and painting that links the dreaming doubt with Descartes's proposal of the evil deceiver. Through the painting analogy, Carriero explains, Descartes instructs the meditator in what is internal to the medium of thought and what enters the mind through the senses. Painting – in particular, its deployment of colour – shifts the meditator's attention from the sensory provenance of mental images to the condition of possibility for the production of those images in the first place.

## BIBLIOGRAPHY

Abbate, Carolyn (2004), 'Music: Drastic or Gnostic?', *Critical Inquiry* 30(3), pp. 505–36.

Althusser, Louis (1997), 'The Only Materialist Tradition Part I: Spinoza', in Warren Montag and Ted Stoltze (eds), *The New Spinoza*, Minneapolis: University of Minnesota Press.

Amacher, Maryanne (1999), 'Head Rhythm 1' and 'Plaything 2', *Sound Characters: Making the Third Ear*, New York: Tzadik.

Augst, Bertrand (1965), 'Descartes' Compendium of Music', *Journal of the History of Ideas* 26(1), pp. 119–32.

Balibar, Etienne (1998), *Spinoza and Politics*, trans. Peter Snowdon, New York: Verso.

Carriero, John (1999), 'Painting and Dreaming in the First Meditation', *Norms and Modes of Thinking in Descartes*, *Acta Philosophica Fennica* 64, pp. 13–46.

Christensen, Thomas (1993), *Rameau and Musical Thought in the Enlightenment*, Cambridge: Cambridge University Press.

Cusick, Suzanne (1994), 'Feminist Theory, Music Theory and the Mind/Body Problem', *Perspectives of New Music* 32(1), pp. 8–27.

Deleuze, Gilles (1988), *Spinoza: Practical Philosophy*, trans. Robert Hurley, San Francisco: City Lights.

Deleuze, Gilles (1993), *Expressionism in Philosophy: Spinoza*, trans. Martin Joughin, New York: Zone.

Deleuze, Gilles, and Félix Guattari (1987), *A Thousand Plateaus: Capitalism and Schizophrenia*, trans. Brian Massumi, Minneapolis: University of Minnesota Press.

Della Rocca, Michael (2008), *Spinoza*, New York: Routledge.

Derrida, Jacques (1985), *The Ear of the Other*, trans. Peggy Kamuf, Lincoln: University of Nebraska Press.

Descartes, René [1618] (1961), *Compendium of Music*, trans. Walter Robert, Middleton, WI: Musicological Studies and Documents.

Donovan, Sarah (2009), 'Re-reading Irigaray's Spinoza', in Moira Gatens (ed.), *Feminist Interpretations of Benedict Spinoza*, University Park: Pennsylvania State University Press.

Gatens, Moira (2009), 'Introduction: Through Spinoza's Looking Glass', in Moira Gatens (ed.), *Feminist Interpretations of Benedict Spinoza*, University Park: Pennsylvania State University Press.

Gaukroger, Stephen (1995), *Descartes: An Intellectual Biography*, Oxford: Oxford University Press.

Gouk, Penelope (2002), 'Harmonics and the Scientific Revolution', in Thomas Christensen (ed.), *The Cambridge History of Western Music Theory*, Cambridge: Cambridge University Press.

Grosz, Elizabeth (2008), *Chaos, Territory, Art: Gilles Deleuze and the Framing of the Earth*, New York: Columbia University Press.

Hahn, Tomie (2007), *Sensational Knowledge: Embodying Culture Through Japanese Dance*, Middletown: Wesleyan University Press.

Hallward, Peter (2006), *Out of this World: Deleuze and the Philosophy of Creation*, London: Verso.

Kassler, Jamie Croy (1995), *Inner Music: Hobbes, Hooke and North on Internal Character*, Cranbury, NJ: Associated University Presses.

Kerman, Joseph (1985), *Contemplating Music: Challenges to Musicology*, Cambridge, MA: Harvard University Press.

Kofman, Sarah, and Madeleine Dobie (1996), 'The Psychologist of the Eternal Feminine (Why I Write Such Good Books, 5)', *Yale French Studies* 87, *Another Look, Another Woman: Retranslations of French Feminism*, pp. 173–89.

Kofman, Sarah, and Françoise Lionnet-McCumber (1987), 'Nietzsche and the Obscurity of Heraclitus', *Diacritics* 17(3), pp. 39–55.

Kravitz, L., and E. Werner (1986), 'The Silence of Maimonides', *Proceedings of the American Academy for Jewish Research* 53, pp. 179–201.

LeGuin, Elizabeth (2006), *Boccherini's Body: An Essay in Carnal Musicology*, Berkeley: University of California Press.

Lloyd, Genevieve (1994), *Part of Nature: Self Knowledge in Spinoza's Ethics*, Ithaca, NY: Cornell University Press.

Macherey, Pierre (1998), *In a Materialist Way: Selected Essays*, ed. Warren Montag, trans. Ted Stoltze, New York: Verso.

McMullen, Tracy (2006), 'Corpo-Realities: Keepin' It Real in "Music and Embodiment" Scholarship', *Current Musicology* 82, pp. 61–83.

Moreno, Jairo (2004), *Musical Representations, Subjects and Objects: The*

*Construction of Musical Thought in Zarlino, Descartes, Rameau and Weber*, Bloomington: Indiana University Press.

Reik, Theodor (1949), *Listening With the Third Ear: The Experiences of a Psychoanalyst*, New York: Farrar Straus.

Sanden, Paul (2009), 'Hearing Glenn Gould's Body: Corporeal Liveness in Recorded Music', *Current Musicology* 88, pp. 7–36.

Sharp, Hasana (2007), 'The Force of Ideas in Spinoza', *Political Theory* 35(6), pp. 732–55.

Spinoza, Baruch (1994), *A Spinoza Reader: The Ethics and Other Works*, trans. and ed. Edwin Curley, Princeton: Princeton University Press.

van Orden, Kate (2002), 'Descartes on Musical Training and the Body', in Linda Phyllis Austern (ed.), *Music, Sense and Sensuality*, New York: Routledge.

# Interlude

LANCE BREWER, 'SHADOWS'

I find Spinoza's famous thesis, that all life is one substance with infinite attributes and modifications, helpful for thinking about photography. Photographs are the attribution and modification of one material – light.

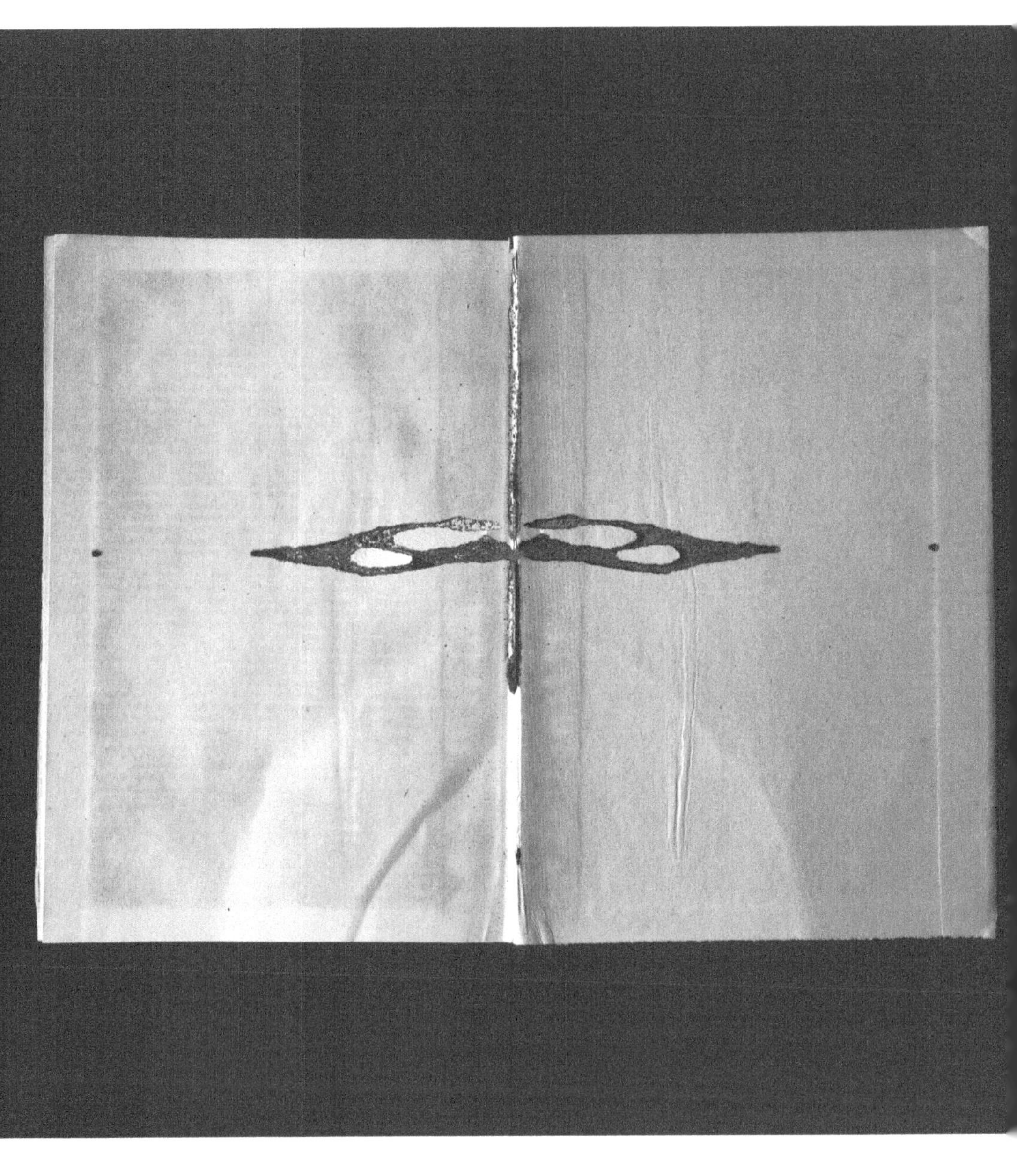

My main interests in photography are the complexities it brings forth between objects and subjects. I do not see the photograph as a simple and locatable object, nor do I see the photograph as a point mirrored off another point: a representation. For me the photograph is a type of connection: a vector between an object, chemistry, a substrate and a perceiver that is irreducible to any point along the line. The Spinozan concept of expression, the coupling of explication and implication that moves substance into attribute and attribute into modality, functions as a bridge between objects and the photographs that transport them into thoughts.

# CHRISTINA RAWLS, 'GREY MATTER(S)'

Recently, dancer and artist Thandie Newton said: 'The cracks have started to show in our constructed world . . . we haven't figured out how to live in oneness.'[1] The power of anomalies and external causes in nature is sometimes greater than can be calculated, imagined or anticipated. When we are among them, we can hardly recognise what direction to step towards next that does not hold some uncertainty. Anomalies also operate according to the laws of nature and when they strike us they always leave a trace, a footprint of some kind. From one encounter to the next, one perspective from another, one interpretation to the other, we attempt to navigate the ground beneath and around us as best we can. The Earth suddenly cracks open, but if we understand why, if we know how to take a different path, if we cherish each event, each encounter, each question as nature unfolding, rupturing, projecting and growing back together, then we can more fully understand that we are both witness to and expression of what it is to truly be alive. Spinoza's philosophy has changed my life, and I realised that the Earth cracked open, not me. I cannot change the perceptions or actions of others, but I can and do understand my own. Beyond his philosophy I move as and with nature to become a more capable and endeavouring expression of what it is to live joyfully amidst the cracking Earth and anomalies. I strive to become someone with tenacity, to listen more carefully, and I affirm more intensely. My ideas can be re-arranged according to the disposition of my body and ideas, I can create a new way among the grey matter(s) of the everyday. This is what Spinoza's philosophy can do. It is a tool for being, for thinking, for doing. It is a set of ideas for moving, a way of creative and dynamic becoming. After that, it is up to you how to use it. For me, I absorb the system fully, ontologically, linguistically, mathematically, socially, biologically, artistically, infinitely. But I do this in order to leave it behind so that I can keep walking . . .

# SHELLEY CAMPBELL, 'MUD BATHERS'

Let us remove qualitative notions from a landscape, a gesture or a still life. No longer will we *interpret* or distinguish clearly between heavy and light, fluid and static, moving and still, air and anvil, midday and midnight, near and far, or light and shade. With a kind of precision that sidesteps – or in a certain way transforms – the effects of contingency, we have the glimmer of a hope of seeing that which falls beneath our gaze. Where individuality 'fades away', as Gilles Deleuze proclaims (2001: 29), in favour of: a life.

If we did really *see* that which we looked at, then our experience of our selves, of our neighbours and of our world would be radically changed. Our moral attitude would be tranquil, our scientific method sharper, and our bias and prejudice weaker or non-existent. This idea transposed on to a canvas is the effect I am trying to achieve in the painting 'Mud Bathers'. In his essay 'Immanence: A Life', Deleuze claims that 'Small children . . . are infused with an immanent life that is pure power and even bliss' (2001: 30). The subject and the technical treatment of this painting seek to demonstrate a Spinozan 'oneness' or non-dualism as a response to how we normally see others and ourselves as individuals within our perceived landscapes.

The light falls on to the child-figures without partiality. As a painter, I want to convey through my practice the thought that the shapes created by environment and object (negative and positive space) are equal in value. In the same way that objects and surroundings create shapes, I propose that shapes are also perceived through the presence and absence of light imparting tonal value (shades and tints) and again, through colour imparting hue. The individuality of the painting's objects is incidental to its arrangement of shapes composed by noting the contingencies of that particular moment. The contingencies through which we judge our vision obscure the boundaries of the individuals. In so doing, they reveal a non-contingent and indivisible nature, that which was always present but *unseen*.

## NOTES

1. 'Embracing Otherness, Embracing Myself', online broadcast at www.ted.com/talks/lang/eng/thandie_newton_embracing_otherness_embracing_myself.html, accessed 10 November 2011.

BIBLIOGRAPHY

Deleuze, Gilles (2001), 'Immanence: A Life', *Pure Immanence: Essays on A Life*, trans. Anne Boyman, New York: Zone, pp. 25–34.

# 6. *Thinking the Future: Spinoza's Political Ontology Today*

MATEUSZ JANIK

With regard to political theory, the difference between Hobbes and myself which is the subject of your inquiry, consists in this, that I always preserve the natural right in its entirety, and I hold that the sovereign power in a State has right over a subject only in proportion to the excess of its power over that subject. This is always the case in a state of nature. (Letter 50 to Jelles, June 1674)

## INTRODUCTORY REMARK

One of the most tempting political questions that one could ask with respect to Spinoza's significance beyond philosophy is to what extent the Spinozan concept of Nature overlaps with the global horizon of contemporary history. This chapter proposes only a possible ground on which such a question could be asked. I want to argue that, in order to provide the answer, one has to elaborate a non-anthropocentric analysis of the collective political agency that can be derived from Spinoza's writings. The political meaning of his philosophy can be derived from his political texts (*Theologico-Political Treatise* and *Political Treatise*), as much as from his theory of affects or critique of theological prejudices. Nevertheless, in each case, interpretation confronts the core philosophical notions which organise the metaphysical horizon of his *Ethics*. One of the main reasons for this philosophical detour is that Spinoza's political anthropology is only a side effect of his ontology. This is not one-direction determination. Spinoza's politics is an effect of his metaphysics as much as the metaphysics is a ground on which articulation of political stakes takes place. For this reason, political concepts such as the *multitude*, and 'right or power', can be clarified by analysis of the way in which they are rooted in the philosophical environment of the *Ethics*. This allows us to avoid the traps of humanist or 'subject-centred' readings of social action, traps indicated by other authors of this volume (see especially Caroline Williams in Chapter 1). Thus, in order to lay the ground for the question of the global dimension of politics in the context of Spinoza, one has to confront the political body as every other body.

This being said, I want to argue that the ontological concept of multitude allows us to introduce the idea of transformation and composition as alternatives to the subject-centred approach within the field of political critique. Such reorientation allows us to grasp more adequately the stakes of the contemporary historical conjuncture. The following chapter consists of four sections. In the first section I indicate briefly the position held by Spinoza within the philosophical discourse of modernity. The second section describes a conceptual context within Spinoza's system that provides a ground for a possible model political ontology that would be independent from modern anthropological discourses. The third section focuses on the relation connecting the historical realm and Spinoza's ontology. In the fourth section, I propose an analysis of the approach toward the political ontology that is established through this relation. All four sections are bound together by the concept of multitude and the question of its critical potential.

## REOPENING THE DEMOCRATIC PROJECT

Ever since it was first established, the notion of democracy has been under constant historical transformation, facing periodic ruptures that force us to rethink not only its conditions of possibility, but also its practical constitution. Today we are in the middle of such a moment, when modern frames of democracy have been shifted again and the constitutive force of democratic discourse has been transformed into a system of mediation, which organises the circulation of social powers in a constant, given way. But if this is so, then the reconstruction of the notion of democracy, understood as the 'material constitution' of the social field, takes the form of a political challenge.

There are many reasons determining the fact that this task situates us in the centre of Spinoza's metaphysics. One of the most important is the powerful fusion of praxis, cognition and ethics present in Spinoza's writings. These three dimensions yield the idea of collective political ontology going beyond the juridical and moral warrants of early modern state theory. The Spinozan reconfiguration of politics' metaphysical basis gives us the opportunity to pose the question of power, not only in terms of its continuity or its solidity, but also in terms of a constant transformation and production. The same fear that organised the Hobbesian concept of sovereignty and the Cartesian restatement of theological absolutism becomes, in Spinoza's writings, a motor of liberation.[1]

However, this specific position occupied by Spinoza in early modernity, which has already earned a rich tradition of studies (especially in post-war France), does not mean that we have to pose the question of Spinoza's currency in terms of 'returning to the sources'. It is not a problem of origin, or the founding moment that has to be comprehended in order to understand the current situation. It is, rather, a matter of a repetition (and difference – to be precise) of a historical conjuncture, or even better, the return of the repressed tradition of materialism. Spinoza's philosophy may be, and in fact is, treated as a sinister sibling of modern political discourse.[2] The modern reflection upon the question of power and genesis of social relationships has made a great exertion to remove from its terrain the problem of ontology, either by replacing it with juridical anthropology or by proposing the transcendent apparatus of political representation (see Montag 2005: 656). The political problem of the constitutive character of being, the core theme of Spinoza's metaphysics, has been pushed into the realm of the unconscious – on both a theoretical and a practical level. Of course, it was still real, and, like every trauma, it was able to produce material effects. However, each time an attempt to articulate this discourse was made, as in the case of Marx, Nietzsche or Freud, it revealed its distortive character. It is because of this suppression that Spinoza returns today as a thinker of the future – in fact, it is almost impossible to think him as anything other than a philosopher of political practice.

## THE PRODUCTIVE MULTIPLICITY

One of the most exceptional aspects of Spinoza's philosophy is that it proposes an infinitely multifarious ontological constitution of existence. The most basic fact of being – the existential 'there is' – is happening always already within the realm of infinite causal production; the God of Spinoza, when referred to the 'created' world, is first of all a productive instance. In theoretical terms, this assertion is located in between three propositions which establish the immanent equivalence between expression, power and causality:

> From the necessity of the divine nature there must follow infinite things in infinite ways (that is, everything that can come within the scope of infinite intellect). (E I16)

> God's power is his very essence. (E I34)

> Nothing exists from whose nature an effect does not follow. (E I36)

This equivalence receives its articulation in the immanent concept of causal power asserted in the famous Proposition 18 of the first part of the *Ethics* ('God is the immanent, not the transitive, cause of all things').[3]

Furthermore, the productive infinity in question is quantitatively differentiated; it is the absolute infinity of attributes ('infinity of ways'), and relative infinity of modes ('infinity of things').[4] The latter is also comprehended as the infinity of causal chains. This initial overdetermination puts in question every individualist interpretation of Spinoza's metaphysics. In fact, each singularity, each individual thing, can be distinguished from the causal flux only by an act of abstraction; Spinoza's singularity is not an individual but a positional being.[5] And even as such, to be conceived adequately, this positional singularity has to be comprehended as plural. This is exactly the kind of adequate abstraction which may be found in the seventh definition at the beginning of the second part of the *Ethics*:

> By individual things [*res singulares*] I mean things that are finite and have a determinate existence. If several individual things concur in one act in such a way as to be all together the simultaneous cause of one effect, I consider them all, in that respect, as one individual. (E IID7)

The idea of *plural individuality*, as the singular position within the causal order, is one of the crucial concepts of Spinoza's ontology, around which all arguments concerning body and practice are built. The fact that the individual is not only an effect of the interaction between singularities, but also is explained in a productive-causal manner, opens the stage of political ontology. This opening takes place simultaneously with an inversion of perspectives, a movement from the establishment of the field of immanent productive order (the above-mentioned chain of propositions from Part I, P16–P18–P34–P36) toward material immanence (Part II of the *Ethics*), constituted by the dynamic relations between bodies forming the multitude of productive instances (the singular positions capable of being conceived as affecting and being affected).

Within this inversion, the passage from the realm of metaphysics to the political dimension of Spinoza's thought is made. It is based on a transition from the multiplicity of being to the idea of the common good. The complex character of being acquires its singularity by a direct, cognitive act of re-composition of material relations constituting adequate knowledge. It is introduced at first under the general name of the 'perceiving intellect',[6] and transformed later into the ethical, active concept of power augmentation. In fact, one may observe in the movement of argumentation from the first to the fourth part of the *Ethics*, a specific process of 'socialization of knowledge' and of intellect as such.

In the first part, the intellect is only a cognitive instance 'perceiving' the content of substance's attributes (i.e. extension and thought). In the second part, cognition and intellect are already explained on the relational level of bodies and their affections.[7] This mode of explanation is characteristic of Spinoza as a thinker of immanence – that is, a thinker of the ontological field organised totally within itself without any external reference determining it. The third part introduces the fully elaborated concept of active being based on the idea of adequate cause; it is through this operation that the intellect becomes involved in the concept of a constitutive practice.[8] Finally, in the fourth part, cognition is presented as founded on the grounds of social cooperation, as something that is happening *between* singularities according to their nature – that is, internal composition:

> [I]f we consider the mind, surely our intellect would be less perfect if the mind were in solitude and understood nothing beyond itself. Therefore, there are many things outside ourselves which are advantageous to us and ought therefore to be sought. Of these none more excellent can be discovered than those which are in complete harmony with our own nature. For example, if two individuals of completely the same nature are combined, they compose an individual twice as powerful as each one singly. (E IV18S)

But this transformation of the notion of knowledge[9] into a practical mechanism of the social execution of power is conditioned by a problem of relation between the historical realm and the metaphysical plane of immanence. The integration of these perspectives plays a crucial role in articulating a political ontology which would not be trapped in a transcendent or transcendental apparatus warranting the consistency of being. We may trace the development of Spinoza's historical discourse in its most direct form already in the *Theologico-Political Treatise*, as well as in the comparative analysis of political regimes in the *Political Treatise* (Balibar 1998: 36–42). The full ontological elaboration of the concepts of power, singularity, imagination and multitude – the latter being the central question of political dynamics and its modalities – can be found only in the *Ethics*. The historico-political dimension has to be explained in ontological terms referring to the materialism of immanence. Accordingly, the concept of multitude must be expressed not in directly political terms, but in physical terms introduced in the course of the presentation of a body and its compositional structure.

## THE GLOBAL HORIZON OF SPINOZA'S ONTOLOGY

I would like to propose a strong comparative thesis that will provide a frame for considering Spinoza's currency. This thesis states that ontological premises that establish the horizon of our thinking of the crisis of modernity in the political dimension have a Spinozan character. To understand the novelty of the current historical situation in respect to modernity, one has to take a theoretical detour via Spinoza and his heterogeneous position in the discursive field of early modernity itself.

This diagnosis becomes meaningful through what, after Immanuel Wallerstein, can be called the global geoculture: a set of norms and general structures determining the form and mode of social practices on the global level – that is, the modality of reproduction of social relationships.[10] One of the main premises of today's political Spinozism is that the modern geoculture is becoming increasingly unstable due to the encounter between the infinite (i.e. global) dimension of the modern world-system (we could call it, using Spinoza's spatial vocabulary, an 'infinity in its kind', for no other macro-structural social formation limits its existence)[11] and the infinite (in the common, cumulative sense) accumulation of capital (Wallerstein 2004: 24). The fact that no economical, political or cultural areas remain unmediated in the global circulation of goods, commodities, money and people opens the realm of absoluteness, based not simply on imaginary identification with some sort of transcendent totality but on a material, immanent totality without any external reference. In this sense, the causality of the global network of production and exchange establishes its own principle of existence, in the sense that it does not refer to any spatial or structural externality (and thus becomes a sort of socio-economic *causa sui*). It was not until the emergence of this global horizon that the sphere of immanence revealed its practical potential.

If Wallerstein's diagnosis of the crisis is correct, then the openness of the system's global structure changes the position of the political practice. It is becoming more and more difficult to speak about any sort of action which could be referred to a quasi-transcendent political structure warranting solidity of its form. In fact, every action becomes self-defining and constitutive of the new forms of organisation (Wallerstein 2004: 77). At the same time, single social action is an effect of global relations and a source of its own constitution. The paradox of Spinoza's ethics finds its material representation: God / Substance / Nature exists in its own effects and through them (E IP18) and, at the same time the thing exists as much as it is dependent solely on its own actions (E IIP13). Not only political practice but also the political subject ceases to be defined as a solid element, deriving its internal composition from the relation it has to the meta-conditions of a stable systemic structure that (still) establishes his or her essence. The problem of the subjective form of political agent gives way to the question of composition. In other words, the problem of the political or social subject ceases to be a problem of distinction or of its *principium individuationis* and becomes a question of inclusion.

How do we approach this paradox from the point of view of critical political theory? Antonio Negri and Michael Hardt propose a new mode of analysis that focuses on the immanent composition of the subject's political body. In the always illustrative language of Marxism, they suggest that the question is not 'what divides waged industrial laborers from the other social classes and groups?', but rather 'what is the composition of the working class and how does it include different social agents?', or even better, 'what is the principle of inclusion of other social groups and individuals in the category of the working class?'[12]

The work of Antonio Negri and Michael Hardt, which has earned the adjective 'neo-Spinozan', allows us to approach the idea of immanence directly through the historical conjuncture of late global capitalism. We will borrow the starting point from Kiarina Kordela's lapidary and uncompromising critique of the Spinozan connotations of the political project proposed by Hardt and Negri. Kordela's argument refers to an assumption made by the authors that 'since there is no exteriority to substance, the same substance must be that which sustains the existing politico-economical system *and* that which undermines it' (Kordela 2007: 3). Kordela objects by saying that this logic is bound to reproduce the Hegelian–Marxist teleological structure of historical movement. The authors of *Empire* simply repeat the argument, stating that the development of capitalism necessarily produces its own conditions of collapse. But this description of Hardt's and Negri's project is unsatisfactory, as long as it is framed in the Spinozan perspective. In fact, it repeats misunderstandings generated by Pierre Bayle's famous article on Spinoza: namely, the identification of modes and substance. Through this mechanism of identification we find ourselves in the realm of the pantheist *Short Treatise* rather than in the field of immanence proper to the *Ethics*. Nevertheless, Kordela's argument indicates the nodal point at which the ethical relation between ontology and history is established. The problem arises when we posit ourselves, going alongside the consequences of her assumption, on the historical level. One of Hardt's and Negri's main arguments is based on the thesis that the whole period of modernity has been marked by a perpetual tension between power (*potentia*) exercised on the level of immanence and what they call the 'transcendental apparatus' (Hardt and Negri 2000: 78–83). While the first term mentioned is supposed to be a proper and direct form of exercising power on the level of social life, visible in sequential revolutionary projects of modernity, the latter, tending to neutralise this spontaneous historical movement by all sorts of institutional and conceptual mediation, is a figure of transitive power (*potestas*) and exploitation.[13] It is important to notice that this transitive form of power includes not only the institutional apparatuses of political representation, but also the mediations determining the proper orders of production. This is the crucial point of Negri's argumentation, since it both deprives modernity of its positive or assertive content, and indicates that it is bound up with the economical structure of capitalist modes of production. This remark is important because, in Negri's and Hardt's proposition, the emergence of historical immanence is happening exactly at the level of productive practice.

Currently, according to Negri and Hardt, we may notice a process of lessening the distance between capital and labour (without dissolution of the antagonism between these two terms), which, in their vocabulary, can be called the transition from industrial to biopolitical production. The argument is based on the thesis that 'traditional' commodity production – that is, production of the means of social life – is supported, and to some extent substituted, by a production of social life as such (Hardt and Negri 2004: 103–15; Virno 2004). The theoretical articulation of this movement towards 'production of life' is possible through the conceptual apparatus of immaterial labour, understood as the organisation of cognitive, communicative and affective abilities embodied in relations between the singular instances of social practice, coming into productive order. This is a process through which the forms of social collaboration, the interaction between individuals and singularities, thus all forms of collective practice, become a 'raw material from which management extracts productivity' (Dyer-Whiteford 2005: 140). In Negri's opinion, the political stake of this process is a transition from the juridical to the ontological basis of the democratic project.

In the Spinozan context, it introduces into the order of politics and its ontological articulation a whole set of problems, known from *Ethics* Parts III and IV. This includes the question of *conatus* and social assembly, and the co-extensivity of the right of a given subject (collective or individual) with its power to act, as presented in the *Theologico-Political Treatise*. In general terms, the well-known passage about the transitive power of kings and the absolute, immanent, power of God (E II3S) is the most direct articulation of the question, repeated constantly in the *Ethics*, about being and its organisation. It occurs later in Part III in the form of passive / active affects, and adequate / inadequate causes of action, and in Part IV in the idea of disagreement and agreement according to one's nature.

This is also the proper context for the question concerning the constitutive power of the multitude. And it is exactly the Problem (capital P), for its ambiguity is evident. It concerns primarily the existential modality of the multitude. The problem is not obvious, since the occurrences of this term in the current philosophical discourse are marked by a certain duality.

On the one hand, there is the already mentioned Negrian line of interpretation emphasising the ontological multiplicity and productivity of being. In Spinozan terms, it indicates an approach based on the logical connection between the absolute productivity of God's power (E IP16) (thus, of being as such, E IP36) and the materialist perspective established by Proposition 13 in Part II. As a theoretical tendency, this approach is prone to a semi-romantic political activism (a quality which does not have to be a disadvantage) and tends to perceive the question of multitude primarily in terms of organisation and production.

On the other hand, we may distinguish an expanded project of anti-humanist philosophical anthropology, developed by authors such as Etienne Balibar and Warren Montag, emphasising the affective dynamics of social practice. This theoretical optics brings forth the problem of the masses and their constitutive role in the realm of politics; as such, it is much more embedded in the theoretical consequences of the famous second paragraph of the third chapter of the *Political Treatise* and enforced by the theory of affects presented in the third part of the *Ethics*. Thus it provides basic concepts for an analysis of the collective nature of social life and of how state apparatuses are constantly subjected to modifications resulting from pressure coming from new forms of mass movement and the masses themselves. The common ground for both theoretical tendencies is the irreducible material reflectiveness of being and its openness for new forms of existence. This openness, the very fact that being is a never totally fixed configuration of elements, determines the exact centre of Spinozan political ontology.

One can see that the multitude, far from being a simple quantitative term, may refer not only to 'all of us' – to use Kordela's phrase – but also to completely different modes of collective singularities: the archetypal 'angry mob', semi-organised crowds (as those which constitute massive migrations), heaps of individuals inhabiting the mythical private sphere, international coalitions of social movements, and classes. In fact, it denotes all sorts of assemblies on all levels of complexity, all at the same time. This simultaneous variety of modes of existence makes it difficult to establish a unified theory or code of description (this is why I prefer to speak about theoretical tendencies rather than about theories as such). It is also the reason why multitude is described as a mode of approach to social existence rather than a concrete form of organisation.

The problem is that the dominant tradition of modern political philosophy was, so to speak, intoxicated with the question of the subject and its involvement in the order of the national state. Thus, in the moment of confrontation with the global horizon of late capitalism, it has faced a drastic lack of conceptual tools, crucial for comprehension of the multiplicity and plenitude of collective existence, and thus inevitably experienced it as chaotic fluctuation of uncoordinated tendencies. This is the main reason why Spinoza is a necessary detour. His ontology, based on the collective perspective, an ontology of the 'body composed of a great number of individual parts' (E IIPost.I), is one of the main conceptual repositories with which we may comprehend the character of multitude. It is, therefore, not by accident that two major philosophical attempts to re-think the modern political stakes in the context of globalisation (namely, that of Balibar and Wallerstein, and that of Negri and Hardt) are carried by thinkers of Spinozan provenience.

## TRANSFORMATION AS AN ETHICAL PRACTICE

Up to this point, I have tried to indicate that there exists a specific type of direct relation between Spinoza's ontology and the field of politics understood as a concrete historical realm. Now I would like to indicate how this relation is established and how it affects Spinoza's metaphysics and political theory. I would like to confront this question through the notion of transformation, elaborated by Balibar in the early 1990s. By transformation I understand a practice proper to material universality: that is, a practice exercised always within the field of the global configuration composed of 'institutions, groups, individuals', as much as of processes involving them – that is, 'circulation of commodities and people, the political negotiations, the juridical contracts, the communication of news and cultural patterns, etc.' (Balibar 2002: 147). Its effects (and stakes) are encapsulated in the horizon of history, without reference to any kind of ideal universality or imaginary identification with political narratives (institutional mediation). The transformation aims at the material conditions constitutive for both aforementioned discourses. In this sense, transformation (ascribed to the order called by Balibar a 'heteronomy of politics') establishes a materialist perspective *par excellence*, indicating the direction we should follow in order to trace the passage between political ontology and history. The Spinozan character of this idea is grounded in the fact that, from the perspective of politics, its own conditions seem to be natural or, to be more precise, non-political. In other words, politics perceives itself as independent from the relations constituting its content and thus posits itself 'outside nature', establishing a sort of *imperium in imperio*. Naturalisation of economic life, of social existence, culture and ecology, is inseparable from the process of institutionalisation and autonomisation of political practice embodied in representative parliamentary democracy. The modern idea of liberal democratic societies is thus a direct counterpoint of political ontology understood in Spinozan terms. The direct consequence of taking the perspective of material conditions of politics (i.e. its heteronomy) as the proper locus of adequate political action[14] is the dissolution of distance between politics and 'non-politics', revealing the fact that the very distinction in question is already a political reminder of material relation. Any adequate attempt to escape this trap of imaginary separation involves, in the last instance, a re-composition of material relations.

We have already said that the practice of transformation involves an intervention dissolving the imaginary distinction, constitutive for the relative autonomy of politics. But from what positions is this intervention made? The explanation may be found in an apparently inconspicuous displacement in Spinoza's line of argumentation.

In the second part of the *Ethics*, the passage from Proposition 13 to 14, one of the most famous, is marked at its initial moment with some hesitation or ambiguity. This ambiguity occurs even earlier, in Proposition 11, where Spinoza asserts that the 'actual being of the human mind is the idea of some particular thing actually existing' (E IIP11). We will not focus here on the instability of Spinozan parallelism, which becomes visible almost immediately after its formulation. We will, instead, turn our attention to the scholium of this proposition: 'Here, I doubt not, readers will come to a stand, and will call to mind many things which will cause them to hesitate' (E IIP11S). This hesitation changes into astonishment as soon as Spinoza informs his readers that this particular thing is the human body. But Spinoza explains quickly: 'The propositions we have advanced hitherto have been entirely general, applying not more to men than to other individual things, all of which, though in different degrees, are animated [*animata*]' (E II13S). But this 'animation' is nothing else than the fact that each body has its idea (or, more precisely, may be conceived from the perspective of the attribute of thought); thus the whole weight of the argument is lying here on the body and its properties, determining the specificity of man in a very characteristic way:

> Therefore, in order to determine the difference between the human mind
> and others and in what way it surpasses them, we have to know the nature
> of its object, that is, the nature of the body [. . .] I will make this general
> assertion, that in proportion as a body is more apt than other bodies to act
> or to be acted upon simultaneously in many ways, so is its mind more apt
> than other minds to perceive many things simultaneously. (E IIP13S)

There is nothing peculiar or unique in this strange combination of
'individuals composing the human body' (E IIP11; translation modified), except the fact that, through their composition, it is capable of
acting in its own way, with its own power (and its own right – it is
worth recalling that this is an ontological equivalent of the argument
about the co-extensiveness of right and power from Chapter 16 of the
*Theologico-Political Treatise*). But if this is so, then we are forced to
abandon *all* imaginary distinctions and limitations. The imaginary
remainder is replaced by material relation. There seems to be no reason
which could restrain us from applying subsequent propositions not
only to man but also to 'other individual things' – except Spinoza's dec-
larations, of course, especially those which are composed from human
individuals themselves.

We can find something even more disturbing in those passages concerning the body's internal composition and the ways in which it may
be affected: namely, the fact that this composite cluster does not have
any sort of a warrant; nothing assures its individuality. Spinoza will
have to use all his conceptual inventiveness to provide some sort of
stability and consistency, through *conatus* and, later in the fourth book,
through the reintroduction of the concept of nature. But on the level of
immanence we know only that 'All bodies are either in motion or at
rest,' that they move either 'more slowly' or 'more quickly', that they
are recoiling from each other. There are only bodies, velocities and col-
lisions (and 'fixed relations', but these are established solely within and
between bodies). The composition of the body is open and conditioned
only by the degree of power that is the actual relations between its parts
– there is only being and its immanent organisation. This is the material premise of equation between the final cause and desire proposed in
the preface to Part IV. There is no final cause primarily because there
is no end or origin in the infinite chain of configurations, constituting
infinitely complex bodies.

The material constitution of a human body – of every singular body,
to be more precise – cannot be separated from the problem of imagination, and in a wider perspective from the cognitive relations proper
to individual bodies. The abstraction which allows us to speak about
an individual is imaginary, but we should not forget that imagination,

even if inadequate, has for Spinoza a positive character. It is worth considering once again the collective character of cognition.

After presenting the general principles organising interactions between bodies, Spinoza returns to the problem of cognition and individuation: 'The idea of any mode wherein the human body is affected by external bodies must involve the nature of the human body together with the nature of the external body' (E II16). The two corollaries to this proposition seem interesting:

> Corollary 1: Hence it follows that the human mind perceives the nature of very many bodies along with the nature of its own body.
> Corollary 2: Secondly, the ideas that the human mind has of external bodies indicate the constitution of our own body more than the nature of external bodies. This I have explained with many examples in Appendix, Part I. (E IIP16 C1–2)

The individual perceives its individuality through the way it is affected; it determines its identity through the relation with other bodies. This is a material condition of the imaginary relation in Spinoza's vocabulary. The latter is described as follows:

> [T]o retain the usual terminology, we will assign the word 'images' to those affections of the human body the ideas of which set forth external bodies as if they were present to us, although they do not represent shapes. And when the mind regards bodies in this way, we shall say that it 'imagines'.
>
> At this point, to begin my analysis of error, I should like you to note that the imaginations of the mind, looked at in themselves, contain no error; i.e., the mind does not err from the fact that it imagines, but only insofar as it is considered to lack the idea which excludes the existence of those things which it imagines to be present to itself. (E IIP17S)

The imagination is inadequate as long as it substitutes an external body in place of an affective relation. The formation of an adequate relation is thus an operation of acquiring an idea which determines whether the external body is or is not present. But at the level of analysis on which Spinoza formulates this assertion, acquiring adequate ideas through an individual body means changing and expanding its ability of affecting and being affected. This means that the notion of individuality loses all its obviousness. Spinoza seems to be confused with the consequences of his theory of composition. He comes back to the problem again in the fourth part of the *Ethics* in another famous passage:

> [H]ere it should be noted that I understand a body to die when its parts are so disposed as to maintain a different proportion of motion-and-rest to one another [. . .] I have no reason to hold that a body does not die unless it turns into a corpse, indeed, experience seems to teach otherwise. It sometimes

> happens that a man undergoes such changes that I would not be prepared
> to say that he is the same person. I have heard tell of a certain Spanish poet
> who was seized with sickness, and although he recovered, he remained so
> unconscious of this life that he did not believe that the stories and tragedies
> he had written were his own [. . .] And if this seems incredible, what are we
> to say about babies? A man of advanced years believes their nature to be so
> different from his own that he could not be persuaded that he had ever been
> a baby if he did not draw a parallel from other cases. (E IVP39S)

It is worth noticing that, on the political level, Spinoza provides a
proposition for overcoming the problem of death. It is an idea of a collective individual – an assembly. This is, for example, the case of the
sufficiently numerous council: 'Kings are mortal whereas councils are
everlasting,' says Spinoza (one could add that 'the sovereign Power that
has once been conferred on a council never reverts to the people'), and
what is more, 'the rule of a king is often precarious by reasons of his
minority, sickness, old age, or for other causes, whereas the power of a
council of this kind remains always one and the same' (TP 8.3).

But even such strong anti-essentialist principles of individuation as
material composition, the degree and range of power, or the 'ability
to affect and be affected' are imaginary in the sense in which they are
always estimated from the perspective of some kind of functionality
or end, some kind of purpose or at least general tendency; in fact, we
are always dealing with an abstraction (which is another name used by
Spinoza for imaginary relation – see E IP15S). So, when Spinoza says
that we do not know what the body is capable of, he simply affirms
that we never know all the relations and configurations in which it is
involved. That we do not know all the capacities of the body means
that we never know with what kind of body we are dealing. The constant transformation of the singular body relation in order to acquire
adequate ideas is a process of infinite expansion from an individual to a
collective position. In other words, we know, or rather we are supposed
to know, that in the last instance, we are dealing with Nature – that
is, absolutely adequate, i.e. ethical being; this *practical* knowledge is
precisely the gist of Spinoza's political project.

The major consequence of this fact is that the multiplicity of the multitude is completely deprived of anthropocentric character. Composite
political organisms are those composed not by human individuals but
by all possible intersections of their bodies composed in concrete forms
staying in a concrete material relation. The proper Spinozan (but probably not Spinoza's) answer to this apparently dead end of political
practice is that the only possible way of making politics goes through
complete dissolution of the imaginary distinction between the social

and the natural (this is why one of the most Spinozan authors today is, probably, Bruno Latour). Thus, the problem of current politics does not concern the search for a successor of a political subject able to reconfigure the field of politics – and even less of a new rule or principle distinguishing the realm of politics from other spheres of activity and practice. It is rather the question of the actual composition of social movements, modes of communication and combinations composing their practical content. In this perspective, the imaginary relations able to produce political identity are supposed to become transformed into material and intellectual connections able to produce an active political stance.

If we say that, in the last instance, there are only bodies and their affections, then their collective character becomes the primary feature of political theory. Politics comprehended in those terms becomes a practice of composition. This opens the horizon of possibilities indicating that Spinoza's ontology allows us to think the future as an actual practical problem. What is more, Spinoza's philosophy, seen from this perspective, turns out to leave no space for non-politics; 'Spinoza's true politics is his metaphysics' (Negri 1991: 266), and vice versa.

At this point we can see more clearly the Spinozan character of the current historical moment. Kiarina Kordela argues that reading history through Spinoza's lenses is likely to fall into the trap of teleology, derived from the Marxist–Hegelian model of historical necessity. While such danger is perfectly real, there is also an aspect of Spinoza's political ontology marked by ultimate openness. It corresponds to another concept, elaborated in the field of social sciences: namely, the already mentioned idea of bifurcation. This term is used by Wallerstein to denote the uncertainty of historical effects of the structural crisis within the world-system. The bifurcation means that the immanent tensions and contradictions of the system lead to its transformation into something unknown yet dependent on current actions. The crisis of the last few decades, according to Wallerstein, has exactly this transformative character. In this context the political practice of transformation may depend solely on the body itself, to use Spinoza's language, or be subordinated to external causes. We may try actively to change the historical output of this crisis or stay passive, exposed to external causes. Such historical activity depends, to a great extent, on the *knowledge* of the true causes, even if this knowledge concerns true causes of imaginary (or abstract) singularities.

If the above argument is correct, then the multitude's existence is located at the intersection of complete dissolution and infinity. As a multiplicity of bodies and their assemblies, as an innumerable swarm of overlapping singularities and instances, the multitude is the body of reality marked by a tangle of affections and fixing its internal relations. As an infinity, multitude is an absolute power, *potentia* that can be organised in many different forms, mediated, recomposed but never alienated, since it is constitutive for the composition as such. Every possible mediation is thus only a loop or fold, which dams up the circulation of power. In this sense, the ethical horizon of multitude is *communio* or *communitas* – participation in power with no exception or mediation. This seems to be the proper stake of today's political ontology, at least as long as we consider it as the realm of ethical practice – that is, as a transformation of the material conditions of existence.

## NOTES

1. This idea refers to the problem of the historical crisis and reactions which it yields. For elaboration on the crisis in seventeenth-century modernity see Hobsbawm (1956). For recent studies see Parker and Smith (1997). The interesting concept of the philosophical reaction to the seventeenth-century crisis was presented by Antonio Negri in *The Political Descartes* (Negri 2006). Spinoza's exceptional approach to the early modern 'fear of the masses' is elaborated in Warren Montag's *Bodies, Masses, Power: Spinoza and His Contemporaries* (Montag 1999).

2. The tradition of presenting Spinoza as a philosophical monstrosity is as old as the reception of his writings (see especially Vernière 1954). The way in which this demonic narration was intercepted by the current 'neo-Spinozan' discourses, and transformed into an indication of his theoretical importance (a truly Spinozist strategy), could become a theme for a separate study.

3. It is worth noticing that Proposition 18 is one of the *Ethics'* complete and absolute points. Spinoza does not refer to this proposition anywhere else.

4. For one of the most precise descriptions of the difference between the modal infinity of singular things and absolute infinity of divine substance, see Deleuze 1992: 218–19.

5. This is an inversion of Kołakowski's argument about the contradictory character of Spinoza's concept of an individual presented in *Jednostka i nieskończoność* (1958), based on Spinoza's correspondence with Tschirnhaus, and those passages from the *Ethics* which defend the more or less unstable concept of parallelism.

6. For example, 'By attribute I mean that which intellect *perceives* of substance as constituting its essence' (E ID4); and more directly: 'The Intellect in act, whether it be finite or infinite, as also will, desire, love, etc., must be related to *natura naturata*, not to *natura naturans*' (E IP31).

7. '[W]hen we say that the human mind perceives this or that, we are saying nothing else but this: that God – not insofar as he is infinite but insofar as

     he is explicated through the nature of the human mind, that is, insofar as he constitutes the essence of human mind – has this or that idea' (E II11C).

8. 'I say we are active when something takes place, in us or externally to us, of which we are the adequate cause' (E IIID2).

9. This transformation is played on two levels simultaneously. One is the transformative movement from intellectual cognition to cognitive practice; the second is a gradual model of three kinds of knowledge.

10. We can, at this point, still only metaphorically describe it in a Spinozan manner, as an 'unvarying relation' according to which 'bodies form close contact' and retain a certain 'rate of speed' (E IIA2″). This holds as long as we keep in mind the idea of nature as a single (global) individual (E IIL7).

11. 'A thing is said to be finite in its own kind when it can be limited by another thing of the same nature. For example, a body is said to be finite because we can always conceive of another body greater than it' (E ID2).

12. The problem of class composition, and the inclusion of new social groups into the content of the traditional Marxist concept of class was also the main interest of Negri's writings in the late 1970s. The context of the Italian Autonomist movement overlaps perfectly with Wallerstein's diagnosis as an exemplary figure (see Negri 2005).

13. Both notions are borrowed from Spinoza's analysis of two concepts of power. In this context, *potestas* is the transitive and limited power ascribed to the individual's possible actions, which is always the power over something or to do something. *Potentia* is the power co-extensive with existence of the singular thing in so far as it is considered as constituted by the infinite and absolute power of God. For a general explanation of Negri's use of the conceptual pair *potentia / potestas* see Hardt's foreword to Negri's *Savage Anomaly* (Negri 1991. xi–xvi). There one may also find an analysis of the relation between the two terms within the *Ethics* (Negri 1991: 59–67).

14. An adequate action is one 'through which its effect can be clearly and distinctly perceived' (E IIID1).


# BIBLIOGRAPHY

Balibar, Etienne (1998), *Spinoza and Politics*, trans. P. Snowdon, New York: Verso.

Balibar, Etienne (2002), *Politics and the Other Scene*, trans. C. Jones et al., London: Verso.

Balibar, Etienne, and Immanuel Wallerstein (1991), *Race, Nation, Class: Ambiguous Identities*, trans. C. Turner, London: Verso.

Deleuze, Gilles (1992), *Expressionism in Philosophy – Spinoza*, trans. M. Joughin, New York: Zone.

Dyer-Whiteford, Nick (2005), 'Cyber-Negri: General Intellect and Immaterial Labor', in Timothy Murphy and Mustapha Abdul-Karim (eds), *The*

*Philosophy of Antonio Negri, Resistance in Practice*, vol. 1, London: Pluto, pp. 136–62.

Hardt, Michael, and Antonio Negri (2000), *Empire*, Cambridge, MA: Harvard University Press.

Hardt, Michael, and Antonio Negri (2004), *Multitude*, New York: Penguin.

Hobsbawm, Eric (1956), 'The Crisis of the 17th Century', *Past and Present 6*, pp. 44–65.

Kołakowski, Leszek (1958), *Jednostka i nieskończoność*, Warsaw: PWN.

Kordela, Kiarina (2007), *$urplus, Spinoza–Lacan*, New York: SUNY.

Montag, Warren (1999), *Bodies, Masses, Power: Spinoza and His Contemporaries*, London: Verso.

Montag, Warren (2005), 'Who's Afraid of Multitude? Between the Individual and the State', *South Atlantic Quarterly* 104, pp. 655–73.

Negri, Antonio (1991), *The Savage Anomaly*, trans. M. Hardt, Minneapolis: University of Minnesota Press.

Negri, Antonio (2005), *Books for Burning: Between Civil War and Democracy in 1970s Italy*, trans. A. Bove et al., London: Verso.

Negri, Antonio (2006), *The Political Descartes*, trans. M. Mandarini and A. Toscano, London: Verso.

Parker, Geoffrey, and Lesley Smith (eds) (1997), *The General Crisis of the 17th Century*, London: Routledge.

Spinoza, Benedict (2002), *Complete Works*, ed. M. L. Morgan, trans. S. Shirley, Indianapolis: Hackett.

Vernière, Paul (1954), *Spinoza et la pensée française avant la révolution*, Paris: PUF.

Virno, Paolo (2004), *A Grammar of the Multitude*, trans. I. Bertoletti et al., New York: Semiotext(e).

Wallerstein, Immanuel (2004), *World-system Analysis: An Introduction*, London: Duke University Press.

# 7. *Spinoza's Empty Law: The Possibility of Political Theology*

DIMITRIS VARDOULAKIS

The evolution of how power is both understood and exercised can be explained in two ways or two distinct narratives.[1] According to the first one, power articulates itself by seeking justification through its relation to the law. I will refer to this as the juridical conception of power.[2] According to the second one, the exercise of power cannot be justified with recourse to the law. I will refer to this as agonistic power because it expresses itself through its antagonism towards juridical power.[3] Clearly, the juridical model has been the dominant one in the Western tradition: that is, in any conception whereby power is different from kingship. However, the agonistic power forms a strong current in the intellectual tradition, one that includes Marx and Nietzsche in the nineteenth century, as well as French post-structuralists such as Foucault, Derrida and Deleuze, and the Frankfurt School and Walter Benjamin in Germany.

It may appear easy to identify and to critique the tradition that understands power from a juridical perspective. For instance, Foucault identified that tradition as the source of our conception of sovereignty, even though he lamented that 'we still have not cut off the head of the king' (1990: 89). The reason that the king's head is still intact may be that the secular conception of sovereignty shares an essential similarity with the agonistic tradition opposed to it – namely, that they both conceive of the law as empty. The emptiness of the law does not mean that power is disconnected from statute. Rather, the emptiness of the law refers to the lack of a foundation to legality as such. For instance, Jean Bodin (1992: 7) argues that sovereignty is given unconditionally, meaning that sovereignty stands above the law of the state and hence the sovereign is entitled to change the law at will. The content of the law is a mere derivate of power standing above the law – or, what is primary is power's relation to, and use of, the law. This idea is present, *mutatis mutandis*, in the entire tradition that understands power from a legalistic perspective – from Locke's insistence on the sovereign prerogative in the *Treatises of Government*, to Rousseau's famous assertion that 'the general will is always in the right,' to the development of the theory of the exception by Carl Schmitt and his followers. At the same time, however, the agonistic tradition, with its opposing emphasis on the lack of any – transcendent or earthly – authority of legitimacy, also conceives of the law as empty. The law is also determined in relation to particular articulations of power. For instance, Derrida (1992), in his essay on Kafka's 'Before the Law', describes the law as constantly vacillating between a universal proscription and its particular application, just as, in the legalistic tradition, Derrida describes the law not in terms of the inviolability or otherwise of its content, but rather in terms of its utility. So how are we to understand this common insistence from two opposing traditions on the emptiness of the law? In this chapter, I will turn to Spinoza, who belongs to the tradition that critiques juridical power, in order to show how, in fact, the emptiness of the law can be used to show some of the salient differences between the two traditions of how we understand power.

Before turning to Spinoza's own position, it is necessary to clarify further the juridical understanding of power. The first significant point is that, even though juridical power articulates itself in relation to law, this does not mean that it is commensurate with law. Rather, juridical power is given in its various relations with legality that lead to justification. According to Antonio Negri, such relation to the law is the criterion for distinguishing three phases of juridical power. There is a first phase where right and sovereign power are united. What characterises the empires of the past, especially the Roman Empire, is, according to Negri, a moralisation of the law. The second, modern phase begins with the secular separation of powers. This entails the separation of right and law, leading to the distinction between the private and the public and ultimately to the Enlightenment ideal of the progression towards a 'perpetual peace' or a universal community of enlightened citizens. The third, biopolitical phase, according to Negri, performs a re-unification of law and right, of institutional formations and eternal moral values. This re-unification effectively means that law is transformed into regulation and procedure – or, in other words, the law pervades every aspect of life.[4] The starting point of Spinoza's critique of the juridical tradition is that the law is empty. This emptiness of the law asserts, as I will argue, agonistic power and allows for a conception of power's monism. We will also see how Spinoza's conception of power leads to his political theology that is determined from two perspectives – either in relation to law's emptiness or in opposition to an understanding of the law as having a content.

A further significant point in clarifying the juridical tradition is to recognise that the juridical tradition itself can appropriate the emptiness of the law that is mobilised by Spinoza precisely in order to deconstruct it. For instance, the emptiness of the law is a defining feature of the discourse of political theology that starts with Carl Schmitt. 'The sovereign is he who decides on the exception,' writes Schmitt (1985: 5). There are two significant aspects in this definition of sovereignty. First, power is articulated through the sovereign, whose function is to stand above the law in such a manner as to be able both to affirm and to suspend the law. The law, according to this tradition of political theology, is empty because it is given by something external, the sovereign, that is without content because he occupies a structural position of exteriority to the law. So, even though he defines the law as empty, Schmitt can still be regarded as working within the juridical tradition since he relies on a justification of power through the law. Thus, in order to argue that Spinoza is indeed opposed to the juridical tradition, his own notion of the law's emptiness must be differentiated from Schmitt's – as well as that of the entire post-Schmittian movement that has dominated political theology in the twentieth century and up to the present through thinkers such as Agamben (see, for example, Agamben 2005). In other words, we need to discover a criterion to distinguish between the two notions of empty law that lead to two different political theologies, one relying on juridical power, the other putting forward agonistic power.[5] And this brings us to the second aspect of Schmitt's definition of the sovereign which has to do with how the exception is understood. It is the figure of the enemy that allows Schmitt to define the exception. The exception arises through sovereignty's response to those that threaten its power.[6] Contrasting Spinoza's definition of agonism to Schmitt's enmity will highlight their divergent understandings of the emptiness of the law and their distinct political theologies. Spinoza's political theology is different from Schmitt's because agonism is not articulated as enmity but rather as a function of love, as we will see shortly. Such construal of agonism in Spinoza entails that there is no outside power. Schmitt requires that outside – indeed, it is precisely the enemy that occupies the space outside the sovereign's power. For Spinoza, on the contrary, there is a sense of power that excludes no one – or, rather, a power to which the binary of exclusion and inclusion does not pertain. In this sense, it is a single all-inclusive power. Thus, the distinctive feature of Spinoza's political theology is that it is both agonist and monist.

In order to delineate clearly Spinoza's political theology, as well as its differentiation from the political theology of Carl Schmitt and the entire juridical tradition of power, it is necessary to show the way that agonism and monism are related. Such a task is only possible by examining in detail Spinoza's conception of the emptiness of the law.

In order to recognise the emptiness of the law as it is conceived in Spinoza, it is necessary to situate his project within the accounts of the formation of the state by the social contract theories of the seventeenth century. There are two aspects of Hobbes's well-known version of the social contract that will help us juxtapose his construction of juridical power to Spinoza's agonistic power. These consist in the way that legitimation and justified violence are understood. According to *The Leviathan*, there is a state of nature where everybody is an enemy to everybody because all are absolutely equal and hence all can desire the same thing. Such a state of nature is defined by an absolute freedom conceived of as man's natural right. The transition to civil society introduces law whose function is the opposite of right: namely, law's function is to delimit freedom, to prohibit, to ban. Whereas the freedom of the state of nature is simply the unharnessed desires of the equal individuals, the law of the social contract regulates desires by referring them to statute, to a written content. In other words, Hobbes's narrative requires the distinction between right and law that, as Hardt and Negri indicate, defines the second or modern configuration of juridical power. This separation of law and right legitimates sovereign power that, in its turn, has recourse to justified violence in order to perpetuate itself. This requires the creation of the outlaw. What happens when people follow their desires – that is, their natural rights – after they have entered the commonwealth? What happens when they seek to re-assert their natural freedom and equality? They contravene the content of the law that legitimated the state. As a consequence, their actions exclude them from the law that founded the commonwealth and the full force of the state can legitimately fall upon them. For instance, Hobbes discusses rebellion thus: 'Rebellion . . . is against reason. Justice therefore, that is to say, Keeping of Covenant, is a Rule of Reason, by which we are forbidden to do any thing destructive to our life; and consequently a Law of Nature' (1999: 103). The rebel contravenes reason because reason is commensurate with the content of the law – which is precisely what the rebel opposed. Therefore, the justification of violence against those excluded from the law, such as the rebel, relies precisely on the fact that the law has a content. This is not an argument peculiar to Hobbes but rather one that permeates the social contract tradition. For instance, a century later, Rousseau, in his own *Social Contract*, despite being in many respects almost antithetical to Hobbes, is still in complete agreement about the violence that ought to be directed against the outlaw. In Chapter 5 of Book II, titled 'The Right of Life and Death', Rousseau unambiguously states: '[E]very wrongdoer, in attacking the rights of society by his crimes, becomes a rebel and a traitor to his country . . . The preservation of the state becomes incompatible with his own' (1994: 71). Foucault (2003: 240) summarises this point by saying that the sovereign prerogative consists in the right of life and death, which 'is actually the right to kill', or the justification of violence against anyone who is deemed to be outside the law. So, according to the contract tradition, the outlaw is, by definition, excluded by the law, and hence can be liquidated. Law justifies violence against the outlaw. In sum, the juridical power arising out of the social contract tradition consists in giving content to the law – first, as a way of separating it from right and, second, as the justification of violence against the outlaw who contravenes the law's content.

Spinoza's description of the emptiness of the law is opposed to the law having a content according to the social contract tradition. Spinoza presents, in the *Tractatus Theologico-Politicus*, his version of the narrative of state formation by opposing the starting premise of the contract theory: namely, that there is a state of nature defined by lawlessness. Spinoza's detailed reading of the Biblical account of the exodus and the formation of the Jewish state in the first thirteen chapters of the *Tractatus*, situated within the context of the theories of state formation in the seventeenth century, ultimately amounts to a single point: *pace* contract theories, power is not articulated with recourse to the institution of law. Giving content to the law – legitimating the state – does not signal the transition from natural lawlessness to socially and politically organised power. More broadly, right and law do not define power simply by distributing their fields of influence within power. Instead, law always already exists – or, more precisely, what always already exists is the law of nature or possibility, which, as will be shown later, leads to an account of power that does not require a justification of violence. So, does this mean that there are no outlaws in Spinoza? Are there no rebels who can oppose the law of the state? And would the state, then, not be justified in exercising violence against those rebels? To tackle these questions, we need to turn first to the role that law – law as empty – plays in the formation of the political.

Spinoza summarises his analysis of the Biblical narrative about religious law and the formation of the Jewish state by writing that 'the aim of Scripture is simply to teach obedience . . . Moses' aim was . . . to bind [his people] by covenant' (TTP Ch. 14, p. 515). The aim of the lawgiver was to bind the people together, as a people. The law makes a community possible. This is radically different from Hobbes's account because the law consists solely in the fact that it must be obeyed, not that its content as such is legitimating.[7] If the sole purpose of religious law is obedience, then the aim of the law is the following of the law. In addition, this is the necessary condition for the creation of a community. The aim of the law is the following of the law and this following is the constitution of a community. Spinoza continues: 'the entire Law consists in this alone, to love one's neighbour ... Scripture does not require us to believe anything beyond what is necessary for the fulfilling of the said commandment' (TTP Ch. 14, p. 515). Spinoza does not regard the 'love of one's neighbour' as *a* commandment – the law does not prohibit or ban, as is the case in Hobbes. Rather, the *entire* content of the law can be reduced to the love of one's neighbour. And this amounts to saying that, from the perspective of obedience, all that can be said about the content of the law is that, in a set of circumstances, a content is given solely with the purpose of facilitating the creation of love as the actualisation of commonality. The law as such is empty, but the giving of a content to create a religious law is dependent on the situation. The moment law is given a content, it becomes *contingent*.[8]

Arguing that law is contingent is not simply an argument against religion or religious law. On the contrary, Spinoza recognises a clear function for religion, which is that the obedience of religious law – the love of one's neighbour – makes a community possible. This function turns religious institutions into temporal authorities. As the story of the Israelites demonstrates in the first thirteen chapters of the *Tractatus*, Moses proposed to them laws that suited their pursuit of a state. Because of contingent circumstances, the love of one's neighbour can be articulated in an indefinite number of ways. Further, in so far as someone participates in a community by loving one's neighbour, then there is no fixed content of the law; there are no eternally true commandments or eternally true dogmas. When religion is politics, little does it matter whether 'god' is omniscient, omnipotent or omnipresent. Instead, 'every man is in duty bound to adapt these religious dogmas to his own understanding and to interpret them for himself in whatever way makes him feel that he can then more readily accept them' (TTP Ch. 14, p. 518). What the doctrines and dogmas say, what the content of the law is, is irrelevant, so long as – and for as long as – it can be accepted. The manner of effecting obedience in order to form a community is entirely contingent, and it is the duty of every man to 'adapt' to these contingent circumstances. The actual laws of the Church and the state are effects of the historical and economic circumstances, no less than the prejudices and imagination (in Spinoza's sense) of the people for whom the laws are written. The following of the law so that a community can be formed – the fact that there must be obedience in order to love one's neighbour – is produced by the law's contingency – the myriad articulations that obedience as well as neighbourly love can take. The law is sharply separated from universality, because it addresses contingent human relations, unpredictable formations of communities.

Spinoza's conception of religious and political law as contingent does not require a radical relativism that rejects truth as such. The contingency of the law is, rather, directed against the belief that there is an end to the law. More broadly, the emptiness of the law for Spinoza means that there is no law of teleology. Since no content to the law is of necessity true, then the truth of the law is that it effects the political. This is not to deny that the law should not be given content in particular configurations of society. Rather, Spinoza's is the much more radical position that whatever content is given to the law, it is necessarily always transformable. The empty law can be given a content if and only if that content is open to challenge when it does not suit the particular circumstances within which the community is formed. An allowing of agonism against the law is necessary for the law to be articulated. As Spinoza himself puts it, 'faith requires . . . dogmas . . . [that] move the heart to obedience; and this is so even if many of those beliefs contain not a shadow of truth, provided that he who adheres to them knows not that they are false. If he knew that they were false, he would *necessarily* be a rebel' (TTP Ch. 14, pp. 516–17, emphasis added).[9] With rebellion, we move from law's contingent modality to the modality of the necessity of challenging the law. Rebellion is necessary in order to guarantee that, after its being given content, the law – or the lawgivers, *potestas* or constituted power – adheres to its own constitutive emptiness and hence its originary contingency. Etienne Balibar (1998: 68) summarises Spinoza's radical conception of the polity thus: '[N]o body politic can exist without being subject to the latent threat of civil war ("sedition").' It is at this point that the category of truth is operative. The law as statute contains 'not a shadow of truth'. It is a category mistake to ascribe truth to the law since that would rob the law of its contingency, giving it a content and a *telos*. The modality of truth is necessity and its articulation in relation to the law is in the form of the possibility of rebellion against the law's articulation of content seeking to pass itself as true instead of as contingent.

The religious and political laws are co-articulated in terms of a mutual dependence of necessity and truth. Rebellion is not merely opposed to obedience but in a sense makes it possible. It is the function – the responsibility – of reason to safeguard that the law's content is not given as a *telos*. Thus, reason is distinguished from obedience. 'The domain of reason . . . is truth and wisdom, the domain of theology is piety and obedience' (TTP Ch. 15, p. 523). The name of the former domain is philosophy and of the latter is religion. The two are distinct, but not opposed: '[I]f you look to its [i.e., religion and obedience's] purpose and end, it will be found to be in no respect opposed to reason' (TTP Ch. 15, p. 523). Sheer obedience, devoid of any resistance or opposition, is, in Spinoza's structure, a contradiction in terms, because it would require that a true content had been found for the law, whereas the law, as already shown, is empty for Spinoza. Rather, it is the role of opposition or resistance to seek the truth of the law – that is, law's contingency.

> I ask, who can give mental acceptance to something against which his reason rebels? For what else is mental denial but reason's rebellion? I am utterly astonished that men can bring themselves to make reason, the greatest of all gifts and a light divine, subservient to letters that are dead. (TTP Ch. 15, p. 521)

It is the illusion of a 'true' content to the law that turns it into a 'dead letter'. In other words, sheer obedience would collapse the distinction between religion and philosophy. Spinoza's political theory requires that these terms are kept distinct but in such a way as to challenge or probe each other, thereby preventing their solidification in an ultimate *telos* – their final death.

We can discern here the otherwise obscure meaning of the title of the *Tractatus*. Political theology does not indicate merely the obvious point that religion is politics – or that the Enlightenment ideal of the separation of powers is just that, an ideal (cf. Lefort 1988). Further, political theology indicates the transformative relation between obedience and reason – a relation that, in Spinoza's sense described above, couples necessity with contingency. More precisely, political theology is the ineliminable agonism between obedience and reason, religion and philosophy – an agonism as the rebellious instability that guarantees the radical openness of the law. The truth of the law is its untruth. This statement recognises both that the law is distinct from truth because it is contingent, and also that the law relies on truth as a function that probes the law and keeps it transformable. Untruth and truth – law and reason, obedience and rebellion – rely upon their mutual agonism in order to produce each other. This agonism is, for Spinoza, political theology.

It is of paramount importance, however, that political theology's agonism is not violent in the sense that it does not operate through exclusions. We can call it an 'agonism of love' in order to distinguish it from the violent exercise of power through the expunging of the outlaw that we encountered as the second characteristic of the construction of juridical power in the social contract theories. It will be recalled that the social contract requires the outlaw against whom violence can be directed so that the content of the law, as the source of the social contract, can both delimit freedom and justify its operation. For Spinoza, conversely, there is no such notion of the outlaw because 'all men without exception can obey [*omnes absolute obedire possunt*]' (TTP Ch. 15, p. 526). This is not merely a religious or political law, but rather a natural law as the condition of the possibility of obedience – that is, of the contingency of religious and political law. Natural law could not be articulated here in the Hobbesian terms of a bifurcation between absolute freedom and law as prohibiting. Instead, Spinoza's conception of natural law is articulated here in terms of possibility – a possibility that is ascribed to the entirety of humanity. Or, more precisely, possibility, or power, excludes no one ('*omnes absolute*'), not even the non-human: 'And here I do not acknowledge any distinction between men and other individuals of Nature, nor between men endowed with reason and others to whom true reason is unknown, nor between fools, madmen and the sane.' Spinoza immediately links absolutely possessed power with right. 'Whatever an individual thing does by the laws of its own nature [*ex legibus suae naturae*], it does with sovereign right [*summo jure*], inasmuch as it acts as determined by Nature, and can do no other' (TTP Ch. 16, p 527). Everyone is subject to the law of nature and, moreover, one's right is determined by the way that natural law allows one to do what is possible for them to do. Everyone is included within this law of nature that is described as the dispensation of possibility.[10]

At this point, the question arises about the relation between, on the one hand, law as obedience and the way that it effects the creation of the community, and, on the other, the law of nature. Or, to reformulate the same question: how can the agonism pertaining to political theology tally with an all-inclusive, and hence all-encompassing, nature? In delineating how the domain of possibility needs to be distinguished from – but not opposed to – the domains of obedience and truth, Spinoza will show the indispensable reliance of the agonistic aspect of power to monism. Spinoza formulates the question as follows:

> Is not our earlier assertion, that everyone who is without the use of reason has the sovereign natural right in a state of nature to live by the laws of appetite, in clear contradiction with the divine law as revealed? For since all men without exception, whether or not they have the use of reason, are

> equally required by God's command to love their neighbour as themselves, we cannot without doing wrong, inflict injury on another and live solely by the laws of appetite. (TTP Ch. 16, p. 533)

In a sense, this question amounts to Spinoza querying the similarity of this theory to that of Hobbes, and in particular his assertion that the state of nature is pure appetite, and therefore lawless. Spinoza responds to the possible objection:

> [T]he state of nature . . . is prior [*prior*] to religion in nature and in time. For nobody knows by nature that he has any duty to obey God. Indeed, this knowledge cannot be attained by any process of reasoning . . . So a state of nature must not be confused with a state of religion; we must conceive it as being apart from [*absque*] religion and law. (TTP Ch. 16, pp. 533–4, trans. modified)

The first crucial term that describes the relation between political theology and nature is 'prior'. The law is articulated in relation to reasoning – not in relation to a putatively lawless state of nature, as is the case with the social contract tradition. The law as contingent is delimited through its agonism with the necessity of truth. In addition, this contingent necessity of political theology is not opposed to the possibility contained within Spinoza's extrapolation of the state of nature. Instead, nature as possibility is 'prior' to political theology. The reason is that, whereas political theology designates the untruth of truth – the *agon* between obedience and truth, or religion and the reasoning of philosophy – power designates a different level that is defined in terms of possibility, as a modality that is more basic (*prior*) to any consideration of truth as its opposite.[11] It is only the fact that everyone without exception ('*omnes absolute*') *can* – has the *power* to – obey that makes untruth and truth, obedience and reason, possible.

The second crucial term in Spinoza's description of the relation between political theology and nature in the above quotation is 'apart'. Spinoza describes the state of nature, not only as being apart from obedience, but also as being of a different kind from 'any process of reasoning'. It would be a mistake to understand this word '*absque*' as indicating a disconnectedness between the three different modalities – contingency, necessity and possibility. Rather, they are both apart and a part of each other.

> Nature's right is co-extensive with her power. For Nature's power is the very power of God, who has sovereign right over all things. But since the universal power of Nature as a whole is nothing but the power of all individual things taken together, it follows that each individual thing has the sovereign right [*ius summum*] to do all that it can do; i.e. the right of the individual is coextensive with its determinate power. (TTP Ch. 16, p. 527)

The power of nature encompasses everything. There is nothing outside nature. Nature's absolute right entails a radical connectedness between things.[12] This means that everything is mediated. Any notion of immediacy in its various manifestations – for instance, as the absolute freedom and absolute equality that characterised Hobbes's state of nature – is incompatible with Spinoza's conception that 'the individual is co-extensive with its determinate power.' Spinoza's power includes the totality of human activity. The 'a-partness' of nature refers to this interconnectedness, as the condition of the possibility of action and thought.

The total interconnectedness of Spinoza's power includes everyone and everything. We can discern here a notion of the exception that is not only very different from the exception that plays such a pivotal role in the standard accounts of political theology, but which also illustrates a second function of the agonism that characterises Spinoza's political theology. According to Spinoza, there are no exceptions to the fact that there is no exception to the totality of power, not even for the sovereign whose power is defined precisely in the same terms as that of nature and the individual: 'the rights of sovereigns are determined by their power' (TTP Ch. 20, p. 567). Thus, Spinoza's conception of political theology appears completely incompatible with, even agonistic against, Carl Schmitt's juridical understanding of power, as well as the entire post-Schmittian movement that includes thinkers such as Giorgio Agamben. For it will be recalled that the exception – a state of lawlessness or a state outside the law, bare life – is the common denominator that defines the standing of sovereignty above the law. But more broadly, and much more importantly, we here arrive at a second way of describing power's agonistic function. It emerges at this point that political theology does not solely stage an *agon* between contingency and necessity, obedience and truth, or religion and philosophy. In addition, it emerges that theologico-political effervescence is itself positioned against all these conceptions of power that seek to deny the third modality – the all-encompassing possibility – that is ontologically prior to, and a-part from, the agonism of the theologico-political. In other words, the theologico-political, as it is conceived by Spinoza, is also agonistic towards any understanding of power that relies on a notion of lawlessness and understands power as juridical power. But, crucially, this is only possible because there is the single, all-encompassing sense of power. Or, to put this the other way around, it is the agonism against juridical power and its various forms of exclusion or exception that point to power's irreducibility to a legalist definition. What emerges here is that agonism and monism empty the law of content, thereby allowing it to transform itself, while at the same time the fact that power can be conceived as independent of the law makes the resistance to juridical power possible. Monism and agonism are the obverse sides of the same notion of non-juridical power in Spinoza.

So, Spinoza separates three modalities – contingency, necessity and possibility – in order to separate three realms that are nevertheless imbricated; religion/politics, reason and power. By describing these modalities and their realms as a-part – apart and yet part of each other – Spinoza can offer an account of agonistic and monistic power as different from, and incompatible with, juridical power. This account relies on the total interconnectedness that characterises possibility. This possibility – the possibility of political theology – shows that the potential that characterises the right of nature is the all-encompassing dialectic of obedience and disobedience. At the same time, however, this is a dialectic devoid of any final synthesis. Rather, it persists in the process of the unfolding of the agonism allowed within its all-inclusive power. This relation between agonism and monism is Spinoza's conception of the theologico-political.

## NOTES

1. I examine these two ways in terms of justification and judgement in my *Sovereignty and its Other*. The entire discussion of Spinoza here draws on my book that provides much historical and conceptual background of and elaboration on the two ways of understanding power. See also my 'Kafka's Empty Law'.

2. In the famous discussion in *The Will to Knowledge* about not having yet cut off the image of the king, Foucault observes that 'we must break free of . . . the theoretical privilege of law and sovereignty, if we wish to analyse power within the concrete and historical framework of its operation. We must construct an analysis of power that no longer takes law as a model and code' (1990: 90). This is not to say that Foucault is opposed to the law. Such a superficial reading of Foucault has been conclusively refuted by Golder and Fitzpatrick (2009).

3. For the concept of the agonistic I am indebted to the work of Chantal Mouffe and Bonnie Honig.

4. See Michael Hardt and Antonio Negri, *Empire* (2000), Part 1, Section 1, as well as the entire Part 2. For a summary of this position, see pp. 11–12. Even though I am relying on Hardt and Negri to refer to the distinction between three different phases of power, I disagree with their account in one significant respect. They describe that transition between the different forms as passages, suggesting that the three forms are successive and that they can be separated. I argue instead that the three forms of sovereign power are in fact mingled, and that one of the main features of biopolitics is that it incorporates the older forms of power.

5. For an analysis of the two different senses of political theology, see Vardoulakis (2010).

6. There is a significant body of literature on the concept of the enemy in Schmitt. Jacques Derrida's critique in *The Politics of Friendship* (1997) remains the decisive argument against it: Schmitt slides between two definitions of the enemy that are mutually exclusive, either as the structural, transcendent other of the sovereign, or as the actual enemy that sovereign power faces. Arguably – although this is not a point that I can take up here in detail – it is the actuality of the enemy that re-introduces a content to Schmitt's conception of the empty law.

7. For an outline of the differences between Hobbes and Spinoza, see Armstrong (2009).

8. According to Lefebvre (2008: 58–9), Deleuze also creates a positive image of the law, or what he calls 'jurisprudence', by developing a similar conception of its parallel contingency and necessity.

9. Such an assertion is incompatible with the liberal insistence on tolerance, as it is expressed, for instance, in Locke's 'Letter on Toleration'. But the importance of the 'necessary rebel' is a point that H. L. A. Hart fully recognises for any conception of the law:

> At any given moment the life of any society which lives by rules, legal or not, is likely to consist in a tension between those who, on the one hand, accept and voluntarily co-operate in maintaining the rules . . . and those who, on the other hand, reject the rules. . . . One of the difficulties facing any legal theory anxious to do justice to the complexity of the facts is to remember the presence of both these points of view. (Hart 1982: 88)

10. Spinoza mentions in the *Tractatus Theologico-Politicus* that a renunciation of one's right in order to enter the polity (that is, the prerequisite of the Hobbesian theory) is impossible. However, this point is not argued for properly until the *Tractatus Politicus*. For a discussion of the relation of the first to the second treatise, see Montag (2005).

11. The distinction between the three modalities and their relation to the law in the *Tractatus* raises the obvious question of the relation of the law to the three levels of knowledge identified in *Ethics*. This is a complex issue that I plan to discuss in detail elsewhere.

12. This absolute connectedness is a motif that will be taken up again by Romanticism, especially Jena Romanticism (see Benjamin 1997; and Kompridis 2009: 251, who expresses this point as the aesthetic problem of philosophy).


# BIBLIOGRAPHY

Agamben, Giorgio (2005), *State of Exception*, trans. Kevin Attell, Chicago: University of Chicago Press.

Armstrong, Aurelia (2009), 'Natural and Unnatural Communities: Spinoza beyond Hobbes', *British Journal for the History of Philosophy* 17.2, pp. 279–305.

Balibar, Etienne (1998), *Spinoza and Politics*, trans. Peter Snowdon, London: Verso.

Benjamin, Walter (1997), 'The Concept of Criticism in German Romanticism', in Marcus Bullock and Michael W. Jennings (eds), *Selected Writings*, vol. 1, Cambridge, MA: Belknap, pp. 116–200.

Bodin, Jean (1992), *On Sovereignty: Four Chapters from the Six Books of the Commonwealth*, ed. and trans. Julian H. Franklin, Cambridge: Cambridge University Press.

Derrida, Jacques (1992), 'Before the Law', in *Acts of Literature*, ed. Derek Attridge, trans. Avital Ronell and Christine Roulston, New York: Routledge.

Derrida, Jacques (1997), *The Politics of Friendship*, trans. George Collins, London: Verso.

Foucault, Michel (1990), *The Will to Knowledge*, vol. 1 of *The History of Sexuality*, trans. Robert Hurley, London: Penguin.

Foucault, Michel (2003), *Society Must be Defended: Lectures at the Collège de France 1975–1976*, trans. David Macey, New York: Picador.

Golder, Ben, and Peter Fitzpatrick (2009), *Foucault's Law*, London: Routledge.

Hardt, Michael, and Antonio Negri (2000), *Empire*, Cambridge, MA: Harvard University Press.

Hart, H. L. A. (1982), *The Concept of Law*, Oxford: Oxford University Press.

Hobbes, Thomas (1999), *Leviathan*, ed. Richard Tuck, Cambridge: Cambridge University Press.

Kompridis, Nikolas (2009), 'Romanticism', in *The Oxford Handbook of Philosophy and Literature*, ed. Richard Eldridge, Oxford: Oxford University Press.

Lefebvre, Alexandre (2008), *The Image of Law: Deleuze, Bergson, Spinoza*, Stanford: Stanford University Press.

Lefort, Claude (1988), 'The Permanence of the Theologico-Political?', in *Democracy and Political Theory*, trans. David Macey, Cambridge: Polity, pp. 213–55.

Montag, Warren (2005), 'Who's Afraid of the Multitude? Between the Individual and the State', *South Atlantic Quarterly* 104.4, pp. 655–73.

Rousseau, Jean-Jacques (1994), *Discourse on Political Economy* and *The Social Contract*, trans. Christopher Betts, Oxford: Oxford University Press.

Schmitt, Carl (1985), *Political Theology: Four Chapters on the Concept of Sovereignty*, trans. George D. Schwab, Cambridge, MA: MIT Press.

Spinoza, Baruch (2002), *Complete Works*, trans. Samuel Shirley, ed. Michael L. Morgan, Indianapolis: Hackett.

Vardoulakis, Dimitris (2010), 'Stasis: Beyond Political Theology?', *Cultural Critique* 73, pp. 125–47.

Vardoulakis, Dimitris (forthcoming), 'Kafka's Empty Law: Laughter and Freedom in *The Trial*', in Brendan Moran and Carlo Salzani (eds), *Kafka and Philosophy*, New York: SUNY.

Vardoulakis, Dimitris (forthcoming), *Sovereignty and its Other*, New York: Fordham University Press.

# 8. *Which Radical Enlightenment? Spinoza, Jacobinism and Black Jacobinism*

## NICK NESBITT

Spinoza's philosophy, Jonathan Israel has argued, was the determinant force in what he has compellingly described as the transnational 'Radical Enlightenment' of the eighteenth century. Israel's argument, for all its encompassing scope, remains firmly limited to the geographic and cultural confines of Western Europe. In fact, Spinoza's political philosophy, enriched, developed and extended by political philosophers such as Rousseau, the late Diderot and Robespierre, influenced not only the French Revolution and its struggle for popular sovereignty and universal natural rights, but also the Haitian Revolution of 1791–1804. In this peripheral colony, at the tail end of the Enlightenment, Spinoza's political theory was suddenly and shockingly retranslated to address the concerns of this marginalised community of African and Creole slaves who literally counted for nothing politically, being recognised as no more than a quantum of bestialised productive labour power on the sugar plantations of Saint Domingue in the age of the so-called 'rights of man'.

Five of Spinoza's basic axioms, in particular, filtered through these and other thinkers of the French Radical Enlightenment, theoretically founded and determined the concept of universal rights and the general will of the 1790s, in Saint Domingue as in Paris. These can be briefly stated as: (1) the axiom of univocity, of a single undivided substance (*Deus sive natura*), (2) the proposition of the immanent self-moving force of any body (*natura naturans*), (3) the ethical directive that any body should and must strive to achieve its maximum power of expression and understanding, (4) the proposition that this perfect maximum (*laetitia*) can only be achieved by humans in society, rather than in a state of nature, and (5) the view that the only proper or true form of society that will allow for this maximum of human expression and reason is what Spinoza calls 'democracy'. Owing to his premature death at the very moment he set out to articulate the precise model of 'democracy' to be deduced from his ontology, it has been left to scholars to speculate as to its form, based upon the more or less articulated comments on the topic elsewhere in his *œuvre*.

Without entering into this discussion, which would demand a book of its own, and without wishing to repeat an argument I have developed elsewhere, in what follows I will argue that this political-democratic dimension of the Spinozan Radical Enlightenment was developed, articulated and instantiated in the political theories and practices of Rousseau, Robespierre and Toussaint Louverture, and in particular in their understanding of concepts including the social contract, popular sovereignty, the general will and universal natural rights.

The Haitian Revolution of 1791–1804, while inextricably linked to the French Revolution and Enlightenment that culminated in the abolition of slavery in 1794, took its place, after the fall of the Jacobins on 9 Thermidor and the subsequent political degradation of Thermidor, the *Directoire* and the *Consulat,* at the vanguard of what Jonathan Israel has called the Radical Enlightenment.[1] This link between revolutionary France and its soon-to-be-former colony is undeniable, if complex and not at all unidirectional (it was, of course, the putatively backward slaves who showed France and the world in proper Hegelian fashion that a slave-free social order was, in fact, and despite the wishes of those many powerful slave states of the era, *real*). The primary participants in that Caribbean revolution explicitly affirmed, on multiple occasions, the role of the revolution's declaration of the rights of man, along with the influence of Enlightenment figures such as Rousseau and Raynal (and through him, anonymously, Diderot), in the radicalisation of a large-scale slave uprising. This local revolt on the periphery of early modern Europe, thanks to that radicalisation, after 1793 became a fully transnational revolution intending (and, within the coming century, eventually achieving) nothing less than the destruction of the early modern world-system of plantation slavery.

Between June 1794 and the Napoleonic invasion of Saint Domingue in 1802, the general, if never straightforward nor unchallenged, trend of French politics to undermine the revolutionary institutionalisation of a politics of popular sovereignty is clear. Less clear, perhaps, is a series of questions that goes to the heart of the relation between the Radical Enlightenment, a largely theoretical and philosophical movement, and the radical revolutionary politics of late eighteenth-century France (and, subsequently, Saint Domingue). To what extent was the French Revolution a product or manifestation of Radical Enlightenment ideas? More precisely, which of the many moments and tendencies in that revolution can be said to remain faithful to the Spinozan democratic ideas that gave the Enlightenment its most radical form?

Two periods immediately come to mind as possible candidates for this trophy. In other words, did the political modality of the Radical Enlightenment culminate in the first declaration of the rights of man and citizen of August 1789, and the subsequent constitutional monarchy (most accurately described, in M. Genty's turn of phrase, as an 'elective aristocracy') from 30 September 1791 to 10 August 1792? Or is the political instantiation of the Radical Enlightenment to be located in the period of Jacobin ascendancy from the fall of the Girondins on 2 June 1793, to the fall of Robespierre one year later, and its attendant assertion of a politics of popular sovereignty, general will, and the struggle for the survival of these imperatives in the face of invasion by and war with the European monarchic powers, betrayal (Varennes, La Fayette and Dumoriez) and internal counter-revolution (Chouans, Vendée) that continues to be known misleadingly as the Terror?[2]

In limiting this question from the outset to *radical* revolutionary politics, I am explicitly excluding from consideration the earlier American Revolution. Though certainly the first instance of modern decolonisation, it should not be considered radical in the full (Spinozan) sense of asserting a single, *undivided* (political) 'substance' or class. Truly radical, to preempt the argument to follow, are those political theories (Rousseau) and struggles (Jacobin and black Jacobin) that draw the full political conclusions of Spinoza's ontology, to assert *universal* popular sovereignty and its expression as the undivided general will. Spinoza's rejection of Hobbes's social contract theory of the alienation of one's power to a third-party sovereign clearly and unmistakably announces Rousseau's further articulation of this in the *Contrat social*. Spinoza asserted that no person 'can so utterly transfer to another his power, and consequently his right, as to cease to be a man; nor can there ever be a power so supreme that it can carry out its every possible wish' (cited in Armstrong 1997: 46). The Hobbesian contract, in Spinoza's view, is literally impossible, for it would imply the annihilation of the contracting subject. Contract serves, instead, for Spinoza, to designate the consensual passage from the state of nature to that of society not as an increase in the power of a third party and the corresponding diminishment of that of the subject of that power, but to the increase in the power of the social totality. 'The power of this Whole', observes Aurelia Armstrong, '*is* actually the collective power of its "parts"' (Armstrong 1997: 46).

If Spinoza himself died before he could articulate the model of democracy to be deduced from the *Ethics*, and while the theoretical and political complexities of such an affirmation of universal popular sovereignty are obviously enormous (and Rousseau and the Jacobins struggled mightily and endlessly with them), still, radical political theory and practice of the period meant only one thing: the militant struggle to institute the natural and universal rights of man both theoretically and in practice within the social order. In place of this, the American Revolution – with virtually no exceptions, and all of them minoritarian until the 1840s – should be characterised as the institution of a broad-based, popular oligarchy premised upon the radical exclusion (and continued systematic domination, disenfranchisement and degradation) of the new nation's subaltern productive class (i.e., African Americans).

To draw the full implications of the historical movement C. L. R. James obscurely – if, in my view, absolutely correctly – called *Black Jacobinism*, it is essential to take a step back to analyse Jacobinism itself in its full radicality. In essence, my argument consists of two basic claims. First, Jacobinism (and by extension, its Caribbean instantiation as black Jacobinism) is the name given in the 1790s to the political struggle to institute the universal rights of man in actually existing social institutions as *undivided* popular sovereignty. Second, this politics of undivided popular sovereignty is theorised in the political sphere of the Radical Enlightenment in a direct line of influence and increasing articulation from Spinoza (above all, in his critique of Hobbes) to Rousseau (as the articulation of Spinoza's social contract theory and the general will), to the late Diderot of the Raynal articles and *Bougainville*, to Robespierre (and to a much lesser extent, the natural law theories of Saint-Just), and finally, and in terms no less, if quite differently, conflicted and problematic than the Jacobin Terror, to the black Jacobinism of Toussaint Louverture that culminates in his world-historical constitution of 1801 and the declaration of independence of Haiti as the world's first slave-free state on 1 January 1804.

If Jonathan Israel's understanding of the Enlightenment is refreshingly transnational, it remains marked by Eurocentrism. Israel has laboured mightily on a research project that spans a range of sources that makes him perhaps the most compelling and original contemporary historian of eighteenth-century ideas. In advance of the publication of the forthcoming and much-awaited *Democratic Enlightenment*, the third instalment of his monumental trilogy, Israel's recent book, *A Revolution of the Mind: Radical Enlightenment and the Intellectual Origins of Modern Democracy* (2010), based on a series of lectures delivered at Oxford in 2008, must be taken as a summary of his understanding of Radical Enlightenment revolutionary politics. In fact, read in this light, the latter book places an unexpected and more problematic twist on his earlier vision of the Radical Enlightenment, as described in that earlier volume (2001).

On the one hand, in pursuing the implications of his earlier book to show the political consequences of Spinozism in the age of the American and French Revolutions (Israel never mentions, as far as I am aware, the Haitian Revolution) Israel argues persuasively that the division between Moderate and Radical Enlightenments was constitutive and unavoidable in the 1780s and 1790s. One was either for or against miracles, divine providence, democracy, equality and other such fundamental questions (Israel 2010: 18). Radical Enlightenment forces a decision on what were apparently undecidable matters. 'Every Enlightenment writer', says Israel, 'had to choose either broadly to endorse the existing structure of law, authority, and privilege, whatever incidental repairs he proposed, or else denounce them more sweepingly' (2010: 29). The full implications of the Radical Enlightenment initiated by the publication of Spinoza's *Theological-Political Treatise* and the clandestine circulation of the *Ethics* entailed, necessarily and from the simplest and most basic axioms, the total destruction of *ancien régime* society, 'a successful revolution of fact,' says Israel, 'leading to an entirely new kind of society' (Israel 2010: 33). It was, Israel concludes decisively, the writings and speeches of the Radical Enlightenment that 'engendered a new language of freedom, the evidence shows, that was the most active and chief factor in shaping the democratic tendency . . . culminating in the French Revolution' (2010: 49).

Most powerfully, Israel critiques an entire tradition of revolutionary historiography in its refusal to accept and explore the fundamental role of ideas in the unfolding of revolution and universal emancipation. 'The real structural shift before 1789 has been broadly missed because it was a "revolution of the mind",' Israel writes, 'an intellectual transformation, bringing with it a huge cultural shift, the essential revolution that preceded the revolution of fact' (2010: 38).

The basic thrust of this argument is clear and overwhelmingly convincing, as well as being refreshingly critical of the anti-conceptual orthodoxy of much of French Revolutionary Studies. Where Israel goes quite wrong, I am convinced, is over the place of Jacobinism in the Radical Enlightenment. When I began my study of the Haitian Revolution, and taking my cue from C. L. R. James's title, it seemed obvious to me that the black Jacobinism of Louverture was directly and explicitly derived from the universalism of Jacobin politics that was the first to refuse in 1793 the absolute right of property, and to mitigate that right to reflect the inalienability of personhood first asserted by Rousseau (in Robespierre's proposal for the 1793 constitution); it was also first to draw the immediate implication of that argument and to ban slavery on 4 February 1794. The task of such a critique required mounting a convincing argument, inspired and influenced by Israel's *Radical Enlightenment*, that a direct line in the history of these radical political ideas could and should be drawn back from the thinkers of the rights of man, Robespierre, Diderot and Rousseau, whom figures like Louverture actually read, to the one they did not: Spinoza. If Israel is right, however, in identifying the thought of Spinoza hidden clandestine behind eighteenth-century radical thought, there is no reason not to call attention to the reception of those ideas in more tropical climates, and to underline the very powerful effects they had upon a struggle utterly foreign to the point of incomprehensibility and inadmissibility to the supposedly enlightened pro-slavery French Metropole. Robespierre himself failed to live up to his own principles, agreeing on this count with Grégoire that the slaves were not 'ready' for immediate emancipation (Boudon 2006: 32). Though hostile to the slave trade, *l'incorruptible* was, on this count, no different from so many other liberal thinkers and *amis des noirs* of the period, repeatedly denouncing immediate emancipation as a recipe for anarchy and disaster.

Israel makes the surprising claim in *A Revolution of the Mind* that Rousseau and his disciple Robespierre are not the culmination of the Radical Enlightenment, but precisely its *betrayal*. Israel is at pains to paint a monochromatic picture of 'the Republican deviationism of Rousseau', and of Jacobinism as a political 'theocracy' (2010: 63, 60). Of course, Rousseau's manifold contradictions included a powerful moralistic anti-intellectualism, a defence of moral immediacy and 'natural sentiment', and recourse to faith in a transcendent God, all decidedly un-Spinozan attacks on the Radical Enlightenment. But this one-sided portrait unconvincingly ignores Rousseau's radical egalitarianism and its profound debt to the Spinozan tradition of universal and unqualified rights that has been well documented since Paul Vernière's *Spinoza et la pensée française avant la Révolution* (1954).

Rousseau's indebtedness to Spinoza's political theory in the *Contrat social* has been a matter of record for many decades, well documented by Vernière.[3] Vernière documents this indebtedness on a number of levels, from the admittedly speculative to documentation of near-verbatim citation. His arguing points include an unpublished note that references Part V of Spinoza's *Ethics* ('The soul can only imagine or remember anything of the past as long as the body persists,' E VP21), a theorem virtually unknown in the eighteenth century, including by Bayle and Boulainviller:

> If a being whose essence is to think, Rousseau writes, no longer remembers being the same being, in fact it no longer *is* the same being. From this, we see that those who maintain, as does Spinoza, that upon the death of a man, his soul is reabsorbed into the great soul of the world, say nothing that makes any sense; they speak pure gibberish. (cited in Vernière 1954: 480, my translation)

Vernière further underlines the similarity in the two thinkers' concepts of the general will. For Spinoza,

> Human society can thus be formed without any alienation of natural right, and the contract can be preserved in its entirety with complete fidelity, only if *every person transfers all the power they possess to society* [. . .] In this way all remain equal as they had been previously in the state of nature. (TTP Ch. 16, p. 200, 202, my emphasis)

Rousseau describes in turn how 'Each of us puts in common his person and all his power under the supreme direction of the general will; and we receive as a body each member as an indivisible part of the whole' (2006: I, 6).

Vernière cites as well what he calls Rousseau's 'undisguised translations of Spinoza':

> Regarding those associated together, they collectively take the name of a *people* and call themselves in particular *citizens* participating in sovereign authority and *subjects* insofar as they submit to the laws of the State. (Rousseau 2006: I, 6)

> We call men citizens insofar as they enjoy all the advantages of the commonwealth by civil right; we call them subjects insofar as they are bound to obey the ordinances or laws of the commonwealth. (TP 3.1)

Finally, against Locke, one could extend Vernière's argument to point out that Spinoza and Rousseau share a structurally identical critique of slavery based on three suppositions:

1. A *negative critique* of Hobbesian tranquillity and peace (to be achieved for Hobbes through political representation and the delegation of sovereignty to a representative) in which both equate the inhumanity of slavery to despotism. 'One lives peacefully in prison,' Rousseau would famously write; 'is this enough [to be fully human]?' (Rousseau 2006: I, IV).
2. Alienation of one's self (in slavery) is, for both Spinoza and Rousseau (as it will be for Robespierre, Kant, Toussaint Louverture and Hegel), a *contre-sens*, in so far as the self is not a property.
3. A truly *human* nature supposes not only the will to (mere animal, Hobbesian) self-preservation, but furthermore, the inalienable

*perfectibility* through *reason* of every human being, a process achievable not in a state of nature, but only in a society in which the power of self-determination is not alienated. Rousseau, like Spinoza before him, never wavered in his rejection of the state of nature as inferior to the developmental possibilities of a true, uncorrupted society such as the one he describes in the *Contrat social* and *Emile*. Here again, the great thinkers of the French Radical Enlightenment and German Idealism are unanimous. Only in (political) society can reason become active and fulfil its real potential. In Spinoza's words, 'The man led by reason is freer in society, where he lives according to common decree, than in solitude, where he only obeys himself' (E IVP73).

Israel's portrayal of Rousseau and Robespierre as the betrayers of the Radical Enlightenment culminates in a prophylactic quarantine of a Rousseauian Jacobinism that, Israel claims, 'discredited the Revolution in the minds of contemporaries in France and abroad just as they have in the minds of modern readers and students ever since' (2010: 230). It is hard to imagine a more simplistic, uncritical reproduction of the received wisdom regarding Jacobinism than this, in which an immensely complex and progressive political sequence is vilified by Israel as nothing more than 'crass demagoguery and murderous violence' (2010: 231). Attention to the ten volumes of Robespierre's writings, the most important of which are the thousand-and-some speeches he made in the five years between 1789 and 1794, reveals one of the great political minds of the modern world, and undoubtedly one of the most original and influential theoreticians of radical democracy. Robespierre's political thought and action are distinguished, above all, by his unwavering ('incorruptible') fidelity to a single imperative: in C. Mazauric's brilliant summation, 'The unceasing activity of Robespierre during the first five years of the revolution was inspired by only one imperative: the will and struggle to institute within the social order the natural rights of man' (Soboul 1989: 916). The unrelenting struggle, in other words, for the very same ethical imperative that Israel celebrates repeatedly in *A Revolution of the Mind*: justice as equality.

If Robespierre sought to achieve this novel goal by any means possible, including the terrible *in*justice of the paranoid law of suspects of 22 *Prarial*, one should conclude only that, in those final days and weeks following the attempt on his life and the turning of the Assembly against him, and in the wake of repeated military victories that should rightfully have lessened the need for restrictive Terror, Robespierre for once allowed the safety of a faction or even a single person (himself) to be placed before that of the universal *Salut public*. Most importantly in regard to Israel's argument, this portrait of uncompromising political radicality in the name of popular sovereignty, a radicality to the point of Terror, however we may ultimately judge it, can hardly constitute a *rejection* of the Radical Enlightenment, but only a last, desperate attempt to save the revolution for popular sovereignty and justice as equality Robespierre had *radicalised* more than any other figure of the age.

As Jean-Pierre Gross has argued, the Jacobins under the leadership of Robespierre undertook a politics in the short period of their power that, while derived from and oriented in reference to a few basic principles such as justice as equality and the imperative to make society the space for the expression of undivided popular sovereignty, was enormously inventive and managed to defend, articulate and begin to implement many of the most basic political accomplishments that we now take for granted. The Jacobins asserted the then-novel human right to life – above all, as a basic right to a minimal nourishment for survival and basic bodily functionality. To do so, they extensively and repeatedly debated the proper line of demarcation between what we might call abject and humanly decent or honourable poverty, and asserted the necessity for all citizens to have access to a general market of exchange that would allow them to live from their labour (Gross 2003: 7).[4] The Jacobins asserted the fundamental right to work and unemployment benefits, and (like the Condorcet Israel so admires) defended and drew legislation for free universal education. More broadly, Jacobin egalitarianism should be understood as an unsettled mix of a defence of the human right to everything necessary for the preservation and minimal flourishing of life (food, shelter, education, labour, justice, political sovereignty), all of which was to be held in common by society, and a proto-liberal right on the part of any citizen to an unlimited potential excess (of wealth and property) beyond that minimum. The Jacobins, despite their reputation for radicality, resorted to only the most gradual means of economic restructuration, such as taxation and redistribution of confiscated property, to the limit of rationing food in the wartime context (Gross 2003: 45, 64; see also Mathiez 2010: 4–5).

The Jacobin-dominated Assembly put through what Gross terms a 'vigorous' programme of land reform, one whose ultimate success may have been uneven, but was nonetheless quite real, culminating in the decision of 2 *Frimaire* to break up émigré plots into smallholdings.[5] Robespierre, like Condorcet, defended progressive taxation and price control (the *maximum*) of bread. One of the most enduring successes of the Jacobin initiative, and one that reflects a radical extension of the high-Enlightenment coffee-house public sphere throughout all levels of society, was the development of a general culture of political sociability in the Jacobin clubs; some 5,332 clubs were spread at their height throughout all of France, open to anyone (Soboul 1989: 589–90).

If Robespierre rightly attacked the inherent elitism common to almost all Enlightenment thinkers, this hardly constitutes what Israel terms an 'anti-enlightenment purge' (2010: 232). Robespierre's attacks on Condorcet and the French materialist atheists were politically rather than intellectually motivated. Robespierre, in fact, notably lacked the anti-Enlightenment discourse of the more conflicted and sentimentalist Rousseau. For Robespierre (like Spinoza), reason is a universal attribute of humanity, and this 'universal reason' is repeatedly claimed to be the seat of the 'principles', such as justice as equality, that orient his political thought. The political logic of Robespierre in this sense develops the political implications of Spinoza's *Ethics*, while prefiguring the universal reason of Hegel's Absolute Spirit. Reason being universal, eternal and invincible, he argues in a speech to the Convention on 2 December 1792, the triumph of the Revolution is itself inevitable. The Revolution is, for Robespierre, the immanent accomplishment of universal human reason in its political, social mode. As it did for Spinoza, reason stands opposed to 'prejudice', 'superstition' and 'fanaticism'. Robespierre was of a piece with this radical dimension of the Enlightenment that Israel has so convincingly distinguished from the moderate equivocations of Leibniz, Newton, Locke, Voltaire and their like. Reason and philosophy, as they never were for Rousseau, were for Robespierre strictly synonymous (Boudon 2006: 54, 559).

According to Albert Mathiez, who knew Robespierre's thought more intimately than perhaps any modern historian, Robespierre had a perfectly Spinozan understanding of the divine. He equated the Supreme Being, quite simply, with nature, but as a politician, not a philosopher, he was committed to the triumph of popular sovereignty, to which all other concerns were secondary. He saw atheism not as false, but as a luxury of a privileged bourgeois and aristocratic education and habitus. To the goal of achieving true popular sovereignty, Mathiez concludes, Robespierre even went so far as to respect this prejudice of the *peuple* (2010: 235).

The fundamental continuity between the political philosophy of Spinoza, Rousseau and the Jacobins lies in the centrality of the concept of a social contract theory based upon the inalienability of popular sovereignty. For all three, the primary challenge of democratic theory lies in articulating the means of preserving popular sovereignty as fully as possible. For each, in turn, the means of doing so lies in the pursuit of justice as equality through the principled expression of the general will in legislation and the creation of egalitarian institutions. Political representation, all three agreed, threatens, perhaps necessarily, popular sovereignty because the people and the representatives, like doctors and patients, necessarily have different *interests*.

In a modern state, this pursuit inevitably, all agree, requires recourse to political representation. While Rousseau famously decries all representation in the *Contrat social*, less known is the fact that he later admitted its necessity in a large modern state like Poland, given necessary safeguards against the alienation of the popular will, such as the revocability of elected officials. Julien Boudon has argued that Robespierre, once he took power and was forced, after 31 May 1793, to abandon his antagonistic claim that *all* representation *necessarily* entailed an alienation of sovereignty, employed two principal tactics in the political struggle to mitigate this alienation of sovereignty: first, he called for the revocability of representatives (or *mandataires*), most notably in the 1793 constitution, which promised to give the citizens, for the first time in a modern state, the real opportunity of making the law, rather than alienating this power to representatives. The laws to be passed by the Assembly were explicitly proposals that required the sanction of the people. This approval was understood to be tacit if no objections were made within forty days; if a sufficient number of citizens protested, a process of referendum was to be initiated. The 1793 constitution, the reference ever since for popular democracies the world over, did not simply give citizens the means to control and survey their elected assembly, but, Pertuć concludes, 'associated them [*le peuple*] directly and magisterially in the creation of the law' (Soboul 1989: 284). Unlike this authentic yet never implemented solution, however, an increasingly pervasive solipsism used by the Jacobins sought to get around the problem of representation as alienation by a more or less sophistic and rhetorical (to the degree that it was or was not true) equation of the representatives with the *peuple* themselves in full immediacy (Soboul 1989: 216, 242). Sustaining this immediacy required that the mandates of the *élus* must be brief, non-renewable, and subject to a strict separation of legislation and the executive.

Second, and though the Jacobins' use of the concept of the general will tended to fluctuate with the political winds of any occasion in the pursuit of its expression, the pursuit of social equality remained a touchstone for Robespierre, as it had been for Rousseau. The latter argues, in the *Contrat social*, that it is only when the plurality of particular *interests* are moderated through sacrifice to social equality, when, in reciprocity, all give up such extremes, that the general will can find expression. This expression, in turn, is manifest in the systematic substitution of the rule of abstract and anonymous law for the rule of individuals such as kings and oligarchs. The general will can only become adequately true (to use Spinoza's distinction) when all are truly equal under the law (Boudon 2006: 132).

Unlike Rousseau and Montesquieu before him, however, the Jacobins saw true, just laws as universal rather than local institutions. Like the universal faculty of reason, laws should not in this view be adapted to the particularities ('vices') of differing climates and mores. A true law, for the Jacobins, was true for all humanity. To argue otherwise, one might add, would be to open the way to the various 'particular' legal regimes that the pro-slavery constituents of the period, from the slave owners of 1791 to Napoleon himself, repeatedly argued should except the Antillean colonies from the 'universal' rights of the Metropole. The challenge of the Jacobin attempt to institutionalise this Radical Enlightenment political theory of popular sovereignty lay in negating the hydra-like tendency of society continuously to form sovereign bodies of privilege separate from the people. Not only *mandataires*, but the military, police, juries and priests, Robespierre argued, should either be elected by the *peuple* or closely monitored by the Assembly (Boudon 2006: 236).

Even more surprisingly than his disparagement of Robespierre and the Jacobins, which in its simplicity of formulation merely borrows from the anti-populist doxa that has passed for truth from Burke and Bentham to Furet, Israel goes on to contrast this putative Jacobin betrayal of the Radical Enlightenment with the regressive regime that replaced it, known to posterity by the infamous epithet of 'Thermidor'. 'Radical Enlightenment writers who survived the Terror', Israel tells us, 'subsequently denounced Robespierre, not just as an abominable and bloody dictator but also [. . .] as a crassly anti-intellectual demagogue and Rousseauist fanatic' (2010: 244). While this may be literally accurate, Israel never stops to ask whether such denunciations were, in fact, true. It is Israel's 'Hail, Thermidor!', I would argue, and not Jacobinism, that is the true betrayal of the Radical Enlightenment. For Israel, the Thermidorian ideologues 'represent the intellectual tradition that kept the radical agenda alive', to the point that it would be 'their principles [that] emerged as the official values of a major part of the world after 1945' (2010: 235). While this may be true, it certainly would not be, as Israel intends it, to the credit of the post-1945 world order.

This is a difficult argument to accept from the world's leading scholar of the Radical Enlightenment. Thermidor is the name we have inherited for all counter-revolutionary terror, the re-imposition of order and privilege after the attempt to restructure society in the name of justice and equality. Michelet, famously, disdained even to continue his magisterial history of the French Revolution beyond the fall of Robespierre. Thermidor names not a beginning, but the systematic destruction of the institutions and practices of the Jacobin hegemony, Albert Mathiez argues in his recently reprinted masterpiece, *La Réaction thermidorienne* (2010: 57).

The Thermidorian constitution of *l'an III* that Israel celebrates replaced the Jacobin attempt to eliminate privilege and oligarchy in the 1793 constitution with their restoration; in place of Jacobin universal emancipation, Thermidor names the post-1789 triumph of the oligarchy of propertied, bourgeois elites over both the *ancien régime* and the *tiers état*. One statistic among many: in place of Robespierre's unyielding, rational and egalitarian attack on the infamous 'marc d'argent' (poll tax), Thermidor restricted suffrage to a mere 30,000 electors for all of 'democratic', 'revolutionary' France. Thermidor began the unfortunate tradition of the parliamentary coup d'état, and managed to erase, for the first time since 1789, any and all reference to the 'natural rights of man' in the discriminatory preamble to the 1795 constitution.

Thermidor witnessed the triumph of a politics of personal interest, passions and resentments. In creating, for the first time, a permanent political class by the gerrymandering of its constitution, the infamous *'république des camarades'*, the Thermidorian Convention, ends in a defence of oligarchic privilege (Mathiez 2010: 367). The particular interest of this new class of political functionaries was united only in their having universally profited from the Revolution, and they defended in their constitution the skeleton of the republic only because, having profited from the sale of émigrés' property and, for many, having voted for the execution of Louis Capet, a return to monarchy would have meant their end, both politically and physically.

In the Thermidorian republic of mediocrity and self-interest, the only politician of principles to stand out was the reactionary royalist, Boissy d'Anglas. His influence on the drafting of the new constitution was 'determinant', in the judgment of Marcel Dorigny, and it was he who, as *rapporteur* for the commission of eleven drafters, summarised in their name the principles it sought to enshrine. Like some evil twin of Robespierre, Boissy too based his politics on a single principle, which he summarised in his speech from 21 *Ventôse*: 'the legislator's work [. . .] must consist in [. . .] establishing wise laws, immutable barriers [. . .] that prevent poverty from violating the property of the rich' (cited in Soboul 1989: 128).

Thermidor, in other words, is not the cessation of Terror, but its redeployment against those excluded from the corridors of power. One must conclude that Thermidor is not a beginning but a closure, the destruction of the rational, undivided egalitarianism of the Radical Enlightenment derived from Spinoza and consummated in the politics of Robespierre and Toussaint. Thermidor names the defence of the Terrorist state and its legitimate violence, a state devoted not to defending the general will of all against royalist regression, but to dominating and excluding the vast majority of the population to the profit of a tiny minority.

Robespierre and Jacobinism, not Thermidor, are the proper names for the politics of the Radical Enlightenment. They undertook the rational destruction of inequality and an unyielding defence of the universal rights of all. These were the pure human rights of actors, Jews and slaves, the principled refusal of exclusion through taxation, a politics of undivided equality and justice derived from the pure Spinozan principle of the construction of a society that allows for the fullest development of the inherent potentiality of all humans. After the fall of Jacobinism, I have argued, along with Laurent Dubois and others, it is the Haitian Revolution and Toussaint Louverture, in particular, that was left to defend a politics of the Radical Enlightenment in the face of bourgeois, Napoleonic and then royalist regression to 1804 and beyond.

How does Israel arrive at what seems so blatantly wrong-headed a conclusion to his magnificent and inspiring reconfiguration and revitalisation of the vast, world-historical project of Radical Enlightenment? I think there exists a fundamental uncertainty in Israel's argument, judging at least from this most recent publication, over the fundamental characteristics of what he identifies as the Radical Enlightenment. On the one hand, and here I think he is exactly right, through the majority of his text Israel consistently identifies the Radical Enlightenment with fidelity to a single overarching cause: what I have called above the axiom of justice as *equality*. The radical tradition, 'following Spinoza', says Israel, 'boiled down [. . .] to the principles of justice based on equality'. 'The principle of equality [. . .] anchored democracy in the moral and political philosophy of the Radical Enlightenment, so it was "equality" that grounded its entire social theory.' 'Justice and benevolence anchored in equality [. . .] became for the *philosophes modernes* the exclusive ground of morality itself' (Israel 2010: 22, 95, 194).

On the other hand, Israel's text occasionally affirms a second set of criteria defining the Radical Enlightenment. These include parliamentary democracy, 'individual liberty of lifestyle; full freedom of thought, expression and the press; eradication of religious authority from the legislative process and education; and full separation of church and state' (Israel 2010: viii): in short, Israel concludes, the 'core democratic values [that] did finally triumph in much of the world after 1945' (2010: ix). In order to prove that the current world order is the actual triumph of the Radical Enlightenment, Israel is forced to abandon the basic criterion of universal justice as equality (in so far as the contemporary world fails to live up to this standard), and to reduce the Radical Enlightenment to the freedoms of faith, discussion and the press.

In short, Israel's is a *moderate* Radical Enlightenment, one made safe for the liberal, parliamentary post-1945 order in power today. The full implications of Spinoza's radical egalitarianism and the destruction of privilege articulated in the Jacobin and black Jacobin Revolutions thus remains safely quarantined, without critical consideration, as 'Rousseauian deviation' and 'abominable' dictatorship, their rightful violence posing no threat to the iniquities of contemporary north Atlantic parliamentary democracies and their notable failures of justice and equality. Israel's is an *idealist* Radical Enlightenment, in which the destruction of privilege remains gradualist and moderate, a mere *Revolution of the Mind*, as his book title so appropriately states, a *Procope* Enlightenment of coffee-house debate among the radical chic intelligentsia of the age. Above all, Israel wants, like those who shrank before the beheading of Louis Capet, a revolution without a revolution, as Robespierre rightly taunted them.

The problem lying at the core of Israel's shrinking before the full political implications is thus precisely that of violence; Radical Enlightenment and the equality it calls for require the destruction of the world of privilege, and it was the Jacobins alone, with the black Jacobins in their wake, who pursued this destruction of propertied privilege (slavery by any other name). Jacobinism names this legitimate violence, the refusal to capitulate before the Allied Monarchies and *Chouans*, who would stop at nothing to re-impose the society of their hierarchical privilege. Likewise, the rightful violence of the Haitian Revolution was the defensive refusal of former slaves to re-enter that state of servitude. Toussaint Louverture warned the Directory, in his famous letter of 1797, that these black citizens of universal rights would die before submitting to re-enslavement, and their struggle from 1802 to 1804 proved his words prophetic:

> Do they think that men who have been able to enjoy the blessing of liberty will calmly see it snatched away? They supported their chains only so long as they did not know any condition of life more happy than that of slavery. But to-day when they have left it, if they had a thousand lives they would sacrifice them all rather than be forced into slavery again ... France will not revoke her principles, she will not withdraw from us the greatest of her

benefits . . . But if, to re-establish slavery in San Domingo, this was done, then I declare to you it would be to attempt the impossible: we have known how to face dangers to obtain our liberty, we shall know how to brave death to maintain it. (Cited in James 1989: 197)

While Spinoza affirmed that, in the state of nature, any being has the 'right' to do whatever is in its power (as big fish eat little fish, to use his own example), this universalisation of right is equivalent to its erasure as tautology: whatever happens happens, and is right because it happens. Rousseau and the Jacobins reject Spinoza's terminology but retain his conclusions regarding violence and insurrection. Given their commitment to the universal *rights of man* (and not, as for Spinoza, right in general), they conclude that it is nonsensical to speak of a *right* to insurrection and defensive violence. Rousseau never wavers; there is no such thing as a *right* to overthrow tyranny, just as there is no right of the stronger. Defensive violence is a *fact* not a *right*, occurring in contexts of force rather than the rule of just (egalitarian, anonymous) law. Where force rules, a people can at any moment respond in turn with force, and need not await the recognition (were it ever to come) of a specious 'right' to revolt (Rousseau 2006: I, III, XVIII; Boudon 2006: 170).

Defensive violence and insurrection, I would argue, are always decisions, 'legitimate' and 'rightful' only in the broadest Spinozan sense that if one has the power to overthrow tyranny, one has the 'right' to. Violence is a sort of transcendental category for humans' being-in-the-world; like language or sociability, it is transcendental in any given situation, and can take an infinite number of forms, modes or orientations (universalist, reactionary, populist, royalist), as attention to an event as complex as the French or Haitian Revolution shows. The decision to struggle for popular sovereignty, universal rights, royalist reaction, or in defence of one's own personal right to garner riches and hegemony is just that, a decision, ultimately ungroundable. Whether one chooses to pursue a Spinozan 'adequately true' society, in which all humans can flourish and develop their fullest potentialities, or whether one struggles for an exclusionary social hierarchy based on the labour and degradation of a 'part with no part', as Boissy d'Anglas in 1795 or Napoleon in 1802 chose, involves not logical proof, but an act of will. Following Spinoza's own logic, if we have the power to create a true, enlightened society, we have the right to, but no less by this measure do we have the 'right' to create a living hell or even to kill ourselves off as a species with atomic weapons and biocide. Spinoza, Rousseau, Robespierre and Louverture can help us to understand how to identify and build an adequately *true* society, but we are still left at every moment with the obligation to choose that struggle rather than any other.

In essence, Israel's *moderate* Radical Enlightenment stands for nothing more than the defence of the virtues of parliamentary *representation* as the apex of democracy. 'The key political tool' devised by the Radical Enlightenment, Israel claims, 'was that of representation as a way of organizing large-scale democracies' (2010: 62). Rousseau's and Robespierre's 'peculiar' concept of the 'general will' is conveniently banished as the 'impossible "chimère" of direct democracy', to be replaced by the 'preference for representative democracy [. . .] designed to produce *experienced* and *qualified* representatives' and '*responsible* leaders' (Israel 2010: 60, 64, 86, my emphasis). Like a latter-day Boissy d'Anglas, Israel's celebration of the oligarchy of the 'experienced' and 'qualified' resonates as much with Hegelian and Habermasian technocratic managerialism as with contemporary attacks on Aristide and Lavalas (cf. Nesbitt 2009). Representation, Rousseau and Robespierre never tired of reminding us, is another name for the alienation of one's power to act, its delegation to another party. It seems plainly wrong to argue, as Israel does, that representation can, in any sense, stand as the fulfilment of Spinoza's political project. Representation is, by definition, the negation of Spinoza's determination (against Hobbes) to preserve natural rights as far as possible and to avoid their alienation to any sovereign body. How one might mitigate that tendency toward alienation in a modern, large-scale democratic state is a political dilemma to which representation is not the solution, but the problem itself. Parliamentary democracy may, in any given iteration, prove to alienate popular sovereignty *less* than another form of government (such as monarchy), and, given certain stipulations (duration of tenure, revocability and so on), may even approach a true expression of the general will, but it is decidedly the latter, as theorised by Spinoza, Rousseau and the Jacobins' concept of popular sovereignty, rather than representation, that is the political fulfilment of the Radical Enlightenment.

Israel's moderate Radical Enlightenment is none other than the top-down, managerial distribution of goods and benefits by the oligarchy of the elite. In this sense, his identification with the Thermidor of Boissy d'Anglas is quite appropriate, though for reasons he might not admit. In place of this neo-Thermidorian managerialism, however, fidelity to the truly *radical* Enlightenment requires defending the single principle of universal equality, including, above all, that of anyone, anyone at all, to participate fully, and not through entitled 'representatives' of their interests, in the pursuit of democracy and the construction of the social order. To conclude, as Israel does following Thomas

Paine, that oligarchic privilege can be overthrown 'by ridicule, by changes in perception and ideas' is to regress to a depoliticised idealism (2010: 99). In his desire to offer a vision of a purified, non-violent Radical Enlightenment, a *moderate* Radical Enlightenment, Israel must weakly conclude that 'embracing revolution, while seeking to minimize disruption and violence, was a classic exhortation of the Radical Enlightenment' (2010: 100). The Jacobin and black Jacobin tradition that was the true culmination of the Radical Enlightenment tells us something different: that there is no right and proper time to overthrow tyranny and slavery, and that it is only by deciding to intervene in an intolerable situation that, in retrospect, we actually create the proper conditions for the progress of universal emancipation.

One should be clear about the political implications of Spinoza's Radical Enlightenment, from Rousseau, the late Diderot of Raynal's *Histoire des Deux Indes*, Robespierre and Toussaint, to C. L. R. James, Fanon, and Aristide and Lavalas today: the critique of miracles, freedom of the press and the like are mere secondary concerns. The Spinozan Radical Enlightenment stands for one thing and one thing alone: the pursuit of undivided, universal equality by whatever means necessary, including the necessary destruction of the violent regimes of privilege that will defend by force of arms the exclusion of the majority from democracy.

## NOTES

1. This is the central claim of my book, *Universal Emancipation: The Haitian Revolution and the Radical Enlightenment* (2008).
2. Misleading because the self-described Jacobin *Terreur* obviously has nothing to do with contemporary understandings of the term, whether referring to genocide, terrorism such as its Russian anarchist or pseudo-Islamic variants, popular violence, or the even affect of terror putatively felt by the Jacobins themselves. Nor, as both Mathiez and Boudon point out, was the *Comité de salut public*, to say nothing of Robespierre himself, ever a 'dictatorship' and the Assembly its rubber-stamp *Politburo*, as anti-Jacobin doxa endlessly intones.
3. As well as in more recent studies, including Maria José Villaverde's article 'Rousseau, lecteur de Spinoza' (1999: 117–40) ,which focuses on Rousseau's appropriation of Spinoza's critique of religion, rather than the political theory that is of interest to me here.
4. In this, as in many other areas, the Jacobins thus stand as clear and distinct predecessors of Jean-Bertrand Aristide's political commitment to the dignity of the Haitian poor.
5. In this regard, the Jacobin land reform points not to the neo-plantocracies

of Toussaint and Christophe, but to the massive and unparalleled (in both scope and success) land reform of Pétion in the wake of Dessalines's assassination and the division of Haiti into Northern and Southern states.

# BIBLIOGRAPHY

Armstrong, Aurelia (1997), 'Some Reflections on Deleuze's Spinoza: Composition and Agency', in Keith Ansell Pearson (ed.), *Deleuze and Philosophy: The Difference Engineer*, Edinburgh: Edinburgh University Press, pp. 44–57.

Boudon, Julien (2006), *Les Jacobins: Une traduction des principes de Jean-Jacques Rousseau,* Bibliothèque Constitutionnelle et de Science Politique, vol. 128.

Gauthier, Florence (1992), *Triomphe et mort du droit naturel en Révolution: 1789–1795–1802,* Paris: PUF.

Gross, Jean-Pierre (2003), *Fair Shares for All: Jacobin Egalitarianism in Practice,* Cambridge: Cambridge University Press.

Israel, Jonathan (2001), *Radical Enlightenment: Philosophy and the Making of Modernity, 1650–1750,* Oxford: Oxford University Press.

Israel, Jonathan (2010), *A Revolution of the Mind: Radical Enlightenment and the Intellectual Origins of Modern Democracy,* Princeton: Princeton University Press.

James, C. L. R. (1989), *The Black Jacobins: Toussaint L'Ouverture and the San Domingo Revolution,* New York: Vintage.

Mathiez, Albert [1929] (2010), *La Réaction thermidorienne,* Paris: La Fabrique.

Nesbitt, N. (2008), *Universal Emancipation: The Haitian Revolution and the Radical Enlightenment,* Charlottesville: University of Virginia Press.

Nesbitt, N. (2009), 'Aristide and the Politics of Democratization', *SmallAxe* 30 (13:3), pp. 137–47.

Robespierre (1965), *Discours et rapports à la Convention,* Paris: Union Générale d'Editions.

Rousseau, Jean-Jacques (2006), *Du contrat social,* Paris: Flammarion.

Soboul, Albert (ed.) (1989), *Dictionnaire historique de la Révolution française,* Paris: Presses Universitaires de France.

Spinoza, B. de (1994), *A Spinoza Reader,* ed. Edwin Curley, Princeton: Princeton University Press.

Vernière, P. (1954), *Spinoza et la pensée française avant la Révolution* (2 vols), Paris: Presses Universitaires de France.

Villaverde, Maria José (1999), 'Rousseau, lecteur de Spinoza', in Tanguy L'Aminot (ed.), *Jean-Jacques Rousseau et la lecture,* Oxford: Voltaire Foundation.

# 9. *George Eliot, Spinoza and the Ethics of Literature*

SIMON CALDER

I

*'The mind does not err from the fact that it imagines'* (E IIP17S). As Moira Gatens has recently emphasised, this phrase is 'uniquely ... underscored' in George Eliot's handwritten manuscript translation of Baruch Spinoza's *Ethics* (Gatens 2009: 79). Spinoza's emphasis on the cognitive role of imagination was of major interest to Eliot, whose first work of fiction was accepted for publication in *Blackwood's Edinburgh Magazine* in the same year, 1856, that her endeavour to publish an English translation of Spinoza's *Ethics* was derailed. Both as a fiction writer and as a self-styled advocate of 'the free and diligent exertion of the intellect', Eliot consistently strove to reveal and to actualise the potential for a particular type of collaboration between 'imaginative' thinking and deductive ratiocination (Eliot 2000: 170). In Chapter 7 of this book, Dimitris Vardoulakis demonstrates that the law as conceived by Spinoza is distinct from the truth as conceived by Spinoza. For Spinoza, the content of the law is always transformable because the function of the law is to make a community possible by addressing a given set of contingent human relations. This chapter illuminates how Eliot's particular endeavour – to create and serve a community of readers – was informed by, yet also critical of, Spinoza's 'dictates of reason'. After assessing Spinoza and Eliot's conceptions of the relation between 'imaginings' and 'necessarily true', or 'adequate', ideas in the first three sections of the chapter, we will address the discontinuity between Spinoza's and Eliot's means of assessing particular 'imaginings' in section 4. Ultimately, we will find that Eliot's fictions aspire not just to instantiate and serve, but also to reassess and refine Spinoza's ethical principles. As such, her rethinking of the relation between imaginative thinking and deductive ratiocination provides the

basis for a new – and especially robust – mode of assessing the ethical merit of fictions.

Since we hope to compare Spinoza's and Eliot's ideas about the relation between *imaginatio* (Spinoza's 'first kind of cognition') and *ratio* (Spinoza's 'second kind of cognition'), we must first recognise that *imaginatio* encompasses sensory perception, sensation and memory, as well as what we call imagination (E IIP40S2; James 1997: 154). In Eliot's translation of the *Ethics*, from which I quote throughout the chapter, 'an imagination is an idea which indicates rather the actual constitution of the human body than the nature of an external body' (E IVP1S). Spinoza states that there is 'no other way' in which the mind can regard external bodies as actually existing (E IIP26). Thus, for example, the sensation that you currently have of holding this book in your hands is no less an 'imagining' than any thoughts you might have about the inhabitants of Middlemarch. The same goes for the 'longing' discussed by George Eliot's partner, George Henry Lewes, below. The following passage first appeared in Lewes's popular biography, *The Life of Goethe*, on which he and Eliot were working in 1854, when Eliot began to prepare her translation of the *Ethics*. Lewes writes:

> It has doubtless happened to the reader in his youth to meet with some entirely novel and profoundly-suggestive idea, casually cited from an ancient author; if so, he will remember the over-mastering influence it exercised, the longing it awakened for a nearer acquaintance with the author. The casual citation of a passage from Spinoza made my youth restless, and to this day I remember the aspect of the page where it appeared, and the revolution in thought which it effected. (Lewes 2001: 174)

Were Spinoza to have read Lewes's 'longing', he would have interpreted it as the desire or appetite to possess a fuller understanding of the *Ethics* nourished by the memory of past encounters with the *Ethics* and counteracted by memories which exclude the existence of that fuller understanding (E III Def.Aff.XXXII). Spinoza would explain that Lewes's longing is not just an 'imagining', but – more specifically – a *passion*, where the passions are 'affections that we experience as we strive to increase our power on the basis of inadequate ideas' (James 1997: 201). Spinoza would explain that the idea instantiated by Lewes's passion is 'inadequate' by virtue of its being relational. Lewes's longing expresses only Lewes's sense of the relation between his body and the *Ethics*; it expresses nothing of the *Ethics* in itself. Spinoza might finally reassure Lewes that, besides these passive emotions (the passions), 'there are other emotions . . . which belong to us considered as active' and that Lewes's passionate longing might yet engender a higher desire, to cultivate a more active, Spinozistic mode of thinking (E IIIP58). It is evident that Lewes's reading of the *Ethics* did not effect so complete a revolution in thought, for in 1856 Lewes's unruly passions compelled him to 'terminate all matters' between himself and the intended publisher of Eliot's translation of the *Ethics*, which was therefore never published in her lifetime (in Atkins 1978: 171).

Seven years before even meeting George Eliot, Lewes had already composed a chapter on Spinoza for his *Biographical History of Philosophy* (Lewes 1857: 423). In that chapter, Lewes introduced British intellectuals to the profoundly suggestive idea that he encountered in Propositions 1 to 8 of Part I of the *Ethics*. Having translated that 'portion of the *Ethica*', Lewes broke off his translation to paraphrase Spinoza's conception that 'there is but one infinite Substance, and that is God ... Everything else is a Mode' (1857: 430). In Spinoza's sense, this idea (of the infinity, indivisibility and unity of Substance) is not an 'imagining' but an 'adequate' idea. For Spinoza, the idea is 'adequate' because it expresses an eternal truth about the nature of reality, as opposed to the idea of some alteration (effected by an external object) in a being's bodily condition. Because Lewes failed to study Spinoza's conception of the difference, and the relation, between 'imaginings' and 'adequate' ideas, he proceeded to offer a rather inadequate assessment of Spinoza's broader philosophical system. Thus, for example, whereas Lewes criticised Spinoza for imagining 'that the mind is ... a passive mirror, reflecting the nature of things', Spinoza's philosophical therapy is founded on the notion that all ideas, even our relatively passive imaginings, are active 'conceptions' (Lewes 1857: 434; E IID3). For Spinoza, it is only through experiencing – and therein enjoying – the activity of thinking that beings become capable of reforming their 'imaginings'.

Three decades later, and two decades into his relationship with Eliot, Lewes's appreciation of Spinoza's philosophical system had radically improved. As Lewes considers the nature of the Cosmos in the second volume of his magnum opus, *Problems of Life and Mind*, below, his writing is suffused by a sense of the difference between relational 'imaginings' and 'adequate' ideas. Lewes writes:

> It is true that our visible Cosmos, our real world of perceptions, is one of various and isolated phenomena; most of them seeming to exist in themselves ... But opposed to this continuous Cosmos perceived, there is the invisible continuous Cosmos, which is conceived as an uniform Existence, all the modes of which are inter-dependent, none permanent. (quoted in Levine 2008: 34)

What Lewes here recognises is that, even (or especially) if the Cosmos is one Substance, we cannot help but read it in two ways. As Spinoza explains, 'quantity is conceived by us in two ways, namely superficially or abstractly, as it is represented in our imaginations; or as substance, which is conceived by the intellect alone' (E IP14S). Eliot was no less affected by this conception and – as the following passage demonstrates – she believed it to be no less applicable to the art of storytelling than it is to the science of astronomy. Here is the epigraph to the sixteenth chapter of Eliot's final novel, *Daniel Deronda*, which was composed in the same year, 1875, that the second volume of Lewes's *Problems* was published. Eliot writes:

> Men, like planets, have both a visible and an invisible history. The astrono-mer threads the darkness with strict deduction, accounting for every visible arc in the wanderer's orbit; and the narrator of human actions, if he did his work with the same completeness, would have to thread the hidden path-ways of feeling and thought which lead up to every moment of action. (Eliot 1998: 139)

Although Spinoza's *Ethics*, Lewes's *Problems* and Eliot's fictions all investigate the relation between the same two modes of thinking ('imag-inings' and deductive ratiocination), Eliot's fictions convey a distinct sense of the ideal type of relation between those two modes of thinking. Ultimately, Eliot's narrators do *not* work with the same completeness as the deductive astronomer; neither, however, do they work with the same single-mindedness. Through analysing Eliot's fiction in light of Spinoza's philosophy, we will see that she habitually and consciously *oscillates* between narrating (by imagining) the visible histories of her characters and narrating (by deducing) the invisible histories of feeling and thought that lead up to every moment of action.

There is no better way to grasp Eliot's conception of the ideal rela-tion between imaginative thinking and deductive ratiocination than to analyse her depiction of the visible and invisible histories of Latimer, who is at once the passionate protagonist and the reflective narrator of Eliot's novella, *The Lifted Veil*, which was composed and published in 1859. Latimer is an ideal experimental subject, for his preternatural prescience and his 'unwilling' awareness of the flow of other minds make him especially cognisant of the 'double-consciousness' at work within each one of us (Eliot 1999: 21). Below, Latimer considers his recalcitrant desire for a woman, Bertha Grant, whom he clearly and distinctly knows will both hate him and harm him in the long run. Latimer reflects:

> Behind the slim girl Bertha, whose words and looks I watched for, whose touch was bliss, there stood continually that Bertha with the fuller form, the harder eyes, the more rigid mouth, – with the barren selfish soul laid bare. (Eliot 1999: 21)

Latimer is able to imagine whatever he desires about 'the slim girl Bertha' with whom he presently interacts, for of all the characters 'in a close relation' to him, she is the only one whose mind he is not compelled to read. Ultimately, nothing positive in Latimer's present imagining (that is, nothing in Latimer's idea of Bertha as she presently affects his body) is nullified by the incontestable evidence of Bertha's 'pitiless soul' that Latimer receives in a 'hell[ish]' prevision of their marital life together (Eliot 1999: 19). Even as the most pitiless of Bertha's present actions provokes 'the shadow of [that] vision' to return, it always passes just as soon as Bertha becomes, once more, 'the object nearest' to Latimer: then '[her] warm-breathing presence again possesse[s his] senses and imagination like a return siren melody' (Eliot 1999: 26).

When one of Eliot's contemporaries, Edith Simcox, came to Lewes in search of some 'moral' for *The Lifted Veil*, Lewes declared that 'the moral is plain enough': Latimer's predicament 'is only an exaggeration of . . . the one-sided knowing of things in relation to the self' that affects all of us insofar as we have not a 'whole knowledge' of the nature of things (quoted in Eliot 1999: xxix). Lewes's implication, that Eliot hoped her readers might actively conceive an affinity between Latimer's – only superficially 'exceptional' – 'mental condition' and their own mental activities, is corroborated by the following passage from Eliot's novella (1999: 3). Below, Latimer requests 'you who read this' to sympathise with him:

> Are you unable to give me your sympathy – you who read this? Are you unable to imagine this double-consciousness at work within me, flowing on like two parallel streams that never mingle their waters and blend into a common hue? . . . You have known the powerlessness of ideas before the might of impulse; and my visions, when once they had passed into memory, were mere ideas – pale shadows that beckoned in vain, while my hand was grasped by the living and the loved. (Eliot 1999: 21)

In the following two sections of this chapter we will review the nature and the content both of Latimer's first stream of consciousness (his 'imaginings') and of Latimer's second stream of consciousness (his reflective ideas). Finally, in Section 4, we will consider what Eliot's fiction suggests about the virtue of restraining our desire to blend these separate streams 'into a common hue'. Whereas Spinoza's philosophical therapy is geared towards uniting the first and second kinds of cognition in intuitive synthesis, Eliot's fiction troubles the Spinozistic idea that our 'one-sided knowing of things' *should*, eventually, give way to an 'adequate' understanding of things as they are in themselves. Only after first considering Spinoza's and Eliot's agreement concerning 'the powerlessness of ideas before the might of impulse' will we be able to assess their disagreement with regard to the virtue of remaining 'grasped by the living and the loved'.

2

In so far as we wish to acquire a true estimation of Latimer's first stream of consciousness, which is comprised of confused cognitions concerning the relation between his body and other modes, we must first attend to Latimer's passions; and in so far as we wish to understand those passions, we must begin by attending to Latimer's desire. For Spinoza, any given being's desire is nothing more nor less than its *appetite attended with consciousness*' (E IIIP9S). As such, we find a perfect starting-point for our investigation in the following passage from the opening pages of Eliot's novella. Here Latimer recalls that, before acquiring his preternatural powers, he had always already been 'hungry for human deeds and human emotions' (Eliot 1999: 3, 6). Latimer reflects:

> I read Plutarch, and Shakespeare, and Don Quixote by the sly, and supplied myself in that way with wandering thoughts, while my tutor was assuring me that 'an improved man, as distinguished from an ignorant one, was a man who knew the reason why water ran down-hill.' I had no desire to be this improved man; I was glad of the running water ... [and] did not want to know *why* it ran. (Eliot 1999: 6–7)

Latimer consciously longs for literature, as opposed to natural philosophy, and for aesthetic experiences as opposed to understanding. In hungering to conceive the magnitude of things *only in so far* as they affect his body ('I could watch [the water] and listen to it gurgling among the pebbles'), Latimer is bound to conceive someone whose ideas are a stream of imaginings as superior to someone whose only mode of conceiving 'running water' is intellectual. Gillian Beer once declared that Latimer's 'will [becomes] paralysed by his prescience' (Beer 1976: 96). Spinoza would contend that Latimer's capacity to be prescient is rather paralysed by his will, or by the closest thing that Latimer has to a will: his degenerate appetite. At four separate points in the novella, Latimer uses the word 'delicious' to express the quality of his (inadequate) thinking about Bertha. He describes 'each day in [Bertha's] presence' as 'a delicious torment', for example, and the moment of Bertha's bodily return as 'a moment as delicious ... as the waking up to a consciousness of youth after a dream of middle age' (Eliot 1999: 17, 27; see also 28 and 31). For the Spinozist, whose prognosis of our protagonist must be extremely bleak, it is precisely because Latimer hungers for such sensations that he cannot construct the concatenation of 'adequate' ideas that would otherwise liberate him from his bondage to passive 'imaginings' (E IIIP9S).

From a Spinozistic perspective, then, Latimer's only hope lies in the possibility that a higher desire for understanding might be engendered by his confused awareness of the shifts, 'from less to greater perfection' (*laetitia*) and 'from greater to less perfection' (*tristitia*), that accompany every being's effort to maintain itself (E III Def.Aff.II and III). Whereas Eliot anticipates Samuel Shirley in translating Spinoza's *laetitia* as pleasure and Spinoza's *tristitia* as pain, I follow Amelie Rorty in translating these terms as elation and dejection on the grounds that Rorty's renderings better convey Spinoza's sense that *laetitia* and *tristitia* are 'expressions of *change*', or 'ideational indicants of bodily thriving or declining' (Rorty 1991: 354). To paraphrase Susan James, desire is our very *conatus*, or endeavour to thrive, but it is complemented by two other principal passions. 'These three principal passions [Desire, Elation and Dejection] . . . are, therefore, our experience of our disposition to try to persevere in our being, and of our victories and defeats in this process' (James 1997: 146–7).

Given that ours is an endeavour to contrast and assess the modes of desire that Spinoza's and Eliot's writings embody and engender, it will be necessary to compare Latimer's striving with the striving of a Spinozistic control subject. We find just such a control subject in Ariadne, the 'protagonist' of Rorty's essay, 'Spinoza on the Pathos of Idolatrous Love and the Hilarity of True Love'. Rorty constructs a Spinozistic narrative about Ariadne, whose actions are at first determined by a series of confused ideas about her lover, Echo, but who eventually comes to govern herself in accordance with 'adequate' ideas (Rorty 1991: 353). Here, and in the remaining two sections of this chapter, we will assess the virtue of the modes of striving that are promoted in Eliot's fiction by reviewing them in light of Ariadne's instantiation of three separate species of striving, each one of which is effected by one of Spinoza's three separate kinds of cognition: *imaginatio*, *ratio* and *scientia intuitiva*.

For Spinoza, every passion is comprised of a particular sensation – of elation, dejection and/or desire – combined with a diagnosis of the cause of that sensation (E IVP56). Thus Rorty describes Ariadne's 'idolatrous love' of Echo as 'a particular sense of health [Elation], with a diagnosis of [Echo as] its cause' (Rorty 1991: 354). Eliot's 'imaginings' of love were also directly informed by Spinoza's definition of love as '[Elation] accompanying the idea of an external cause' (E III Def. Aff.VI). Focusing, for instance, on Latimer's account of his love for his mother, who died when he was young, we note that all he distinctly recalls about her is that she 'kept [him] on her knee' and nursed him back to health when he was once afflicted by blindness as a child (Eliot 1999: 5).

Latimer's declaration that he is 'a being finely organised for pain' is corroborated by the fact that there are far more recollections of hatred (i.e. of dejection 'accompanying the idea of an external cause') than there are recollections of love in *The Lifted Veil* (Eliot 1999: 24; E III Def.Aff.VII). Here we focus only on the most 'intense' of those hatreds: that which Latimer feels for his elder brother, Alfred. Latimer first introduces Alfred as 'a handsome self-confident man of six-and-twenty – a thorough contrast to my fragile, nervous, ineffectual self' (Eliot 1999: 14). To appreciate fully the quality of the dejection generated by Latimer's conception of this contrast, we must consider Spinoza's idea that 'any emotion of one individual differs from the emotion of another to the extent that the essence of the one individual differs from the essence of the other' (E IIIP57S). To illustrate this point, Spinoza claims that, although both a man and a horse are 'carried away by lust to procreate', the latter is carried 'by equine lust' and the former is carried 'by human lust' (E IIIP57S). What pains Latimer is the idea of a discrepancy between the nature and origin of his passions and the nature and origin of Alfred's passions. When Alfred recommends 'a run with the hounds' as 'the finest thing in the world for low spirits', Eliot's portrayal of Latimer's response is clearly informed by Spinoza's reflections on the difference between 'human' and 'equine' (i.e. *in*human) emotions:

> 'Low spirits!' I thought bitterly, as he rode away; 'that is the sort of phrase with which coarse, narrow natures like yours think to describe experience of which you can know no more than your horse knows. It is to such as you that the good of this world falls: ready dullness, healthy selfishness, good-tempered conceit – these are the keys to happiness.' (Eliot 1999: 25)

Already plagued by the idea that his higher desires are much harder to satisfy than Alfred's 'lower' appetites, Latimer is particularly pained by the recognition that *his* love and Alfred's love share a common object: Alfred's fiancée, Bertha Grant. (It is worth noting that, for the Spinozist, this too can be no coincidence, for 'we imitate the affects of others'; James 1997: 148.) This situation causes Latimer to be affected by a strong form of the composite emotion, jealousy, which – for Spinoza – is 'nothing else than a fluctuation of feeling arising from the simultaneous experience of love and hatred [towards a beloved being] conjoined with the idea of a third person who is envied' (E IIIP35S). As Spinoza proceeds to explain that the jealous man will be all the more powerfully afflicted by this disempowering passion if he has had previous cause to hate his present rival (as is the case in this instance), we begin to recognise quite how mutually supportive and cumulatively destructive these confused interpretations of life – the passions – can become. We can now see why it might be necessary for the narrator of human actions to thread the hidden pathways of feeling and thought with something akin to the 'completeness' of the deductive astronomer, for it is by such pathways that the passions travel. Before considering how (and how far) the adoption of such an attitude might remedy the problems posed by the passions, and how far both Latimer and Eliot seem willing to go towards implementing Spinozistic 'remedies of the passions', we will review the virtue of interpreting the passions in the manner that Spinoza and Eliot do.

The first thing to note here is that, in demonstrating that the passions are confused cognitions 'which follow from the common laws of nature', Eliot and Spinoza differentiate themselves both from those who imagine the domain of humanity to 'lie beyond the domain of nature' and from those who 'prefer detesting or ridiculing human emotions and actions to understanding them' (E IIIPref.). Our Spinozistic reading of Latimer's passions has enabled us to recognise that those passions are 'part of nature, not aberrations from it' (Lloyd 1994: 77). Naturally, the idea that Bertha is possessed by Alfred impels Latimer to act in a manner that departs from the dictates of reason.

A second point to note is that Spinoza and Eliot make the passions not just interpretations of life, but also modes of determining life, or 'ideas [by which] . . . the mind is determined to one thought rather than another' (E III Def.Aff.). For example, Latimer admits that 'jealousy impelled' him to act in ways that could never have served his best interests (Eliot 1999: 18). As we will see in the final two sections of this chapter, Eliot also concurred with Spinoza in recognising that many emotions can have beneficent effects, since 'an emotion can neither be restrained nor destroyed except by a contrary and stronger emotion' (E IVP7).

Finally, this Spinozistic mode of reading the passions enables us to capture the essence of particular passions without losing sight of their singularity. Although Spinoza defines a finite number of emotion types (Part III ends with a list of forty-eight General Definitions), he insists that 'the species of emotions . . . are as multitudinous as the species of objects' and that 'all modes in which any one body is affected by another body, result at once from the nature of the body affected and from the nature of the body affecting' (E IIIP56S; IIA1″). The rationale behind Spinoza's decision 'to omit the definitions' of composite emotions such as – significantly – jealousy from his list of General

Definitions will be assessed in the remaining two sections, where we will review what 'good' might come from studying 'bad' emotions, like Latimer's passions (E III Def.Aff.).

3

Near the end of Eliot's novella, Latimer wonders whether 'some remedy' for his intense susceptibility to pain might lie in the science of Charles Menuier, a faithful friend with a 'large and susceptible mind' (Eliot 1999: 12). That Charles's knowledge of 'the psychological relations of disease' might have some curative effect on Latimer seems immediately plausible, given our awareness of the extent to which he is agitated by entirely natural, and potentially controllable, passions (Eliot 1999: 18). The fact that Charles's knowledge is a knowledge of 'relations' is extremely significant, for, as Beer asserts, 'George Eliot constantly seeks *relations*' (Beer 1976: 94). In her essay, 'Myth and the Single-Consciousness: *Middlemarch* and *The Lifted Veil*', Beer emphasises Eliot's sense of the ethical salience of the 'search for understanding' by quoting the following passage from *The Mill on the Floss* (1976: 94). The narrator of that novel reflects:

> In natural science, I have understood, there is nothing petty to the mind that has a large vision of relations, as to which every single object suggests a vast sum of conditions. It is surely the same with the observations of human life. (Eliot 2003b: 284)

It is surely the same with the observation of Latimer's passions, each of which suggests a vast sum of conditions to the active, relation-seeking mind. In so far as Latimer successfully transposes his disparate memories and confused cognitions into a coherent story about the nature, causes and effects of his passions, he reveals that he has (or that he *is*) such a mind. Accepting Beer's general thesis about the ethical salience of relation-seeking, I want to challenge her interpretation of *The Lifted Veil*. Whereas Beer asserts that 'in *The Lifted Veil* we have only the single, authoritative self-pitying insight of Latimer to guide our reading of the world,' I hope to demonstrate how, in that novella, we encounter Eliot's most sustained attempt to estimate the virtue of developing a second reading of the world, a reading comprised of *ideas about* our pre-reflective 'imaginings' (Beer 1976: 98).

By the end of the second section of Rorty's Spinozistic ascent narrative, Ariadne 'knows *what it is to be a mind*' (Rorty 1991: 363). This she knows as a result of having come to conceive herself as *A*, 'a set of ideas of a compound body (vulgarly called *hers*) which is itself

a reflection of the interaction between her compound body and other
sections of extension, including that compound vulgarly called Echo'
(Rorty 1991: 362). Rorty does not number the ways in which Ariadne
overcomes her original, confused cognitions. However, we will find it
useful to pinpoint some five mindful mechanisms by which *A*/Ariadne
liberates herself from her idolatrous love. These five mechanisms can be
mapped on to the five distinct 'remedies of the passions' that Spinoza
lists below:

> It appears that the power of the mind over the passions consists
> I.   In the knowledge of the emotions . . .
> II.  In the separation of the emotion from the idea of external causes which
>      we imagine confusedly . . .
> III. In time, by means of which emotions relating to things that we under-
>      stand, triumph over those relating to things we conceive in a confused
>      and mutilated manner . . .
> IV.  In the multitude of causes by which the emotions relating to the
>      common properties of things, or to God, are encouraged . . .
> V.   In the order in which the mind can arrange its emotions and link them
>      together. (E VP20S)

In the Preface to Part V of the *Ethics*, Spinoza 'suppose[s] all men to
have in some degree experienced, but not to have accurately observed
or distinctly perceived' these remedies (E VPref.). Rorty has observed
them closely, for *A*/Ariadne's capacity to achieve liberation can be said
to consist in these five facts about her constitution and capacities:

1.  *A*/Ariadne's 'capacity for and energy toward clarity in reflection'
    enable her to recognise that 'idolatrous love, focused on a particu-
    lar individual, necessarily involves misperception'.
2.  *A*/Ariadne's 'idea of the causes of her elation' changes as she
    detaches her elation from the confused idea of an independent
    substance called Echo.
3.  *A*/Ariadne's 'power – her elation – is increased by her knowledge of
    the unqualifiedly necessary properties of bodies', because 'universal
    and timeless truths about the basic structure of Nature' become,
    in due time, *more affective* than confused ideas about contingent
    bodies.
4.  In coming to see and to love 'Echo-as-a-particular-expression-of-
    the-vast-network-of-individuals that have affected him', *A*/Ariadne
    comes to relate her love for Echo to her conceptions of the common
    properties of things and to God.
5.  Through becoming less enslaved to particular objects, *A*/Ariadne
    develops 'well-formed attitudes' (attitudes formed from adequate

ideas) from which 'well-formed action[s]' necessarily follow. (Rorty 1991: 357, 358, 363–4, 366, 370)

Through considering Latimer's storytelling in light of each of these five ways in which *A*/Ariadne liberates herself, we will be able to assess how far Eliot went towards integrating Spinoza's five 'remedies of the passions' into her fictions.

A crucial stage in Spinoza's philosophical therapy occurs in Proposition 2 of Part V, where it is observed that *if* we 'disjoin an emotion or affection of the soul from the [inadequate] idea of an external cause', then 'the form of love or hatred is removed likewise; and therefore these emotions, and all arising from them, are destroyed' (E VP2). Now, in Eliot's novella, the storytelling Latimer clearly replaces his original 'imagining' of Alfred as the 'onlie begetter' of a particular sense of dejection, *D*, with the more accurate conception that *D* was determined by a vast sum of conditions, including Latimer's melancholic disposition, the preferential treatment that Alfred received from the boys' father, Alfred's possession of Bertha, and so on. Like Ariadne, Latimer therein discovers that 'there is no better cure for idolatry than the analysis of its causes and objects' (Rorty 1991: 359). As such, Eliot implies that some kind of cure for 'bad' passions can be found (I) 'In the knowledge of the emotions' and (II) 'In the separation of the emotion from the idea of external causes which we imagine confusedly'.

At the next stage of Rorty's Spinozistic ascent narrative, *A*/Ariadne completely 'detaches her love from her confused imagistic thought of Echo, and concentrates instead on understanding how her emotions formed an interdependent pattern' (Rorty 1991: 361). Latimer regularly generates precisely this type of shift in focus, away from particular bodies to the general forms – and the relations between the general forms – of emotion. Consider the transition effected below, from Latimer's reading of his own particular 'suspense' to his expression of a general truth about Suspense. Latimer here reinterprets the affliction that affected him whilst he was waiting to discover whether or not his first prevision, of a particular bridge in Prague, was accurate. Latimer's hope was that his party might tire before arriving at the bridge: 'That would give me another day's suspense – suspense, the only form in which a fearful spirit knows the solace of hope' (Eliot 1999: 22).

Note how Latimer's general idea of the Form of Suspense, as related both to a fearful spirit and the solace of hope, chimes with the explanation that Spinoza attaches to his General Definitions of hope and fear in Part III of the *Ethics*. From the idea that 'Hope is an inconstant pleasure [Elation] arising from a past or future thing concerning the issue of which we are in some degree doubtful' and the idea that 'Fear is an inconstant pain [Dejection]' arising from the same species of idea, Spinoza deduces that 'there is no hope without fear and no fear without hope. For he who is in a state of suspense and . . . doubts whether what he hates will come to pass, imagines something which excludes the existence of what he hates' (E III Def.Aff.XII and XIII). Through undergoing his own form of the third mental mechanism undergone by *A*/Ariadne, Latimer is able to treat his particular memories of hope, fear and suspense as raw material from which to derive universal ideas about these emotions and about their necessary relation to other emotion-types. Ultimately, Latimer is affected by a 'sudden overpowering impulse to go on at once to the bridge, and put an end to the suspense [he] had been wishing to protract' (Eliot 1999: 22) Eliot thus implies that (III) emotions relating to things that we understand (e.g. the dependence of fear on suspense) eventually triumph over emotions relating to things that are conceived in a confused and mutilated manner.

Spinoza's fourth remedy for the passions concerns the encouragement of 'emotions related to the common properties of things'. As Genevieve Lloyd and Moira Gatens have elucidated, Spinoza's concept of common properties or common notions 'explains how human collective life is able to make a *qualitative* leap from relations built on hope and fear to those built on reason and fellowship' (Gatens and Lloyd 1999: 94). Thus, were *A* to read *The Lifted Veil*, her knowledge of common properties would stop her from supposing that Latimer and Alfred were ever essentially united by their desire for Bertha. Discussing scenarios such as this one, wherein one man (Peter) is the indirect cause of another man's dejection because he has something that the other man (Paul) desires, Spinoza denies that men can hate each other 'as a result of loving the same thing, and consequently of their agreeing in nature' (E IIIP34S). Crucially, we are here 'supposing that Peter [or Alfred] has an idea of the loved thing as now in his possession, while Paul [or Latimer] has an idea of the loved thing lost to him' (E IIIP34S). It is because he has an idea about Bertha that is radically different from Alfred's (that is, an idea of Bertha as possessed by himself) that Latimer hates Alfred. We can draw a stark distinction, then, between the previous scenario, wherein we would err in conceiving a desire for Bertha as a common property, and the following scenario, wherein Latimer adequately conceives that he, his father and all other humans are united by a common nature: 'In the first moments when we come away from the presence of death,' Latimer universalises, 'every other relation to the living is merged . . . in the great relation of a common nature and a common destiny' (Eliot 1999: 31). Latimer explicitly states that, following this cognition, his passion for

Bertha is 'completely neutralised by the presence of an absorbing feeling of another kind' (Eliot 1999: 31). As such, Eliot suggests that (IV) an increase in the yield of 'emotions relating to the common properties of things' will – other things being equal – overpower our egoistic impulses and that disempowering 'imaginings', like Latimer's idolatrous love, can and should be vanquished by (V) the proper cultivation of our power to 'arrange . . . emotions and link them together' (E VP20S). In the final section of this chapter we will consider both the nature of and the difference between Spinoza's and Eliot's efforts to facilitate this rational reordering of their readers' appetites and affections.


4

> That which constitutes the form of the human body consists in this, that
> its parts communicate their motions to each other in a certain ratio.
> (E IVP39)

In her 'Notes on Form in Art' of 1868, Eliot asserted that the 'highest' literary forms are intimately related to the 'highest Form' of existence known to us: the human organism (Eliot 2000: 356). Having already observed the congruence between Spinoza and Eliot's ideas about the power of 'the passions' and 'the power of the mind', we can here conclusively assess the relation between the 'form' of the human organism as conceived by Spinoza and Eliot and the structure and philosophical content of their writings. Through pursuing Eliot's suggestive idea that there is a vital continuity between the striving of particular organisms and the structure of the 'forms' that they create and consume, we will be able to grasp the ethical salience of the difference between Spinoza's and Eliot's literary forms and the modes of striving that they each promoted. Thus we will find that Eliot's fiction provides the basis for an especially robust mode of practical deliberation and of ethical literary criticism.

Eliot once asserted that her fictions were 'simply a set of experiments in life – an endeavour to see what our thought and emotion may be capable of – what stores of motive, actual or hinted as possible, give promise of a better after which we may strive' (Eliot 1954: 216–17). Like Spinoza, then, Eliot was consciously committed to fostering her readers' intellectual and emotional capabilities and to demonstrating the promise, not just of present or 'actual', but also of latent or 'possible' motives. There is, however, a radical discontinuity between Spinoza's and Eliot's modes of ethical inquiry: whereas Spinoza believed that a man can only 'understand his essence, i.e. . . . his power . . . so far as [he] knows himself through the medium of true reason', Eliot held that she could only 'help others to see . . . through the medium of art'

(E IVP53; Eliot 1954: 217). As Eliot's own ideas about the congruity between literary forms and modes of striving enable us to appreciate, the effect of this departure from Spinoza's approach had a far from superficial effect upon Eliot's conclusions about 'the good of the whole man' and on the ethos and effects of her writings.

As Martha Nussbaum has recently argued, any endeavour to 'embody ideas about the emotions' in a 'novelistic' mode would be unlikely to effect anything like the degree of liberation from the passions that Spinoza strove to facilitate through composing the *Ethics* (Nussbaum 2003: 508–9). Nussbaum is right to emphasise Spinoza's insistence that 'his own highly abstract geometrical way of writing is the correct way to show relations and objects as they exist from the point of view of a cured and God-oriented understanding' and that 'narration . . . focuses the mind too insistently on particulars' to meet Spinoza's approval (2003: 510). Rorty's Spinozistic story can be fruitfully conceived as the exception that proves Nussbaum's rule: although Rorty shows us that 'to understand [Spinoza's conception of] the pathos of love, we must . . . begin with a particular story', her endeavour to illustrate how A/ Ariadne liberates herself from idolatrous love eventually necessitates a shift away from 'the realm of *imaginatio*', populated as it is by 'vulgar stories' and by 'sound but incomplete generalizations' (Rorty 1991: 353, 360–3, 352). This is what makes Eliot's case so interesting, for in Eliot we have a story-teller who accepted many of Spinoza's ideas, but who refrained from supplementing the 'psychological and historical generalisations' that Latimer and her other narrators amass with that more 'adequate' set of 'explanations' that Rorty believes *ratio* (Spinoza's 'rationally demonstrative science of extension') can afford us (Rorty 1991: 363). The case becomes yet more compelling as we begin to consider how Eliot's prose explodes Nussbaum's distinction between particular-oriented 'novelistic' writing and 'nexus of the universe'-oriented, Spinozistic writing. In the fifteenth chapter of *Middlemarch*, for example, Eliot's narrator asserts that she will *not* disperse her focus 'over that tempting range of relevancies called the universe'; as she endeavours to introduce the 'new settler', Lydgate, to her readers, however, a Spinozistic commitment to tracing invisible histories clearly remains (Eliot 2003a: 141). Eliot's narrator asserts:

> I at least have so much to do in unravelling certain human lots, and seeing how they were woven and interwoven, that all the light I can command must be concentrated on this particular web. (Eliot 2003a: 141)

Throughout this final section of the chapter, we will endeavour to grasp both the salience and the scope of Eliot's uniquely web-oriented writing.

In so far as Eliot's webs are 'particular', the nexus that she unravels and observes is not the same as the universal nexus of interlocking modes that Spinoza encourages us to study; yet in so far as the particulars that Eliot studies are conceived as 'webs' (as opposed to independent substances), there is a vital continuity between Spinoza and Eliot's modes of composition. Whereas Nussbaum's staunchest criticism of Spinoza's ascent narrative is that it liberates *A* from bondage 'only by leaving behind the sight of the real-life individual', I will illustrate how much of the power and the virtue of Eliot's web-oriented writing arises from the fact that it is informed by Spinoza's understanding of the true structure and compossibility of real-life individuals (Nussbaum 2003: 524).

Throughout Spinoza's and Eliot's writings, 'the human organism' is conceived, not as an independent substance, but, in Eliot's words, as 'a varied group of relations' bound up into 'a wholeness' so complex that no part of it 'can suffer increase or diminution [i.e. elation or dejection] without . . . a consequent modification of the organism as a whole' (E IIL1; Eliot 2000: 356–8). As Spinoza explains, it is not only possible but also common for one part of the body to be so strengthened 'by the force of [an] external cause' that that part 'prevails over the rest' of the organism (E IVP60). Thus, for example, as certain parts of the section of extension that constitutes Latimer's body are so affected by the 'web' of 'scarcely perceptible signs' of interest that Bertha 'weaves' for it, those parts might be said to acquire an appetite for *titillating* pleasures (i.e. for elations that are demonstrably poisonous for the section conceived as a whole; Eliot 1999: 29). By drawing a stark distinction between titillation (as a mode of elation that affects 'some parts' of the body) and hilarity (as a mode of elation 'that [affects] all parts of the body alike'), Spinoza indeed endeavoured to demonstrate that only hilarity-induced desires will 'relate to the good of the whole man' and that titillation-induced desires must be 'excessive and evil' to the extent that their 'power . . . predominate[s] over the other actions of the body' (E IVP60; IVP42). After having drawn an analogous distinction between two separate modes of dejection – melancholy and anguish – Spinoza in turn deduces that 'melancholy is always evil,' since it is a mode of dejection that causes 'the body's power of action [to be] absolutely diminished or restrained', and that anguish can be 'so far good as titillation or [elation] is evil' (IVP43). With that foundation in place, Spinoza felt able to prove certainly the relative virtue or vice of every one of the other passions, since he conceived every passion to be a derivation of elation, dejection and/or desire. In so far as Spinoza and Eliot were both committed to demonstrating and to remedying the fact that '[our] desire to preserve our existence often manifests itself in a way inconsistent with our entire well-being,' both authors strove to equip their readers with a concatenation of ideas about the nature and dynamics of elation and dejection, in light of which set of ideas they might reorder their 'imaginings' and re-educate their *conatus* (E IVP60; IVP60S). Through now concluding our comparative analysis of *The Lifted Veil* and Rorty's story, we will see how Eliot and Spinoza developed two extremely different therapies of desire, despite their fundamental agreement about the cognitive nature of the passions and despite their agreement that 'bad' passions can only be remedied by the power of that 'idea of the body' that is the mind.

Returning to *The Lifted Veil*, we immediately encounter evidence of a deep uncertainty on Eliot's part, either about the virtue of Spinoza's method of categorising the emotions or about the virtue of her own novella, for when she first informed John Blackwood of its existence, in March 1859, she explicitly described *The Lifted Veil* as 'a *jeu de melancholie*', and within the novella itself Latimer declares that his habits of reflection engender no more than 'a sort of pitying anguish over the pathos of [his] lot' (Eliot 1999: x, 24). At first, then, the contrast between Eliot's and Rorty's narratives appears to be absolute; whereas Rorty's is a story about superseding 'the Pathos of Idolatrous Love', the protagonist of Eliot's story is only able to *recognise* that pathos, and whereas A/Ariadne achieves 'the hilarity of integration', Latimer can only ruminate on his *melancholie* (Rorty 1991: 370; Eliot 1999: 24). As we have seen, however, *The Lifted Veil* essentially documents the conversion – by Latimer – of a set of sorrowful 'imaginings' into a concatenation of reflective ideas about the nature, causes and effects of a number of passions. As such, Eliot's story lends credence to Spinoza's idea that 'the knowledge of good and evil is nothing else than the idea [of elation or dejection] which follows necessarily from the very emotion [of elation and dejection]' (E IVP7). Indeed, Eliot's is a narrative about the heightening of an individual's 'self-consciousness' to 'that pitch of intensity in which our . . . emotions take the form of a drama . . . and we begin to weep, less under the sense of our suffering than at the thought of it' (Eliot 1999: 24). Recalling Spinoza's assertion that anguish can be 'conceive[d] . . . such as to restrain titillation, . . . and so far . . . prevent the body from having its capabilities diminished', Eliot's novella can be seen to perform a relatively modest, yet vital, Spinozistic function, in impelling melancholic bodies to become anguished bodies by way of provoking them to construct a series of ideas about themselves (E IVP43).

Some of Spinoza's most fundamental conclusions concerning the *necessary relation* between emotions of a certain species and our fundamental endeavour to thrive are fully supported by Latimer's imaginative reflections on the drama that his emotions enact. Thus, for example, Spinoza's assertion that no good can come from 'emotions which belong to hatred or arise from it [e.g. envy, derision, contempt, anger, revenge]' is corroborated by Eliot's rendering of the process by which 'repulsion and antipathy harden into cruel hatred' within Bertha's soul, transforming her into a being that '[gives] pain only for the sake of wreaking itself' (E IVP45C1; Eliot 1999: 32) Our present reading of *The Lifted Veil* enables us to see that Eliot was willing to go only this far with Spinoza, however. Whereas Spinoza deduces that *all* emotions that are derived from dejection (i.e. all emotions that involve a 'transition from greater to lesser perfection') are 'directly evil', Eliot consistently presents *some* derivations of dejection as constitutive components of the well-lived life and of the procedure by which the nature of that life might be determined (E IVP41). Thus, for example, whereas Spinoza reasons that 'compassion in a man who lives according to reason, is in itself evil and useless', Eliot suggests that Latimer's being is essentially enhanced by the 'softening influence' of compassion and, indeed, that it is only because a 'pity . . . for every living thing' has, by the end of the story, forged itself within Latimer's soul that Latimer is *able to cognise* that Bertha's hateful spirit is 'surrounded by possibilities of misery' (E IVP50; Eliot 1999: 28). Thus, whereas *A* becomes committed to preserving the set of ideas that she is by constructing a set of 'good', because non-passionate, emotions, Latimer generalises that the soul 'need[s] . . . something hidden and uncertain for the maintenance of that doubt and hope and effort which are the breath of its life' (Eliot 1999: 29). For Eliot, as for Latimer, passions such as timidity, hope and compassion and mental states such as doubt (the intellectual analogue of 'vacillation' between passions) must be maintained on the grounds that *they* are constitutive components of well being.

Thus, Latimer's mode of governing himself shares some common properties with the mode of *A*/Ariadne, whilst also incorporating some very un-Spinozistic components, such as a conscious celebration of 'doubt'. However, just as Latimer's mature consciousness is thus beginning to distinguish itself, evidence of an alternative way in which 'imaginings' might *form themselves* into hardened schemes of thought is thrust upon Latimer's mind in the form of Bertha's suddenly unveiled cognitions. Significantly, both Latimer and Bertha are stripped of certain illusions as Latimer observes 'the light floating vanities of the girl defining themselves into the systematic coquetry, the systematic selfishness of the woman'; just as Latimer witnesses 'petty artifice and mere negation where he had delighted to believe in coy sensibilities and in wit at war with latent feeling', so Bertha discovers that she is becoming increasingly 'powerless' to affect her husband, 'powerless, because [he] . . . was dead . . . to all the incentives within the compass of her narrow imagination, and [he] lived under influences utterly invisible to her' (Eliot 1999: 32).

Eliot's astute presentation of the causes and effect of the absolute inversion of Latimer's and Bertha's capacities to read and affect one another invites a Spinozistic interpretation: as Latimer becomes 'compelled to share the privacy of [Bertha's] motives, [and] to follow all the petty devices that preceded her words and acts', his greater knowledge of the order of Bertha's affections is accompanied by a greater power to guard himself against her web and to determine his own streams of thought (Eliot 1999: 32). At the same time, from the same Spinozistic perspective, Bertha's underlying *conatus* is revealed to be cruder, and her sense of her own boundaries narrower, than those of the idolatrous Ariadne; whereas Ariadne always desired to form a broader whole with Echo, Bertha is fundamentally unable to recognise that 'promoting the real . . . welfare of an extended self properly arises', as Rorty puts it, 'from a rational recognition of interdependence' (Rorty 1991: 370). It is important not to miss a peculiarly Eliotic component of this demonstration of Bertha's disempowerment, however. Rather than emphasising how much Bertha is impeded by her absolute failure to construct a concatenation of 'adequate' ideas about the human good, what Eliot stresses is the fact that Bertha finds Latimer's affections to be 'unmanageable forces': 'with the essential shallowness of a negative, unimaginative nature, she was unable to conceive the fact that sensibilities were anything else than weaknesses' (Eliot 1999: 32). Bertha's is not just a failure to think rationally, but also – and, indeed, more explicitly – a failure to cultivate the capacity to imagine and to feel.

As Spinoza and Eliot have demonstrated, our passions and other 'imaginings' are not unmanageable forces. Although the 'influences' that Latimer lives under are 'utterly invisible', his sensibilities are determined by two unchanging orders: the order of affections and the order of 'adequate' ideas. As soon as our 'imaginings' are afforded an active role in *determining the content* of the exemplar of human nature that we set before ourselves, it becomes far harder to determine which parts of the organism 'should' lead and which parts of the organism 'should' follow (or even be eradicated) than it is for the Spinozist, who endeavours to make her affections acquiesce with the order of 'adequate' ideas. Eliot's fictions therein reveal the virtue of oscillating between two incommensurable modes of ('adequate' and 'inadequate') judgement. As the very endeavour to govern ourselves in accordance with the dictates of reason and the desire to remain informed by our 'partial', passionate interpretations of the world mutually assess one another, that oscillation must neither dissolve into a battle nor resolve itself into a synthesis. Philosophers and ethical literary critics would do well to emulate Eliot's endeavour to maintain that mode of double-consciousness wherein 'adequate' ideas and sound 'imaginings' inform and assess one another, but never blend into a common hue.

## BIBLIOGRAPHY


Atkins, Dorothy (1978), *George Eliot and Spinoza*, Longwood.

Beer, Gillian (1976), 'Myth and the Single-Consciousness: *Middlemarch* and *The Lifted Veil*, in *This Particular Web: Essays on* Middlemarch, Toronto: University of Toronto Press, pp. 90–115.

Eliot, George (1954), *The George Eliot Letters*, vol. 1, ed. Gordon S. Haight, New Haven, CT: Yale University Press.

Eliot, George (1998), *Daniel Deronda*, Oxford: Oxford University Press.

Eliot, George (1999), *The Lifted Veil* and *Brother Jacob*, Oxford: Oxford Paperbacks.

Eliot, George (2000), *Selected Critical Writings*, Oxford: Oxford University Press.

Eliot, George (2003a), *Middlemarch*, Harmondsworth: Penguin Classics.

Eliot, George (2003b), *The Mill on the Floss*, Harmondsworth: Penguin Classics.

Gatens, Moira (2009), 'The Art and Philosophy of George Eliot', *Philosophy and Literature* 33(1), pp. 73–90.

Gatens, Moira, and Genevieve Lloyd (1999), *Collective Imaginings: Spinoza, Past and Present*, London: Routledge.

James, Susan (1997), *Passion and Action: The Emotions in Seventeenth-Century Philosophy*, Oxford: Clarendon.

Levine, George Lewis (2008), *Realism, Ethics and Secularism: Essays on Victorian Literature and Science*, Cambridge: Cambridge University Press.

Lewes, George Henry (1857), *The Biographical History of Philosophy: From its Origin in Greece down to the Present Day*, London: John W. Parker.

Lewes, George Henry (2001), *The Life of Goethe*, Adamant Media.

Lloyd, Genevieve (1994), *Part of Nature: Self Knowledge in Spinoza's* Ethics, Ithaca, NY: Cornell University Press.

Nussbaum, Martha C. (1992), *Love's Knowledge: Essays on Philosophy and Literature*, Oxford: Oxford University Press.

Nussbaum, Martha C. (2003), *Upheavals of Thought: The Intelligence of Emotions*, Cambridge: Cambridge University Press.

Rorty, Amelie (1991), 'Spinoza on the Pathos of Idolatrous Love and the Hilarity of True Love', in Arthur Coleman Danto et al. (eds), *The Philosophy of (Erotic) Love*, Lawrence: University Press of Kansas, pp. 352–71.

Spinoza, Benedictus (1981), *Ethics*, trans. George Eliot, Salzburg: Institut für Anglistik und Amerikanistik, University of Salzburg.

# *10. Coleridge's Ecumenical Spinoza*

NICHOLAS HALMI

In contrast to most of the essays in this collection, mine will neither analyse Spinozan texts nor employ Spinozan concepts nor affirm a continuing Spinozan legacy. While thoroughly grounded in texts, it will have very little directly to say about Spinoza, although in that respect, at least, it has something in common with the Enlightenment reception of Spinoza. Its modest aim is to narrate, with running commentary, a chapter in Spinoza's *Rezeptionsgeschichte*, one whose historical interest consists in both what it contains and what it does not contain.

Let me begin with this latter. One of Samuel Taylor Coleridge's most significant contributions to the intellectual life of nineteenth-century Britain was to serve as a conduit, from German exegetes such as Johann Gottfried Eichhorn, of the so-called higher criticism of the Bible (see Shaffer 1975 and Harding 1985). It might be taken as a sign of how thoroughly this historico-philological analysis of scripture, which provoked the first anti-Spinozan polemics in England in the 1670s because it rejected the normative assumption of divinely inspired authorship, had been assimilated by the early nineteenth century that Coleridge himself passed almost in silence over Spinoza's seminal contribution, in the *Tractatus Theologico-Politicus*, to the development of the higher criticism. But, in fact, Coleridge's aim of reconciling contextualising exegesis with a belief in divinely inspired prophecy was incompatible with Spinoza's consistent rationalism, which rejected the possibility either of special knowledge on the part of the prophets or of any supernatural agency in the composition of scripture (TTP Ch. 8, p. 155).[1]

When he alluded to the *Tractatus* in the *Aids to Reflection*, an elaboration of his 'Spiritual Philosophy', Coleridge was tellingly selective in his recollection, invoking Spinoza by way of differentiating theological mystery from logical absurdity: 'I abide by a maxim, which I learnt at an early period of my theological studies, from Benedict Spinoza. Where an Alternative lies between the Absurd and the Incomprehensible, no wise man can be at a loss which of the two to prefer' (Coleridge [1825] 1993: 338–9). Coleridge was probably referring to Spinoza's refutation of the claim that scripture never expressly contradicts itself (TTP Ch. 15, p. 184), but he could not have endorsed Spinoza's conclusion – in the same chapter of the *Tractatus* – that reason and theology have separate domains, the former concerned with truth and wisdom (*ratio regnum veritatis, & sapientiæ*), the latter with piety and obedience (*Theologia autem pietatis, & obedientiæ*). Although Coleridge was careful to specify, in a work of biblical hermeneutics composed in 1824 and published posthumously under the title *Confessions of an Inquiring Spirit*, that he understood inspiration not as divine dictation but as the revelation of the truths that the scriptural writers expressed of their own accord and by their own means, even this qualified affirmation of inspired authorship implied, as Coleridge himself acknowledged, the 'inappellable authority' of 'whatever is referred by the sacred Penmen to a direct communication from God' (1995: 1130–1).

Equally noteworthy, if unsurprising, is the absence in Coleridge's response to Spinoza of reference to the programmatic concerns that we identify with the Radical Enlightenment, such as the advocacy of religious tolerance, freedom of speech, and democracy. These political commitments will have been no more congenial to Coleridge, as his disillusionment with the course of the French Revolution gradually hardened into a reactionary conservatism, than the uncompromising rationalism of Spinoza's biblical interpretation. Hence the restrictedness of Coleridge's interest to the metaphysical aspects of Spinozism, by which term I mean a congeries of monistic philosophical systems which he or others of his time happened to label Spinozistic, not excluding Spinoza's. Although he shared with Radical Enlightenment figures some of their enthusiasm for Spinozism, the narrow focus of Coleridge's attention, especially with respect to the Spinozan corpus itself, was more characteristic of his late Enlightenment and Romantic era contemporaries in Germany, whose responses to Spinoza were shaped by the so-called *Pantheismusstreit*, the prolonged controversy of the 1780s and 1790s involving many prominent German intellectuals, including Moses Mendelssohn, J. G. Herder, Goethe and, indirectly, Kant.

As for my title, the word *ecumenical* has two principal meanings: the more general one is *belonging to the whole world*, while the more specific one is *belonging to the whole Christian world, or universal church*. The present collection, with contributors from four countries addressing subjects as diverse as music, architecture, literary ethics and the

Haitian revolution, itself testifies to how Spinoza is ecumenical in the broader sense. But I shall address the question of how he was, as interpreted by Coleridge, ecumenical in the narrower sense. Throughout the first three decades of the nineteenth century, Coleridge sought repeatedly to identify Spinoza in one way or another with Christianity and to rescue him from the prolonged anathematisation that, already by the end of the seventeenth century, had made his name synonymous with the word *atheism*. Lecturing on philosophy in London in March 1819, Coleridge informed his auditors that

> the theologic hatred of his name is one of the most incomprehensible parts of philosophic researches; for Spinoza was originally a Jew, and he held the opinions of the most learned Jews, particularly the Cabalistic philosophers. Next, he was of the most pure and exemplary life, and it has been said of him, if he did not think as a Christian, he felt and acted like one. ([1818–19] 2000: 578–9)

To be sure, Spinoza's early biographers had given some licence to the attempt to associate him with Christianity. Johann Colerus, whose biography was reprinted in the edition of the works that Coleridge annotated (Spinoza 1802–3: vol. 2, pp. 591–665), quoted Spinoza's reassurance to his Lutheran landlady that her religion was a good one and she needed no other to be saved (1706: 41–2), while Pierre Bayle, in his *Dictionnaire critique et historique*, reported that Spinoza had 'publicly profest Christianity, and frequented the Assemblies of the Mennonites, or those of the Arminians of Amsterdam' ([1697] (1710): 2799). In the *Tractatus Theologico-Politicus* Spinoza himself, albeit in an exposition of scripture, referred to Jesus as Christ and to his teachings as the assumption of divine wisdom in human nature (*dicere possumus, Sapientiam Dei . . . naturam humanam in Christo assumpsisse*) (Ch. 1, pp. 20–1), thereby prompting Henry Oldenburg to request a clarification of his Christological views (Letter 71 to Spinoza, 15 November 1675).[2]

But as Coleridge will have known at least by November 1813, having read and extensively annotated a set of the *Opera* which included the correspondence with Oldenburg, Spinoza understood the resurrection of Christ to be merely allegorical (Letter 78 to Oldenburg, 7 February 1676) and confessed that the notion of the Incarnation seemed no less absurd to him than the squaring of a circle (*non minus absurdè mihi loqui videntur, quàm si quis mihi diceret, quòd circulus naturam quadrati induerit*) (Letter 73 to Oldenburg, December 1675).[3] Moreover, Coleridge never claimed that Spinoza had actually been a practising Christian, or that his metaphysics were finally conformable to Trinitarianism – on the contrary, he observed consistently and regretfully that they were not. Indeed, this was the case even before the year of his most intensive study of Spinoza: when, for example, he borrowed the *Opera omnia* from his friend Henry Crabb Robinson in November 1812, Coleridge, according to Robinson's diary,

> kissed Spinoza's face at the title-page, said his book was his gospel, and in less than a minute added that his philosophy was, after all, false ... Did philosophy commence in an IT IS instead of an I AM, Spinoza would be altogether true; and without allowing a breathing-time he parenthetically asserted, 'I, however, believe in all the doctrines of Christianity, even of the Trinity.' (Robinson 1938: vol. 1, p. 112)

All the stranger, then, that Coleridge should have sought to mitigate Spinoza's supposed errors on the grounds of his proximity to Christianity, as he did in his philosophical lecture of 22 March 1819:

> And if we come at last to the man's own professions and service, I have no doubt they were [sincere] ... that not only the immediate publishers of Spinoza's writings, but that Spinoza did think that his system was identical with but that of Christianity, on so subtle a point that at least it was pantheism, but in the most religious form in which it could appear. (2000: 578)

Why the importunate appeals to his Christian mode of life; the fierce denunciations of his detractors as less Christian, or at least no more orthodox, than Spinoza himself; the insistence that 'that right Track was glimmering before him, just as it pleased Heaven to remove him' (Coleridge 1995: 610) – which suggests a certain carelessness on the part of the infinite intellect? The most plausible answer, I think, is to be found in Coleridge's conflicted attraction to philosophical monism.

Though large in number and diverse in medium – notebooks, manuscript fragments, marginalia, letters, public lectures, published books – Coleridge's comments on Spinoza are relatively restricted in content and remarkably consistent. Their interest consists less in their exegetic value, for indeed they do not constitute a sustained analysis of the philosophical writings, than in their illustration, on the one hand, of the complexity of Spinoza's *Rezeptionsgeschichte* and, on the other hand, of a fundamental, unresolved conflict of Coleridge's own intellectual life. To the extent that he sought to assimilate Spinoza to Christianity, or at least maintained that the two were not absolutely incompatible, Coleridge confirmed the applicability to himself of the observation he attributed to an unnamed Englishman of his acquaintance: 'I never yet knew ... a single person, whom Spinoza had ever converted to his way of thinking; but I know half a dozen at least who have converted Spinoza to theirs!' (1995: 620).

It was ever thus. In a recent survey of Spinozan scholarship, Simon Duffy has cautioned, by way of criticising Jonathan Israel's assertion of the centrality of Spinoza's philosophy in the Radical Enlightenment, that intellectual history, which examines ideas in their cultural contexts, should not be confused with the history of philosophy, which studies the internal coherence and 'intellectual architecture' of philosophical arguments (2009: 120). For it advances our understanding neither of the philosopher's own thought nor of the powerful associative resonance of his name in the Enlightenment and afterwards to conflate, as Israel is wont to do, what Spinoza actually wrote with what was called Spinozism, which in the event derived largely from Pierre Bayle's hostile presentation of Spinoza as a 'Systematical Atheist' who, in common with many other ancient and modern philosophers, made no distinction between God and the totality of finite things ([1697] 1710: 2781–2; cf. Colie 1957: 67 and Bell 1984: 3–5). The wide diffusion of this account is particularly ironic in light of Bayle's own concession that 'All those, who have little Religion, and don't much scruple to own it, are call'd *Spinozists*' ([1697] 1710: 2798).

Critical attention to the process of reception is especially warranted in Spinoza's case precisely because this process was conducted as much by his antagonists as, or indeed more than, by his admirers. Although you scarcely encounter the terms *atheist* and *pantheist* in academic monographs on Spinoza published in the last forty years, these epithets – especially the former – were frequently applied to him in the eighteenth century and, in turn, strongly affected Coleridge's own response to him. If the reception of Spinoza's philosophy in the century-and-a-half after his death was largely, as Jean-François Moreau has described it, a process of looking into a mirror and finding one's own contradictions revealed in the distorted image (1996: 408), then the image Coleridge confronted was doubly distorted by what earlier generations had claimed to have encountered. Or to change the metaphor: he examined the works of the lens-grinder through lenses ground by others, and we must now retrieve those lenses, long since discarded, if we are to comprehend what he saw.

I have said that Coleridge's view of Spinoza remained remarkably consistent, which is to say conflicted and characterised by special pleading, and this is true of the last three decades of his life, from about 1803 to his death in 1834. But he had become interested in Spinoza even earlier, certainly by the late 1790s, when he was espousing Unitarianism and consequently had no reason to be preoccupied with Spinoza's relation to Christian orthodoxy. The evidence from this period is somewhat sparser than for the richly documented later years of Coleridge's life, and seemingly contradictory. A letter of 30 July 1797, in which Coleridge tells his brother-in-law, Robert Southey, that he is 'sunk in Spinoza' and remains 'as undisturbed as a Toad in a Rock' (1956–71: vol. 1, p. 534), implies that he was reading the philosopher's works at that date, whereas a letter of 7 June 1800 to the chemist Humphry Davy implies that he was planning to do so but had not yet had the opportunity. When, in a letter of Christmas Eve 1799 to Southey, Coleridge professes himself a Spinozist, he does so jokingly: 'My Spinosism (if Spinosism it be and i' faith 'tis very like it) disposed me to consider this big City [Bristol] as that part of the Supreme *One*, which the prophet Moses was allowed to see' (1956–71: vol. 1, p. 551). Eighteen years later, in an anecdote about the government spy sent to monitor him and his friend William Wordsworth in the summer of 1797, Coleridge again made a joke of his Spinozan interests, but this time in order to insinuate the insignificance of his former political radicalism:

> At first [the spy] fancied, that we were aware of our danger; for he often heard me talk of one *Spy Nozy*, which he was inclined to interpret of himself, and of a remarkable feature belonging to him; but he was speedily convinced that it was the name of a man who had made a book and lived long ago. ([1817] 1983: vol. 1, p. 194)

Admittedly that anecdote is too contrived to be entirely plausible, although the spy was real – he reported back to the Home Office that the two democrats were harmless – and the feeble pun on Spinoza's name had appeared in Coleridge's notebooks as early as 1799 (1957–2002: vol. 1, no. 422).

However unreliable the evidence from Coleridge himself concerning his early engagement with Spinozan or Spinozistic thought, it is supplemented by that from Clement Carlyon, an Englishman who met Coleridge in Göttingen in 1799 and described their conversations in the first volume of his autobiography of 1836. Not only were 'the doctrines of Spinoza' said 'to prevail . . . among the literati of the North of Germany' (i.e. Lutheran Germany), the scandalised Carlyon recalls, but they were frequently discussed by Coleridge, who explained to his friends that the

> great principle of Spinozism is, that there is nothing properly and absolutely existing but matter, and the modifications of matter; among which are even comprehended thought, abstract and general ideas, comparisons, relations, combinations of relations. (1836: 194)

As a recreation of conversations conducted almost four decades earlier, Carlyon's extract will not bear close analysis. But taken in conjunction with the 'concentrated definition of Spinozism' that he attributes to Coleridge – namely, that 'Each thing has a life of its own, and we are all one life' (Carlyon 1836: 193) – the reference to 'combinations of relations' suggests that the source of Coleridge's 1790s version of Spinozism was less likely Spinoza's works themselves than Joseph Priestley's elaboration of David Hartley's associationism (Perry 1999: 112–16).

Whereas Hartley himself, fearful of having to abandon the idea of the immaterial soul, had been unwilling to commit himself fully to a materialist theory of consciousness, Priestley had no compunction about doing so, arguing that man is composed of a single substance comprising both material and mental attributes (1782: vol. 1, pp. xix–xx). Coleridge will have been initially attracted to Priestley's theory because it seemed to resolve the problem of mind–body dualism, as Hartley's qualified materialism manifestly did not. A letter of 1794 to Southey makes Coleridge's allegiance explicit: 'I go farther than Hartley and believe the corporeality of *thought* – namely, that it is motion' (1956–71: vol. 1, p. 137).

What followed from this materialist explanation of thought was a materialist explanation of divinity. For if, Priestley reasoned, we cannot account for our own thought except in terms of the properties and powers of matter (since to do otherwise would be to admit an insuperable dualism), then still less can we account for God in other terms (since to do so would be to deny the distinction between the immaterial and the material). The 'Divine Being' (Priestley's preferred term for the deity) and the world are not essentially different because he, or it, could not act upon the world if he were not also in some sense material; and everything that exists and happens in the world must be owing to him: 'matter is, by this means, resolved into nothing but the divine *agency* exerted according to certain rules' (1782: vol. 1, p. 39). And if, Priestley continued with studied casualness, 'every thing is really *done* by the divine power, what material objection can there be to every thing *being* the divine power?' (1782: vol. 1, p. 40). Just as the individual consciousness is one with the world, so the world is one with God. In 'Religious Musings', a poem of 1794, and in his contribution to *Joan of Arc*, a poem of 1795 co-written with Southey, Coleridge versified the Priestleyan conception of divinity and its implication for human self-understanding: ''tis God | Diffus'd thro' all, that doth make all one whole,' he explained in 'Religious Musings' (lines 139–40, in Coleridge 2003: 25), and ''Tis the sublime of man, | Our noontide Majesty, to know ourselves | Parts and proportions of one wond'rous whole!' (lines 135–7). Hence the effusion of *Joan of Arc*:

Glory to Thee, FATHER and Earth and Heaven!
All-conscious PRESENCE of the Universe!
Nature's vast ever-acting ENERGY!
In will, in deed, IMPULSE of All to all.

> (2.442–5, in Coleridge 2001: vol. 1, p. 223; cf. Piper 1962: 32)

Priestley published the first edition of his *Disquisitions Relating to Matter and Spirit* in 1777 and the second, from which I have been quoting, in 1782. One notable addition to the second edition is a sentence expressly dissociating Priestley's monism from Spinoza's:

> Nor indeed, is making the deity to *be*, as well as to *do* every thing, *in this sense*, any thing like the opinion of Spinoza; because I suppose a source of infinite power, and superior intelligence, from which all inferior beings are derived; that every inferior intelligent being has a consciousness distinct from that of the supreme intelligence, and that they will for ever continue distinct. (1782: vol. 1, p. 42)

Notwithstanding this disclaimer, of which he may in the event have been unaware, Coleridge evidently did consider Priestley's metaphysics to be a kind of Spinozism, and he became increasingly critical of it in the latter half of the 1790s because of what he considered its lack of self-consistency and its unsatisfactory provision for explaining the existence of evil. (He also grew dissatisfied with his own 'Religious Musings', fearing, he acknowledged, that it could 'easily be misconstrued into Spinosism' (Coleridge 1956–71: vol. 3, p. 467).) Precisely by trying to reduce thought to matter, and thereby transforming matter into 'a mere modification of intelligence', as Coleridge later elaborated in the *Biographia Literaria*, Priestley had undermined his own stated position: 'He stript matter of all its material properties; substituted spiritual powers; and when we expected to find a body, behold! we had nothing but its ghost! the *apparition* of a defunct substance' ([1817] 1983: vol. 1, p. 136).

Already in March 1796, when he was still calling himself a necessitarian, Coleridge confided in a letter his difficulty reconciling Priestley's theism with his materialist monism: 'How is it that Dr Priestley is not an atheist? – He asserts in three different Places, that God not only *does*, but *is*, every thing. But if God *be* every thing, every Thing is God: – which is all, the Atheists assert – ' (1956–71: vol. 1, p. 192). The pressure of that question grew more insistent in the following years, and finally intolerable in April 1799, when Coleridge, then attending lectures in Göttingen, received word that his infant son Berkeley (named after the philosopher) had died back in England. In a consolatory letter to his wife he wrote, 'But the living God is every where, & works every where – and where is there room for Death? . . . I confess that the more

I think, the more I am discontented with the doctrines of Priestley'
(1956–71: vol. 1, p. 482). This reflection augurs a crucial turning-point
in Coleridge's intellectual life, after which he was no longer prepared
to accept what Thomas McFarland has unkindly called Priestley's
'bargain-basement Spinozism' (1969: 169).

After returning from Germany in July 1799 with a good command of
the language, Coleridge, while maintaining an interest in British theolo-
gians, devoted himself increasingly to the study of Continental, particularly German, philosophers, from Fichte and Kant in the first decade
of the nineteenth century to Schelling and various *Naturphilosophen*
associated with Schelling in the second decade. A serious, if as yet
unspecific, interest in Spinoza manifested itself in Coleridge's plan,
sketched out in notebook entries of November 1799 and October
1803, to compose a poem on the Dutch philosopher that would address
the possibility of multiplicity, or 'multeity' to use Coleridge's own
word, within unity:

> If I begin a poem of Spinoza, thus it should begin /
>   I would make a pilgrimage to the burning sands of Arabia, or &c &c to
> find the Man who could explain to me there can be *oneness*, there being
> infinite Perceptions – yet there must be a *oneness*, not an intense Union but
> absolute Unity . . . (1957–2002: vol. 1, no. 556; cf. no. 1561)

Presumably Spinoza is the man he would have encountered. But
whether it was a lack of sufficient knowledge of his works or the sheer
improbability of encountering him in the Arabian desert that dissuaded
Coleridge from realising his plan, I don't know. That he quoted a
sentence, without discussion of its context, from Spinoza's *Tractatus
Politicus* in a newspaper article of 12 October 1802 – *Sedulo curavimus
humanas res et actiones humanas non ridere, non lugere, neque dete-
stari; sed intelligere* ('We have taken care not to ridicule, deplore or
denounce human affairs and actions, but to understand them') – may
or may not indicate that he had access to a copy of the *Opera post-
huma* by that date (TP 1.4; Coleridge 1978: vol. 1, p. 363). What is
certain, however, is that by the end of the decade Coleridge recognised
in Spinoza's monism the only intellectually viable alternative to Kant's
transcendental idealism: 'Only two *Systems* of Philosophy – (sibi con-
sistentia) possible 1. Spinoza 2 Kant, i.e. the absolute & the relative,
the κατ' οντα, and the κατ' ανθρωπον. or 1 ontological, 2 the anthropological' (1957–2002: vol. 3, no. 3756). That is one of three notebook
entries devoted to Spinoza in the spring of 1810, and the defensiveness
on Spinoza's behalf in the others (one of which I shall discuss presently)

indicates that he felt himself on the horns of a dilemma, compelled but reluctant to make a choice and therefore taking provisional refuge in a fudge. Here, then, we can mark the beginning of his Christianisation of Spinoza, an effort that, however implausible in itself, becomes comprehensible when considered in the broader context of Coleridge's intellectual life.

In the first volume of the *Biographia Literaria*, a self-justificatory exercise that far outgrew its originally intended function as the preface to an edition of his collected poems, Coleridge presented his philosophical investigations up to 1815, the year he dictated the work, as a search for 'a total and undivided philosophy' ([1817] 1983: vol. 1, pp. 282–3) in which, on the one hand, the original identity of subject and object could be assumed as the ground of knowledge, and, on the other hand, free will could be assumed as the ground of ethics. Retracing his path from associationism and materialism ('unintelligible') through Cartesian dualism ('long since exploded') and hylozoism ('the death of all rational physiology') to Fichte's subjective idealism ('crude egoismus') and finally to Schelling's identity philosophy, in the last of which he finds for the time being a 'genial coincidence' with his own conclusions ([1817] 1983: vol. 1, p. 160) – a coy reference to the numerous plagiarisms from Schelling in the *Biographia* – Coleridge distinguishes two broadly opposed classes of philosophical system, the realist and the idealist.

Appropriating Coleridge's own homelier designations for these classes from the remark to Crabb Robinson that I quoted earlier, Thomas McFarland argues that Coleridge was able to settle the competing claims of the principles of 'it is' and 'I am' only by foregoing systematic philosophy for an emotional commitment to Trinitarian Christianity. In this account, the conflict Coleridge described in the *Biographia*, that 'my head was with Spinoza, though my whole heart remained with Paul and John' ([1817] 1983: vol. 1, p. 201), contained within itself the eventual resolution to his fundamental philosophical dilemma. But in so far as Kant's critical philosophy, by opposing philosophical dogmatism and excluding metaphysics from the realm of knowledge, urged Coleridge towards his *confessio fidei*, the 'Trinitarian resolution', as McFarland calls it, amounted to a victory for the philosophy of 'I am': 'Christianity, as an expansion of the "I am", was Coleridge's lifelong commitment, in philosophical as well as religious terms' (McFarland 1969: 251). To McFarland, whose attitude towards Coleridge is rather like that of a spectator shouting encouragement to an exhausted runner in the final stretch of a marathon, the concept of the Trinity not only anchored Coleridge's 'complete system

... in an extramundane ground without abandoning the reality of the natural world', but also deepened his understanding 'of the "I am" starting-point' (1969: 227).

Attractive as this interpretation is in its neatness, it exaggerates the clarity of Coleridge's distinction between the 'it is' and 'I am' philosophies, and hence between Spinozism and Christianity. To be sure, McFarland follows Coleridge himself in tending to treat the classification *pantheist* as a natural kind, hence self-explanatory, which is why he can refer to 'the pantheist tradition' with no more self-reflexivity than Coleridge displays in collocating 'the Proclo-plotinian Platonists' and 'their Spinosistic imitators, the nature-philosophers of the present Germany' under the rubric of pantheism (1980–2001: vol. 3, p. 909; cf. 1957–2002: vol. 3, no. 4497). Both in this respect are the indirect heirs of Bayle, who began his article on Spinoza by declaring that 'the substance of his Doctrine was the same with that of many Ancient and Modern Philosophers, both in *Europe* and in Eastern Countries' ([1697] 1710: 2782). The consequence of such a capacious conception of pantheism can readily be seen, to take a non-Spinozan example, in Coleridge's inability to appreciate that Plotinus maintained the absolute transcendence of the One from which he considered the world to emanate. (Arguably, Plotinus's hostility to Christianity on the one hand and to Gnosticism on the other impelled him to resort, by way of distinction, and however reluctantly or qualifiedly, to the metaphorics of emanationism, with its appearance of an ontological monism.) A more restricted conception, or at least one that did not, in effect, serve as the hermeneutic instrument of an inherited prejudice, might have spared Coleridge some of the intellectual quandaries he suffered when he read thinkers to whom he was attracted but of whom he thought he ought not to approve. Still, his response to Spinoza himself was often more complex than McFarland acknowledges.

It would be consistent with the account of a Trinitarian resolution to the choice between realism and idealism if Coleridge, having been content to call himself a Spinozist in his Unitarian youth, and probably before having read Spinoza, had then been at pains to reject Spinozism in his Trinitarian maturity, and especially after having read the philosopher's works. But the facts do not conform so tidily to that narrative. Consider, for example, a comment on F. H. Jacobi's *Über die Lehre des Spinoza*, the book (first published in 1785, though Coleridge read the expanded second edition of 1789) which inaugurated the *Pantheismusstreit* by revealing that the much-admired, recently deceased playwright, G. E. Lessing, an exemplary figure of the German Enlightenment, had professed himself a Spinozist in private conversations with Jacobi. Jacobi's own primary concern had been neither Lessing nor Spinoza, but rationalism, of which he took Spinoza's *Ethics* to be the most perfect expression. Assuming the universal applicability of the principle of sufficient reason, a consistent rationalism must be deterministic and fatalistic, Jacobi asserted, and thus incompatible with the belief in a self-caused God and the freedom of the will. Spinozism could not therefore be dismissed as a harmlessly obscure and incoherent metaphysical doctrine, for, in fact, it made manifest the atheism latent in all rationalist philosophy. Thus its espousal by someone considered a representative of Enlightenment, an assessment with which Jacobi did not disagree, was a sign precisely of the Enlightenment's moral bankruptcy.

Now one would expect Coleridge to have found this a compelling argument, not least because he had rejected Priestley's necessitarianism on account of its ethical implications. But instead Coleridge sought either to defend the Dutch philosopher from the charge of atheism or, when he himself made the same charge, to qualify it strongly. Responding to Jacobi in the margin of Robinson's copy of Spinoza's works (rather than in his own copy of *Über die Lehre des Spinoza*), Coleridge insisted, with regard to the finite causality affirmed in the *Ethics* (E IP28), according to which every finite thing is determined by an infinite series of finite causes,

> If these finite Causes can be said to act at all, then that on which they act has an equal power of action – : and even as tho' all in God *essentially*, we are yet each *existentially* individual, so we must have freedom in God in exact proportion to our Individuality. It is most necessary to distinguish Spinosism from Spinosa – i.e. the ~~imaginary~~ consequences of the immanence in God as the one only necessary Being whose essence involves existence, with the deductions from Spinosa's own mechanic *realistic* view of the World. Even in the latter, I cannot accord with Jacobi's assertion, that Spinosism as taught by Spinosa, is Atheism / for tho' he will not consent to call things essentially disparate by the same name, and therefore denies human intelligence to ~~the~~ Deity, yet he adores his *Wisdom* . . . It is true, he contends for Necessity; but then he makes two disparate Classes of Necessity, the one identical with ~~Freedom~~ Liberty (even as the Christian Doctrine, 'whose service is perfect Freedom') the other Compulsion = Slavery . . . (Coleridge 1980–2001: vol. 5, pp. 207–8; cf. Jacobi [1785] 2000: 118)

Coleridge seems here to infer from Proposition 28 of Book I a distinction that Spinoza did not explicitly make, between absolute or logical necessity and merely causal necessity. The *essential* is that which, as an attribute of substance or an infinite mode from which a law of nature follows, could not be otherwise, whereas the *existential* is that which, although the result of a particular series of causes, is not itself necessitated by the general features of the universe and could conceivably, given a different causal series, be otherwise. From this possibility of the contingency of particularities in the universe – a possibility whose admissibility is still contested among interpreters of the *Ethics* (see, for example, Curley 1988: 49–50 and Bennett 1996: 74–6) – Coleridge comes as close as he was ever to do to detecting in the *Ethics* a provision for individual freedom of will, such freedom being the basis of the individual's expression, through moral action, of a love of God. Having identified this mitigation of Spinoza's necessitarianism, Coleridge is momentarily content to explain away the rest by reference to the contemporary philosophical context: 'But never has a great Man been so hardly and inequitably treated by Posterity, as Spinosa – No allowance made for the prevalence, nay, universality of Dogmatism & the mechanic System in his age' (1980–2001: vol. 5, p. 208). Evidently Spinoza's necessitarianism followed necessarily from his philosophical milieu.

The observation of Spinoza's refusal to concede personhood to God, even in a metaphorical sense, anticipates what would soon become Coleridge's fundamental objection to Spinoza's metaphysics. But his special pleading on behalf of that metaphysics did not cease after he had returned the *Opera omnia*, now heavily annotated, to Crabb Robinson in November 1813. The differentiation of Spinozan monism from conventional pantheism figures in the *Biographia Literaria*, where Spinoza is unexpectedly aligned with the theosophist Jakob Böhme and the Quaker George Fox, 'mystics' whom Coleridge credits with having enabled him 'to skirt, without crossing, the sandy deserts of utter unbelief' ([1817] 1983: vol. 1, pp. 149–50). To McFarland this means no more than that both Böhme and Fox were, like Spinoza himself, representatives of the errant philosophy whose temptations Coleridge successfully resisted (1969: 245–6, 249–51). That is the negative version of an interpretation to which Frederick Beiser would offer the positive counterpart: what McFarland and Beiser share is the broad understanding of pantheism characteristic of the late Enlightenment itself. To Beiser the linking to Spinoza of Böhme and Fox, both of whom express their inner conviction of God's presence, would be perfectly comprehensible because he regards the rise of Spinozism in the German Radical Enlightenment as the secular reassertion of the Protestant Counter-Reformation: if Spinoza had undermined the authority of the Bible, he had also preserved the possibility of realising Luther's ideal of the immediate subjective experience of God. Indeed, Spinoza enhanced that possibility, Beiser argues, precisely because he removed the obstacles of a transcendent deity and a difficult sacred text (1987: 50–2).

Coleridge's Spinoza, however, is not secular, and if not exactly Protestant, is trying to be so. His connection with the mystics, then, likely consists in Coleridge's sense that the geometric demonstration of the unity of God and nature demanded an affective supplement, which is exactly what the mystics, with their intuition of the divine presence, supplied. This interpretation would also account for Coleridge's frequent references to Spinoza's system as a '*Skeleton* of the Truth' (for example, [1818] 1969: vol. 1, p. 54n, and 1956–71: vol. 4, p. 775). Just as Kant, in the third *Critique*, conceded to aesthetic judgement the possibility of enabling a transition in thinking from knowledge to morality, thus making the suprasensible ideas of reason real in the sensible world, so perhaps Coleridge hoped that feeling would make intuitible what reason had established to be necessary. In other words, the mystics' feeling might make Spinoza's 'dry Bones live' (1956–71: vol. 4, p. 548). If that is correct, then the pairing of Fox and Böhme with Spinoza – a pairing that Coleridge made on at least two occasions in addition to that in the *Biographia* – would attest to the same need that found expression, not only in Coleridge's writings but also pre-eminently in Goethe's and Schelling's, in the theorisation of the natural symbol in which sign and meaning are ontologically connected: that is, the aesthetic objectification to the subject of its theoretically posited unity with the world of objects (see Halmi 2007). Yet it was one thing to argue for the theoretical necessity of such a symbol, as a constitutive element in the structure of nature itself, and another altogether to see it actually manifested in natural phenomena. To the extent that a Spinozistic monism permitted the assumption of the primordial unity of subject and object in the infinite substance, it promised a solution to the impasses represented by Kant's dualism and Fichte's subjectivism. But it was still susceptible to the same objection, *mutatis mutandis*, that Hans Blumenberg once noted as counting against the architectonic of Fichte's *Wissenschaftslehre*: explaining the world as the self-objectification of the subject in reflection does not guarantee that the world will conform to one's wishes (1979: 298).

To return to the *Biographia*, the logic of Coleridge's alignment of Spinoza with the mystics is peculiar, for he concedes, on the one hand, that the thought of the latter 'is capable of being converted into an irreligious PANTHEISM' – a point he makes also in his marginalia on Böhme – and insists, on the other, that Spinoza's *Ethics* is not '*in itself* and *essentially* . . . incompatible with religion, natural or revealed' ([1817] 1983: vol. 1, p. 152). Are we meant to conclude that the ostensibly atheist Spinoza is actually more amenable to religious belief – or, more specifically, provides a more compelling assurance of the divine presence in the world – than the avowedly religious mystics? It is as if, having skirted the desert with Böhme and Fox, Coleridge were now prepared to plunge into it in search of Spinoza.

Perhaps he was engaging in the rhetorical equivalent of a bait-and-switch tactic, transferring the association with pantheism from Spinoza to the Christian mystics in order to render the contemplation of Spinoza's system more acceptable. If so, it is a stratagem to which he resorted again in letters condemning '*Modern* Calvinism' as a kind of Spinozism that lacks 'the noble honesty, that majesty of openness, so delightful in Spinoza, which made him scorn all attempts to varnish over fair consequence' (1956–71: vol. 4, p. 548), and Unitarianism (which he had long since disavowed) as 'far, very far worse . . . than the Atheism of Spinoza' (1956–71: vol. 6, p. 893). Better a wolf in wolf's clothing.

> Why in the instance of Spinoza alone [Coleridge fumed in a manuscript note of 1817–18] should [it] be thought *suspicious* to extract the medicinal and praise what is praise-worthy? Or is he fixed at the summit of the temple of Heterodoxy as a Conductor, which attracting all the Lightning of our Odium Theologicum towards itself procures an immunity for the Fabric at large . . . ? (1995: 616)

What he meant by 'the Fabric at large' is explained by a notebook entry in which he contrasted Spinoza favourably with 'the Voltaires, Humes, and the whole mob of *popular* Infidels' – Hume, in particular, deserving such opprobrium because, in the *Treatise of Human Nature*, he had mischievously invoked Spinoza's 'universally infamous' doctrine of the single substance in order to ridicule the idea of the immortality of the soul ([1739] 1978: 240–1). Yet, as Richard Berkeley has noticed, Coleridge's appeals to Spinoza's Christian virtues are curiously irrelevant, in that they do not pertain to the content of his metaphysics except in excusing its errors as the consequence of his purported innocence (2006: 8–9).

An extraordinary passage from a note Coleridge left in manuscript serves synecdochically to illustrate this point. Composed in 1817–18, the note draws on Colerus and defends Spinoza by referring not only to his saintly life but to his rebarbative writing style, calculated to ward off casual seekers of heterodoxy:

> Consult his Life by COLERUS, who knew Spinoza personally, lived near him, and collected his materials on the Spot. Himself a strictly orthodox Divine, he speaks of Spinoza's Opinions . . . with at least sufficient Horror: but he did not therefore omit to refute every charge, every calumnious rumour, against his Character as a *man*: and . . . he records the blameless innocence of his Life, his inobtrusive sincerity and his solicitude not to disturb, nay, his anxiety to second, the unquestioning faith and pious

exercises of the simple-hearted . . . Nay, he expressed not only his doubts, but his reluctance to the publication of his MSS . . . in the most innoxious way, namely, in Latin & in the driest, austerest, and most inattractive form, adopted from the method of Geometry, and so free from the least wanton offence against the feelings of his age and [country], so reverential in his use of terms held in reverence by others, that Ludovicus Meyer, the Editor, appears to have seriously believed the tenets of his Master to be in all essentials co-incident with the doctrines of Christianity, as declared in the Gospel of John, and the epistles of S[t] Paul: nor do we possess any satisfactory proof, that Spinoza himself thought otherwise. (1995: 610)

Coleridge's defence is thus founded on two distinct claims: first, that in his innocence and single-minded philosophical rigour, Spinoza formulated a metaphysical doctrine without regard to its implications for the foundations of morality; and second, that the resultant 'errors' of this doctrine were venial in nature. Variations of this defence, as we have seen, recur throughout Coleridge's later writings, and as late as 1830 – in the same conversation from which I quoted in note 3 – he is supposed to have expressed his conviction that Spinoza 'was on the borders of truth, and would no doubt had he lived have attained it' (1990: vol. 1, p. 557).

In the event, however, Coleridge's enduring attraction and insurmountable objection to Spinoza's metaphysics were both rooted in its demonstration of the logical necessity of the single substance. This dilemma found expression in a characteristically Coleridgean footnote to a letter of 1815 to the publisher John Gutch:

> Spinoza's is a World with one Pole only, & consequently no Equator. Had he commenced either with the natura naturata, as the Objective Pole, or at the 'I per se I' as the Subjective Pole – he must necessarily in either case have arrived at the Equator, or Identity of Subject and Object – and thence instead of *a* God, = the one only Substance, at which all finite Things are the modes and accidents, he would have revealed to himself the doctrine of The Living God, having the Ground of his own Existence within himself, and the originating Principle of all dependent Existence in his Will and Word. (Coleridge 1956–71: vol. 4, p. 548)

While satisfying what reason demanded, the dissolution of subject–object dualism, Spinozan monism denied what morality required, a voluntaristic conception of God. For once Coleridge had determined that the only possible guarantor of the free will of individual humans was that of a transcendent but personalised deity, he could never fully accept Spinoza's allegedly unipolar conception of God. Referring in a note of c. 1817–18 to the 'unica Substantia infinitis Attributis' as defined in the *Ethics* (although that particular formulation is never used in the work), Coleridge lamented that Spinoza's 'error consisted not so much in what he affirms, as in what he has omitted to affirm or rashly denied . . . that he saw God in the ground *only* and exclusively, in his *Might* alone and his *essential* Wisdom, and not likewise in his moral, intellectual, existential and personal Godhead' (1995: 609). In short, the *Ethics* lacked the theoretical basis for an ethics.

As we saw earlier, it follows from the distinction between the essential (unconditionally necessary) and the existential (contingently necessary) – a distinction that Coleridge himself, with perhaps excessive interpretive generosity, conceded to the *Ethics* – that the Spinozan God, as the eternal actualisation of the universe, need not impinge upon the temporal actualisation of events, so that individual *qua* finite mode might indeed possess the freedom to actualise itself. But to Coleridge this possibility, to the extent that he seriously entertained it, was insufficiently consolatory because it excluded the existential from the deity itself: the infinite substance required the supplement of an absolute will. Accordingly, Coleridge sought in the abortive *Opus Maximum*, the broad aim of which was to reconcile faith with reason, to demonstrate the necessary existence of the divine will ([1819–23] 2002: 11). But in so far as that will was conceived by analogy to human will – 'the same power but in a higher dignity', as Coleridge himself asserted ([1819–23] 2002: 11), the Coleridgean God exhibited exactly the anthropomorphism that Spinoza had ridiculed in the Appendix to Part 1 of the *Ethics*. What Coleridge wanted, finally, was an infinite substance with a human face.

In that respect, his self-contradictory Christianisation of Spinoza was consistent with his engagement with systematic philosophy generally, and particularly with Schelling's. The fundamental conflict in Coleridge's mature intellectual career was, as Christoph Bode has accurately summarised it, the systematic incompatibility of his religious convictions with 'the philosophical materials [he] assembled from various sources to give substance to his own deliberations or to impress his audiences and readership' (2009: 610). The true object of the special pleading that Coleridge conducted on Spinoza's behalf was not the Dutch philosopher, therefore, but the Highgate sage himself. For it was Coleridge's persistent, if unrealised and indeed unrealisable, hope to become himself the Christian Spinoza, giving Christianity a systematic philosophical foundation while deriving systematic philosophy from a Trinitarian conception of a personalised God. The wistful hope of squaring the circle, so to speak, in a philosophically coherent and religiously satisfying way continued to manifest itself in Coleridge's statements about Spinoza to the end of his life. While acknowledging in a notebook of March 1832, 'If like Spinoza, I had contemplated God as the infinite Substance (Substantia Unica) as the incomprehensible mindless, lifeless, formless *Substans* of all Mind, Life and Form – there would be for me neither Good nor Evil – Yet Pain, & Misery would *be* – & would be hopeless' (1957–2002: vol. 5, no. 6659), Coleridge could nonetheless express in a letter of the same month, without obvious irony, the hope of encountering Spinoza's spirit in heaven, 'with St. John and St. Paul smiling on him and loving him' (1956–71: vol. 6, p. 893). The implication, which hardly needed to be stated, is that Coleridge himself hoped to be equally smiling and smiled on.

If Coleridge was consistently drawn to dichotomising, to the extent that his most enduring contributions to critical theory are the distinctions he formulated himself or adapted from others (e.g. imagination versus fancy, imitation versus copy, organic versus mechanical form, symbol versus allegory), he was just as consistently unable to constrain his thought by a dichotomous logic. Having identified two mutually exclusive intellectual positions, he might try simultaneously to adopt both while nonetheless accepting the truth of their mutual exclusivity. Coleridge's engagement with Spinoza is one example of such a situation, the 'it is' and 'I am' circling each other endlessly, the finite modes, one might say, of his infinite irresolution.

## NOTES

1. Spinoza's writings and letters to him are cited from Spinoza 1925.
2. The interpretive difficulties presented by Spinoza's obscure pronouncements on Christ in the *Tractatus Theologico-Politicus* and correspondence with Oldenburg are discussed by Mason 1997: 209–23 and Nadler 1999: 290–1.
3. In a conversation of 1830 recorded in his posthumously published *Table Talk*, Coleridge alluded to Spinoza's incomprehension of the Incarnation:

> he said that if the Logos could be manifested in the flesh, it must converse and act as Jesus did. At the same time his notions of a God were very Pantheistic . . . He had no notion of a Conscious Being of God – but with these ideas to talk of God becoming flesh appears to me very much like talking of a square circle. (1990: vol. 1, pp. 556–7)

## BIBLIOGRAPHY

Bayle, Pierre [1697] (1710), 'Spinoza (Benedict de)', in P. Bayle, *An Historical and Critical Dictionary*, London: for C. Harper [et al.], vol. 4, pp. 2781–805.

Beiser, Frederick (1987), *The Fate of Reason: German Philosophy from Kant to Fichte*, Cambridge, MA: Harvard University Press.

Bell, David (1984), *Spinoza in Germany from 1670 to the Age of Goethe*, London: Institute of Germanic Studies.

Bennett, Jonathan (1996), 'Spinoza's Metaphysics', in D. Garrett (ed.), *The Cambridge Companion to Spinoza*, Cambridge: Cambridge University Press.

Berkeley, Richard (2006), 'The Providential Wreck: Coleridge and Spinoza's Metaphysics', *European Romantic Review* 14, pp. 457–75.

Blumenberg, Hans (1979), *Arbeit am Mythos*, Frankfurt am Main: Suhrkamp.

Bode, Christoph (2009), 'Coleridge and Philosophy', in F. Burwick (ed.), *The Oxford Handbook of Samuel Taylor Coleridge*, Oxford: Oxford University Press, pp. 588–619.

Carlyon, Clement (1836), *Early Years and Late Recollections*, London: Whittaker.

Coleridge, Samuel Taylor (1956–71), *Collected Letters*, ed. E. L. Griggs, 6 vols, Oxford: Clarendon.

Coleridge, Samuel Taylor (1957–2002), *Notebooks*, ed. K. Coburn, M. Christensen and A. J. Harding, 5 vols, London: Routledge.

Coleridge, Samuel Taylor [1818] (1969), *The Friend*, ed. B. Rooke, 2 vols, Princeton: Princeton University Press.

Coleridge, Samuel Taylor (1978), *Essays on His Times*, ed. D. V. Erdman, 3 vols, Princeton: Princeton University Press.

Coleridge, Samuel Taylor (1980–2001), *Marginalia*, ed. G. Whalley and H. J. Jackson, 6 vols, Princeton: Princeton University Press.

Coleridge, Samuel Taylor [1817] (1983), *Biographia Literaria*, ed. J. Engell and W. J. Bate, 2 vols, Princeton: Princeton University Press.

Coleridge, Samuel Taylor (1990), *Table Talk*, ed. Carl Woodring, 2 vols, Princeton: Princeton University Press.

Coleridge, Samuel Taylor [1825] (1993), *Aids to Reflection*, ed. J. Beer, Princeton: Princeton University Press.

Coleridge, Samuel Taylor (1995), *Shorter Works and Fragments*, ed. H. J. Jackson and J. R. de J. Jackson, Princeton: Princeton University Press.

Coleridge, Samuel Taylor [1818–19] (2000), *Lectures on the History of Philosophy*, ed. J. R. de J. Jackson, Princeton: Princeton University Press.

Coleridge, Samuel Taylor (2001), *Poetical Works*, ed. J. C. C. Mays, 6 vols, Princeton: Princeton University Press.

Coleridge, Samuel Taylor [1819–23] (2002), *Opus Maximum*, ed. T. McFarland and N. Halmi, Princeton: Princeton University Press.

Coleridge, Samuel Taylor (2003), *Coleridge's Poetry and Prose*, ed. N. Halmi, P. Magnuson and R. Modiano, New York: Norton.

Colerus, Johann (1706), *The Life of Benedict de Spinosa*, London: Benjamin Bragg.

Colie, Rosalie (1957), *Light and Enlightenment: A Study of the Cambridge Platonists and the Dutch Arminians*, Cambridge: Cambridge University Press.

Curley, Edwin (1988), *Behind the Geometric Method: A Reading of Spinoza's 'Ethics'*, Princeton: Princeton University Press.

Duffy, Simon (2009), 'Spinoza Today: The Current State of Spinoza Scholarship', *Intellectual History Review* 19, pp. 111–32.

Halmi, Nicholas (2007), *The Genealogy of the Romantic Symbol*, Oxford: Oxford University Press.

Harding, A. J. (1985), *Coleridge and the Inspired Word*, Montreal: McGill-Queen's University Press.

Hume, David [1739] (1978), *A Treatise of Human Nature*, ed. L. A. Selby-Bigge and P. H. Nidditch, 2nd edn, Oxford: Clarendon.

Jacobi, Friedrich Heinrich [1785] (2000), *Über die Lehre des Spinoza in Briefen an den Herrn Moses Mendelssohn*, ed. M. Lauschke, Hamburg: Meiner.

Mason, Richard (1997), *The God of Spinoza: A Philosophical Study*, Cambridge: Cambridge University Press.

McFarland, Thomas (1969), *Coleridge and the Pantheist Tradition*, Oxford: Clarendon.

Moreau, Jean-François (1996), 'Spinoza's Reception and Influence', in D. Garrett (ed.), *The Cambridge Companion to Spinoza*, Cambridge: Cambridge University Press, pp. 408–33.

Nadler, Steven (1999), *Spinoza: A Life*, Cambridge: Cambridge University Press.

Perry, Seamus (1999), *Coleridge and the Uses of Division*, Oxford: Clarendon.

Piper, H. W. (1962), *The Active Universe: Pantheism and the Concept of Imagination in the English Romantic Poets*, London: Athlone.

Priestley, Joseph (1782), *Disquisitions relating to Matter and Spirit*, 2nd edn, 2 vols, Birmingham: for J. Johnson.

Robinson, Henry Crabbe (1938), *Henry Crabb Robinson on Books and their Writers*, ed. E. J. Morley, 3 vols, London: Dent.

Shaffer, E. S. (1975), *'Kubla Khan' and 'The Fall of Jerusalem': The Mythological School in Biblical Criticism and Secular Literature, 1770–1880*, Cambridge: Cambridge University Press.

Spinoza, Benedictus de (1802–3), *Opera quae supersunt omnia*, ed. H. E. G. Paulus, 2 vols, Jena: Akademische Buchhandlung.

Spinoza, Benedictus de (1925), *Opera*, ed. Carl Gebhardt, 4 vols, Heidelberg: Carl Winter.

# Notes on Contributors

**Lance Brewer** lives and works in Oakland, California. He was educated at the Skowhegan School of Painting and Sculpture (where he was also artist-in-residence) and the California College of the Arts. He has recently exhibited his work at galleries in Oakland and Skowhegan and at the San Diego Art Fair.

**Simon Calder** is a lecturer at the University of Minnesota. In 2011 he completed a doctoral thesis on George Eliot, Ludwig Feuerbach and Baruch Spinoza in the Faculty of English at the University of Cambridge. He is currently composing a book on George Eliot and the ethics of fiction-making.

**Shelley Campbell** is a doctoral candidate in Philosophy at the University of Gloucestershire. For her thesis, she is researching the kind of humour that generates so-called 'bad jokes', taking a jointly ethical and aesthetic approach. Her wider interest in aesthetics has led her to publish and present papers on gender issues, among them issues raised by Marcus Harvey's painting *Myra*. She has reviewed the book *Aftershock: The Ethics of Contemporary Transgressive Art*, by Kieran Cashell, in the October 2011 issue of the *Journal of Critical Realism*.

**Amy Cimini** earned her doctorate in Historical Musicology at New York University in 2011. Her research focuses on twentieth-century music and philosophy, with special emphasis on theories of the body and experimental practice. She currently holds a Mellon Post-Doctoral Teaching Fellowship in Music Theory at the University of Pennsylvania. She is developing a monograph that uses a Spinozistic framework to theorise late twentieth- and early twenty-first-century musical experimentalism as political intervention on the distinction between matter and life, focusing on the work of Maryanne Amacher, Alvin Lucier,

Anthony Braxton and others. Amy maintains an active performance career as a professional violist.

**Nicholas Halmi** is Professor of English and Comparative Literature at the University of Oxford and Margaret Candfield Fellow of University College, Oxford. His research is concerned with British and Continental (especially German) literature, philosophy, science, and visual arts of the seventeenth to nineteenth centuries; literary theory and history; and the modern reception of classical antiquity. He is the author of *The Genealogy of the Romantic Symbol* (Oxford University Press, 2007) and editor or co-editor of, among other works, S. T. Coleridge's theological treatise *Opus Maximum* (2002) and Norton Critical Editions of *Coleridge's Poetry and Prose* (2003) and *Wordsworth's Poetry and Prose* (forthcoming). His current projects include books on Coleridge and on the relation between history and genre in Romantic thought.

**Mateusz Janik** is a PhD candidate in the Graduate School for Social Research, Institute of Philosophy and Sociology, Polish Academy of Sciences. He works in the field of philosophy and social theory with special emphasis on political ontology and materialist ethics. He is the author and translator of texts devoted to Spinoza, Althusser and critical theories of modernity.

**Michael Mack** is Reader in English Literature and Medical Humanities at Durham University. Formerly, he has been a Visiting Professor at Syracuse University, a Fellow at the University of Sydney, and Lecturer and Research Fellow at the University of Chicago. He is the author of *How Literature Changes the Way we Think* (Bloomsbury/Continuum, 2012), *Spinoza and the Specters of Modernity* (Continuum, 2010), *German Idealism and the Jew* (University of Chicago Press, 2003), which was shortlisted for the Koret Jewish Book Award 2004, and *Anthropology as Memory* (Niemeyer, 2001, Conditio Judaica Series).

**Nick Nesbitt** is Professor of French at Princeton University. He is the author of *Voicing Memory: History and Subjectivity in French Caribbean Literature* (Virginia, 2003) and *Universal Emancipation: The Haitian Revolution and the Radical Enlightenment* (Virginia, 2008), editor of *Toussaint Louverture: The Haitian Revolution* (Verso, 2008) and co-editor of *Sounding the Virtual: Gilles Deleuze and the Philosophy of Music* (Ashgate, 2010).

**Peg Rawes** is Senior Lecturer at the Bartlett School of Architecture, University College London. Her teaching and research focus on inter-disciplinary links between architectural design, philosophy, technology and the visual arts, and examine spatiotemporality and embodiment, 'minor' traditions in geometric and spatial thinking, new aesthetic and material practices, and relational architectural ecologies. Her recent publications include *Relational Architectural Ecologies* (forthcoming, 2013); *Space, Geometry and Aesthetics* (2008); 'Spatial Imagination', *Designing for the 21st Century* (2008); 'Sonic Envelopes', *Senses and Society* (2008); *Irigaray for Architects* (2007); and 'Second-order Cybernetics, Architectural Drawing and Monadic Thinking', *Kybernetes* (2007).

**Christina Rawls** is completing her doctorate in Philosophy on Spinoza's dynamic theory of knowledge at Duquesne University. Her areas of study include early modern philosophy and the history of ideas, critical race theory, philosophy of psychology, and the problem of increased international organised crime and identity theft in an age of rapidly advancing technology. Christina has recently published philosophical poetry in the graduate art journal, *:lexicon*.

**Anthony Paul Smith** is Assistant Professor in Religion at La Salle University and a Research Fellow at DePaul University's Institute for Nature and Culture. He is the translator of François Laruelle's *Future Christ: A Lesson in Heresy* (Continuum, 2010), and the co-editor of *After the Postsecular and the Postmodern: New Essays in Continental Philosophy of Religion* (Cambridge Scholars, 2010) and *Laruelle and Non-Philosophy* (Edinburgh University Press, 2012).

**Dimitris Vardoulakis** teaches Philosophy at the University of Western Sydney. He is the author of *The Doppelgänger: Literature's Philosophy* (Fordham University Press, 2010). He has edited *Spinoza Now* (University of Minnesota Press, 2011) and co-edited *After Blanchot* (University of Delaware Press, 2005) and *Freedom and Confinement in Modernity: Kafka's Cages* (Palgrave, 2011). Forthcoming books include *Sovereignty and its Other* (Fordham University Press) and the co-edited volume, *'Sparks Will Fly': Benjamin and Heidegger* (SUNY).

**Caroline Williams** is Lecturer in Politics in the School of Politics and International Relations, Queen Mary, University of London. She is author of *Contemporary French Philosophy: Modernity and the*

*Persistence of the Subject* (2001). She has also published widely on Spinoza and on aspects of contemporary continental philosophy. She is currently completing a monograph on Spinoza.

# *Index*

EU Authorised Representative:

Easy Access System Europe Mustamäe tee 50, 10621 Tallinn, Estonia

gpsr.requests@easproject.com


Printed and bound by CPI Group (UK) Ltd, Croydon, CR0 4YY

10/06/2026

02133496-0001